Resident Foreigners

Resident Foreigners

A Philosophy of Migration

Donatella Di Cesare

Translated by David Broder

polity

First published in Italian as *Stranieri Residenti* © Bollati Boringhieri 2017
This English edition © Polity Press, 2020

Via Val d'Aposa 7 – 40123 Bologna
seps@seps.it
www.seps.it

The translation of this work has been funded by SEPS Segretariato Europeo per le Pubblicazioni Scientifiche.

Polity Press
65 Bridge Street
Cambridge CB2 1UR, UK

Polity Press
101 Station Landing
Suite 300
Medford, MA 02155, USA

ISBN-13: 978-1-5095-3354-1
ISBN-13: 978-1-5095-3355-8 (pb)

A catalogue record for this book is available from the British Library.

Library of Congress Cataloging-in-Publication Data
Names: Di Cesare, Donatella, author.
Title: Resident foreigners : a philosophy of migration / Donatella Di Cesare.
Other titles: Stranieri residenti. English
Description: English edition. | Medford, MA : Polity, 2019. | Includes bibliographical references and index.
Identifiers: LCCN 2019014899 (print) | LCCN 2019980058 (ebook) | ISBN 9781509533541 (hardback) | ISBN 9781509533558 (pbk.) | ISBN 9781509533572 (ebook)
Subjects: LCSH: Emigration and immigration--Philosophy.
Classification: LCC JV6035 .D4913 2019 (print) | LCC JV6035 (ebook) | DDC 304.801--dc23
LC record available at https://lccn.loc.gov/2019014899
LC ebook record available at https://lccn.loc.gov/2019980058

Typeset in 10.5 on 12 pt Times New Roman
by Fakenham Prepress Solutions, Fakenham, Norfolk NR21 8NL
Printed and bound in Great Britain by TJ International Limited

The publisher has used its best endeavours to ensure that the URLs for external websites referred to in this book are correct and active at the time of going to press. However, the publisher has no responsibility for the websites and can make no guarantee that a site will remain live or that the content is or will remain appropriate.

Every effort has been made to trace all copyright holders, but if any have been overlooked the publisher will be pleased to include any necessary credits in any subsequent reprint or edition.

For further information on Polity, visit our website:
politybooks.com

To my grandfather Francesco La Torre,
anarchist and socialist,
who set off from Marseilles
and landed, clandestinely,
at Ellis Island in 1925

Contents

Introduction: In Short

In this book, the reader will find no 'answers' to questions like 'how migration flows ought to be governed', what criteria should be used to 'distinguish between refugees and economic migrants', or how they should be 'integrated'. Rather, this work poses a fundamental challenge to such questions. For they are all inscribed in a politics that, while it claims to be pragmatic, responds only to the self-immunizing logic of exclusion. No solutions are to be found along these lines. This politics, which goes so far as to portray even barring entry to the migrant as an expression of concern for her wellbeing, and her rejection as an act of consideration towards her, aims only to defend the state's territory, understood as a closed-off space under collective ownership. But the nation cannot invoke any *ius soli* as a reason to deny hospitality, any more than it can a *ius sanguinis.* It is no surprise that two ancient spectres – the blood and the soil, which have forever been the linchpins of discrimination – have re-emerged in Europe in recent years.

Today's world is subdivided into multiple states that face one another, confront one another, and support one another. For the children of the nation, the state appears as a natural, almost eternal entity; since birth, they have shared the dominant state-centric perspective, which still holds firm. Migration is, then, a deviance to be held in check, an anomaly to be got rid of. The migrant at the outer margin reminds the state of its historical becoming and discredits its mythical purity. That is why any reflection on migration must also rethink the state itself.

This book is the first of its kind to outline a 'philosophy of migration'. Not even philosophy has thus far recognized the migrant's citizenship rights. Only recently has it accepted her within its borders – and even then it keeps her under strict surveillance, ready to push her away again with the first expulsion order.

The first chapter reconstructs a debate between the partisans of closed borders and the champions of open borders – a very intense debate in the Anglophone and German contexts. These two positions each correspond in their own way to liberalism, and indeed reveal liberalism's impasse: one of these positions supports sovereign self-determination, while the other demands an abstract freedom of movement. This book, for its part, is not willing to gaze out at the shipwreck from the shore. It sets itself at a distance from both positions.

A philosophy that starts out from migration, and which makes the reception of immigrants its first theme, allows migrating – released from *arché*, the founding principle of sovereignty – to become the point of entry, and lets migrants become the protagonist of a new and anarchic landscape. The migrant's point of view cannot but have effects on politics as well on philosophy, as it re-energizes both.

To migrate is not a biological drive, but rather an existential and political act. But the right to migrate is yet to be recognized. This book is intended as a contribution to the demand for a *ius migrandi*, in an age in which there is such a breakdown in human rights that it seems quite legitimate to ask whether the end of hospitality has already been sealed.

Looking back at our own time, future history books will not simply indulge today's hegemonic narrative. They will have to say that Europe – the homeland of human rights – denied hospitality to people who were fleeing war, persecution, abuse and rape, desolation and hunger. The potential guest was instead stigmatized *a priori* as an enemy. In the pages of these future history books, those who were safe and protected by state borders will bear the burden and the responsibility for the lives – and deaths – caught up in this history.

As well as the land, the sea has an important place in these pages. It is an in-between space that both unites and separates. It is a passageway that steers clear of borders, erases any trace of appropriation, and preserves the memory of another clandestinity – the clandestinity of opposition, resistance and struggles. This is clandestinity not as a stigma – 'the illegals' – but rather as a choice. The sea route points to the overturning of order, to the challenge of the elsewhere and the other.

For too long, philosophy has wallowed in the edifying use of the word 'other'. It has upheld an idea of hospitality as an absolute and impossible demand, unbound from politics and relegated to the level of religious charity or ethical engagement. This has had fatal results. Anachronistic and out of place, the acts of hospitality carried out by 'humanitarians' – those beautiful souls who still believe in justice – have been the target of derision and denunciation. They are first of all targeted by that politics which believes that it must govern in obedience to welfare chauvinism and the cynicism of 'securitarianism'.

In this book, the migrant enters the gates of the City as a *resident foreigner*. In its attempt to understand what role this latter figure can play in a politics of hospitality, this book takes a path back in time, albeit one that does not follow any chronological order. The stages along this road are Athens, Rome and Jerusalem: three types of city and three types of citizenship which still obtain today. Distinct from Athenian autochthony, which explains many of today's political myths, was Rome's open citizenship. Foreignness reigns sovereign in the Biblical City, where the *ger*, the resident foreigner, is the corner-stone of the community. *Ger* literally means 'he who resides'. This contravenes the logic of the solid fences that assign residency to the indigenous, to the citizen. The short-circuit contained in the semantics of *ger*, which attaches the foreigner to residency, in fact alters both terms. To inhabit does not mean to establish oneself, to settle in, to make a permanent home, or to become as one with the land. From this derive the questions that regard the meaning of 'inhabiting' and 'migration' in the present galaxy of planetary exile. Without recriminating over rootlessness, but also without glorifying wandering, it is possible to glimpse the possibility of a return. And pointing the way is the resident foreigner, who lives in the furrow of separation from the unappropriable earth and within the bond with the citizen, who, in turn, discovers that she herself is also a resident foreigner. In the City of foreigners, citizenship coincides with hospitality.

In the post-Nazi era, the idea that it is legitimate to decide with whom we should cohabit has held firm. 'To each their own home!' It is here that populist xenophobia finds its greatest strength; crypto-racism is its springboard. However, it is often unknown that this is a direct legacy of Hitlerism, i.e. the first project at a biopolitical remodelling of the planet, and one which purported to fix stable criteria for cohabitation. The discriminatory act claims an exclusive place for itself. Whoever accomplishes this act erects himself as a sovereign subject who, fantasizing about a supposed identity between himself and that place, demands his rights of ownership. As if the other, who has always already preceded him, did not have any rights or had never even existed.

To recognize the other's precedence in the place in which one lives means opening up not only to an ethics of proximity, but also to a politics of cohabitation. The *co-* (*con* – with) implicit in such cohabitation should be understood in its broadest and deepest sense, not only meaning participation but also indicating simultaneity. This does not mean rigidly standing right next to each other. In a world criss-crossed by the combined paths of so many exiles, to cohabit means to share the spatial proximity in a temporal convergence, where the past of each person can be articulated in the common present – indeed, in the perspective of a common future.

1

MIGRANTS AND THE STATE

In this world, shipmates, sin that pays its way can travel
freely, and without a passport; whereas Virtue, if a pauper, is
stopped at all frontiers.

H. Melville, *Moby Dick*

1 Ellis Island

They journeyed for weeks across the ocean waves, in the depths of
the hold, almost under the waterline, massed in dark dormitories
of ever shabbier aspect, squeezed onto old straw mattresses –
men, women and children, as many as 2,000 passengers. Only the
third-class ones disembarked at Ellis Island. For those who had
enough money to afford first or second class, there were but a few
quick checks carried out on board the ship by a doctor and a civil
registrar.

Imperious steamers and mighty transatlantic liners set out
from Hamburg and Liverpool, Naples and Marseilles, Riga and
Antwerp, Thessaloniki and Copenhagen, heading towards one same
destination: the Golden Door of a fairy-tale America. After an
exhausting crossing, when the ship finally entered the waters of the
Hudson River, and the shore of New Jersey could be made out at
a distance, the passengers headed up onto the bridge so that they
could see the Statue of Liberty. It was the welcome that they had
dreamed of. Emotion won out over their strains, their worries and
their tiredness. Kafka describes in near-epic tones the arrival of Karl
Rossmann, protagonist of his novel *Amerika*:

As the seventeen-year-old Karl Rossmann, who had been sent to America by his unfortunate parents because a maid had seduced him and had a child by him, sailed slowly into New York harbour, he suddenly saw the Statue of Liberty, which had already been in view for some time, as though in an intenser sunlight. The sword in her hand seemed only just to have been raised aloft, and the unchained winds blew about her form.[1]

The Statue of Liberty has a unique history. Brought to the New Continent as a French donation and a token of European values, over time it became a symbol of welcome for the damned of the Old Continent, the exploited and enslaved, decimated by famine, wars, misery and the hatred to which they had fallen victim. The Jewish poet Emma Lazarus called the statue the 'Mother of Exiles' in her 1883 sonnet, which was engraved on the pedestal of the statue. 'Keep, ancient lands, your storied pomp', the statue shouts with her mute lips: 'Give me your tired, your poor, Your huddled masses yearning to breathe free, The wretched refuse of your teeming shore. Send these, the homeless, tempest-tost to me, I lift my lamp beside the golden door!'

Until 1875, there was open entry onto US soil. Here these outcasts could find redemption by becoming pioneers in a virgin territory, the builders of a just society, and citizens of the New World. In this early period, Castle Garden, the old fort in Battery Park in south Manhattan, was designated as a sorting centre. Then restrictive measures began to be applied, leading to the establishment of the Ellis Island centre on 1 January 1892. Having first been unlimited, immigration became institutionalized. Nonetheless, a large influx was still allowed, and between 1892 and 1924 over 16 million people passed through Ellis Island. From 5,000 to 10,000 a day. Few of them, around 2 per cent, were turned away – almost nothing compared to today's figures. But still around 250,000 people. There were more than 3,000 suicides.

Ellis Island emerged, through the haze, from behind the Statue of Liberty. New York, the promised land, was right there, just a short stretch across the sea. But the third-class passengers knew that their journey was not over. They were separated from the New World by that small island, almost a relict of the Old World, a transit site where everything was still in play, where those who had set off had not yet arrived, and those who had left everything behind still had nothing.

The Mohegans called it Seagull Island; the Dutch rebaptized it Oyster Island, before the merchant Samuel Ellis bought it and imposed his own name, a marker of his possession of this narrow sandbank in the Hudson. The name remained, whereas ownership passed to the city of New York, which expanded the island thanks to the landfill created with ships' ballast and the earth removed from the tunnels for the subway.[2]

For the migrants, it was simply the Island of Tears – indeed, in the languages of all the peoples who passed through it: *isola delle lacrime, île des larmes, isla de las lágrimas, ostrov slez* and so on. The lucky ones would spend just a few hours in the Federal Bureau of Immigration. Enough time, that is, to be subjected to medical checks. The symptoms of possible illnesses, or the parts of the body to be checked, were denoted by letters of the alphabet: C for chest, or tuberculosis; E for the eyes; F for the face; H for the heart; K for hernia; L for lameness; SC for scalp; TC for trachoma; and X for 'mental disease'. Making a chalk mark, the sanitary officials would draw a letter on the shoulders of these passengers, who, having been assigned for closer medical examination, were held on the island for days, weeks or months. But when they diagnosed either a contagious disease, tuberculosis, trachoma or ringworm or 'mental disease', there followed immediate repatriation.

In their testimonies, the passengers recount their long and anguished wait, the confused noise, the painful uncertainty, and the shame felt over the marks chalked on their shoulders. Those who had passed the medical checks joined the line for the legal desk. It was here, with an interpreter's aid, that they had to answer the twenty-nine questions that were fired point-blank by the inspector on duty: 'What is your name? What country are you from? What is your final destination in America? How much money do you have with you? And where? Show it me. Who paid for your passage? Are you meeting a relative here in America? Who? Can they provide a guarantee for you? Are you coming to America for a job? Where will you work? Are you an anarchist?' If the inspector was satisfied, he then stamped the migrant's visa and bid them 'Welcome to America!' If that was not the case and he instead had doubts, he wrote two letters on a piece of paper – 'SI', meaning Special Inquiry. The passenger was then sent on to a commission made up of three inspectors, a typist and an interpreter. The interrogation resumed – this time more exacting and detailed.

Those who had passed all the inspections and questions hurried along to the ship that would take them to New York. Thus, in the course of a few hours, having gone through a couple of checks and a few vaccinations, a Lithuanian Jew, a Sicilian or an Irishman could become an American. For them, the Golden Door, the Eldorado of modernity, was open. Each of them could make a fresh start, leaving behind the past, their own history and that of their ancestors, the country to which they owed their birth, but which had denied them life. Soon, however, many must have had second thoughts. America was not the land of freedom of which they had dreamt, and nor were the streets paved with gold. Those who had arrived first had already appropriated everything and very little remained to be shared out, except for jobs in the factories of Brooklyn and the Lower East Side where workers toiled for fifteen hours a day. As for the streets, at this point they were largely yet to be built, together with the railroads and the skyscrapers.

Those who entered the United States at the dawn of the twentieth century nonetheless ought to have considered themselves privileged. Those were the years in which the peak of migrant numbers was reached. In 1907 alone, 1,004,756 migrants passed through Ellis Island. The First World War would soon contribute to reducing the great influx, but what slowed immigration were above all the measures that the federal government took to restrict it. The Chinese and other Asians had already been barred since 1870. The ban was, however, only made official in 1917 with the Immigration Act – or Asiatic Barred Zone Act – which extended the 'undesirable' label also to anarchists, homosexuals, the insane, vagrants and so on. This was also called the Literacy Act, because it stipulated that immigrants would have to prove that they could read and write in their own language, as well as be subjected to intelligence tests. A few years later, the number of entrants was further reduced, first with the 1921 Emergency Quota Act, and then the 1924 National Origin Act, which imposed an annual limit of 150,000 entrants. This latter, particularly, was a self-evidently racist measure, for it sought to put up barriers to immigration from the countries of Southern and Eastern Europe. The Italian quota, at first as much as a quarter of the total, was then reduced to 4 per cent. It is hardly surprising that, in the 1930s, these laws could also inspire Nazi politics.[3]

Ellis Island, where a psychiatric hospital and a prison had been built, ended up becoming a detention centre for irregular immigrants, and, in the interwar period, was transformed into a prison for suspected anti-US activists. In 1954, the government closed the sorting centre on the island.[4] The island and its name remained inscribed in the autobiographies of many of the children and grandchildren of this great migration. At least 40 per cent of US citizens today have an ancestor who disembarked on Ellis Island.

The America that had in little more than a century increased its population from 188 million to 258 million inhabitants – in large part of European origin – without too many scruples, then chose drastically to reduce the numbers of new entrants and to close its borders.

But how could immigration laws be reconciled with the ideals of the US Constitution, which were meant to be universal? How come some people could be rejected as 'undesirables' if the Declaration of Independence itself asserted that all men are created equal?

This conflict was at the heart of Ellis Island, a crossing to hope yet also a centre of discrimination. Between its lights and shadows, the island – this unique non-place of exile – reflects the contradiction of all US policy. The initial openness of the frontiers, which could rely on widespread consensus, was followed by the introduction of restrictive criteria when the first 'native' Americans born on the soil of the New Continent imagined that, with their birth, they had thus acquired the right to decide whom they would grant the title of 'American citizen'. Not everyone in the world seemed suitable – despite the words, engraved at the foot of the Statue of Liberty, which Emma Lazarus had directed to the outcast and the lowliest. It was then that the nation that had emerged from Ellis Island forgot about its own exile and preferred to exercise its sovereignty. Controlling the borders became the key to fortifying and strengthening the unity of the nation-state, based on homogeneity. Ellis Island is thus the contradictory symbol of modern migration.

2 When the migrant unmasks the state

Upon her arrival, the migrant faces a state that stands up in all its supremacy. These two are the main actors, the two protagonists on this stage. The migrant's rights, starting with her right to move, crash up against the sovereignty which the state exercises over the nation and over its territorial dominion. Here we see the conflict between universal human rights and the division of the world into nation-states.

In the state's eyes, the migrant constitutes an intolerable anomaly, an anomie in its internal space and in the international space, a challenge to its sovereignty. She is not only an intruder, an outlaw, an illegal. Through her very existence, she transgresses the foundational principle that the state is built around, and undermines the precarious interconnection – standing at the basis of the world order – between the nation, the soil and the monopoly of state power. The migrant hints at the possibility of a different arrangement of the world: she represents deterritorialization, the fluidity of movement, autonomous crossing, the hybridization of identity.

Asserting its sovereign power, the state stops the migrant at the site of conflict and confrontation *par excellence* – the border. It can admit the migrant into the space it governs – after the stipulated controls, that is – or else reject her. And, to that end, the state is prepared to blatantly violate human rights. The border thus becomes not only the rock that so many lives are shipwrecked on, but also the obstacle that is set up against any right to migrate.

This contradiction is all the more strident in democracies. Notwithstanding the fact that upon their historical emergence they proclaim the Rights of Man and the Citizen, at the same time they base their own sovereignty on three quite other principles. These three are: the idea that the people self-determines and is both the creator and target of its own laws; the criterion of national homogeneity; and the postulate of territorial belonging. These latter two principles, in particular, frustrate mobility.

Migrants' movements thus bring to light a constitutive dilemma that undermines liberal democracies' very foundations. The philosophical dilemma gives rise to an open tension at the political level, between state sovereignty and the commitment to human rights. A democracy rooted within the nation-state's borders is caught in the web of this double bind. The irreconcilability between human rights and state sovereignty paradoxically also crops up in universal conventions and international legal documents – hence, alas, their impotence.

Migration – in the forms and means in which it manifests itself in the new millennium – is a phenomenon proper to modernity, for it is closely bound to the modern state. Seeking to keep watch over their borders, guard their territory and control their populations, nation-states discriminate and set up the barrier between citizens and foreigners. This does not mean that the empires, monarchies or republics of the past did not defend their borders. But these latter were much softer and more precarious than the borders juridically established and militarily monitored by the modern state.

The clash between the migrant and the state thus extends beyond the protagonists themselves. And it is thus possible to understand why reflection on migration also means rethinking the state. Without that discrimination, already carried out in advance, the state would not exist. Borders take on an almost sacred value and point back to a semi-mythical origin. For they are both the result and the proof of its distinctive task, its mission of drawing boundaries. It is thanks to this task of definition and discrimination that the state context can establish itself, maintain its strength and stability – or, indeed, be a *state*. A state is the exact opposite of mobility. The more imperative this task is – as in the case of the nation-state – the more tenacious the aspiration to homogeneity and integrity proves to be. For the sons and daughters of the nation, who have shared the state's internal outlook from birth, the state has an obvious immediacy. It is an internal fact, whose natural character seems beyond dispute.

The migrant, however, unmasks the state. From its external edge, she interrogates its very foundations, pointing an accusing finger against discrimination. She ties the state back to its historical emergence and discredits the myth of its purity. And she thus insists that the state itself be reconsidered. In this sense, migration bears a subversive charge.

3 The state-centric order

Today's world is subdivided into a multiplicity of bordering nation-states, which both adjoin and confront one another. This state-centric order is assumed to be normal. Everything that happens is considered and judged within the confines of a state-based perspective. Migration is also seen within the terms of the state and its territorial rootedness, and is thus itself considered a contingent and marginal phenomenon. If the state is the essential fulcrum of the political order, migration is an accident.

This world order has begun to be profoundly shaken by the recent, epoch-defining waves of migration. The state-centric outlook nonetheless holds firm and remains dominant. This is the reason why the viewpoint of those who belong to a state and look out from within that internal position, entrenched behind barriers, is always tacitly assumed when the questions raised by the 'migrant crisis' are discussed in public debate. It is no accident that the question marks revolve only around the ways of governing and regulating the 'flows' of migrants. Such differences as do exist, at most, separate those who see immigrants as an opportunity – something useful – from those who instead warn that they represent a danger. The state-centric outlook is always also a normative one. Citizens, those who belong to the state, are recognized *a priori* as having the right to decide, the prerogative to either welcome or exclude the foreigner knocking on their door.

The sovereign power to say 'no' seems to stand beyond doubt or challenge. States claim the capacity to establish who can enter within their borders and who must instead be stopped at the border. In a state-centric global order threatened by migration, the right to exclude thus becomes the means of asserting and cross-checking the state's sovereignty. For it is a proof and measurement of the state's power. Nation-states assert their claim to manage their own territorial and political borders also by resorting to force. Whoever transgresses the borders runs the risk of being interned, as she awaits expulsion. Even if she is let in, it is again up to state authority to decide whether to recognize her as a new member of the community or to reject her.

International law and its norms do nothing but confirm and validate the prerogative to which states lay claim. It is possible to become an expatriate, to leave the national territory, just as it is possible to move within it.[5] But one cannot freely transfer to another state, become part of that state or make one's home there. The principle of *non-refoulement* is the exception that confirms the rule: it establishes that the asylum-seeker cannot be expelled into those countries 'where his life or freedom would be threatened on account of his race, religion, nationality, membership of a particular social group or political opinion'.[6] This is, however, a very limited principle, which moreover applies only to those who are already on the soil, or under the control, of the (putative) country of asylum.

Border policy is a dominion reserved to sovereign states. Jealous of their own powers, determined not to give in, and backed up by international legislation, they claim the right to preclude entry onto the national soil. But if their right to do so is legal, can it also be said to be legitimate? Can states impede or limit immigration?

4 A fundamental hostility

It is not difficult to guess why, in this state-centric context, the conditions that restrict and limit hospitality are dictated by an implicit and fundamental hostility. The migrant who turns up at the border is first of all perceived as a dangerous foreigner, a hidden and secret enemy, an invading savage, a potential terrorist – and certainly not a guest.

In political-media discourse – in which the meanings of words are hollowed out, if they not twisted into their very opposite – 'hospitality' today has no meaning outside the context of private morality or religious faith. Stripped of its political value, it becomes a symptom of a naïve do-gooderism. This allows the flaring-up of the rival term that has always inhabited hospitality – namely, hostility.

'Migrant reception policy' is the formula twisted to indicate the very opposite – that is, a policy of exclusion and expulsion, a police management of migrant flows, a control of the borders which stretches so far as to impose its oversight over the domestic administration of the citizenry. If openness is judged guilty of being naïve, ridiculous, migrant reception – made a taboo, as its real meaning is banished – is disfigured. It is reduced to providing a hypocritical cover, a farcical corrective, to a cynical securitarianism.

What dictates the law is the principle of state sovereignty. This principle makes the nation the norm, and migration a matter of deviance and irregularity. It is articulated in the grammar of the possessive, around which political consensus coagulates. It is the grammar of 'we' and 'ours', of what is 'our own' – property, belonging and identity. Calculation, control and selection become obvious criteria to use. Just as closedness becomes an almost incontrovertible postulate.

This principle of sovereignty operates in concert with a fundamental hostility, because it is exercised over territory, *'our* country', of which the citizens hold themselves to be the legitimate owners, and thus authorized to deny or limit access to it by foreigners, according to the conditions that they can establish in sovereign fashion. The right to property over the territory is combined with the privilege of belonging to the community and the prerogative of monitoring the borders. All this seems absolutely natural. Each citizen must then feel obliged to respond firmly, to support closing the borders, precisely in order to meet the demands of an 'open society'. The paradox of this position, however, remains well hidden.

Backed up by welfare chauvinism and the parochialism of 'our own', state xenophobia is able to cast its shadow over migrant reception. And it does so by invoking the pretext of pragmatic realism and the impossibility of political action. Reception is always read in light of a looming threat, as the foreigner is passed off as an intruder and her arrival as an invasion. Through these undue confusions, these subtle slips, citizenship becomes equivalent to owning the land, and belonging becomes equivalent to the guarantee of equal rights. Thus, in the name of defending a social justice limited within national borders, hospitality reveals its troubling connection with hostility.

Even where it does provide some show of tolerance, the sovereign community cannot do without this prior hostility. Thus, citizens are called on to be the unchallenged referees, the supreme judges, whose responsibility it is to exclude – or else let in – newcomers. This takes place on the basis of the evidence they offer: meaning, for candidates for asylum, proof of persecution and abuse; proof of their usefulness, in the case of economic migrants; and, for all the rest, proof of their will to integrate. Foreigners' human rights are suspended by administrative accounting, while the privileges, the advantages, the immunities of citizens are upheld.

5 Beyond sovereignty: a marginal note

The state – or, better, state sovereignty – is the obstacle that prevents us even thinking about migration. In modernity, this sovereignty has been the epicentre of politics, drawing its map, tracing its limits and thus separating the domestic sphere – subjected to sovereign power – from the external one, which is, instead, given up to anarchy. In this dichotomy, it is sovereignty that prevails, in its positive value.

Sovereign power is exercised in an exclusive way, by way of a single authority, within a defined territorial space. By definition, it cannot recognize any higher powers. It is established in order to overcome the chaos of nature which, according to Hobbes's well-known narrative, could continue to spark civil conflict. In this reading, it is thus the fruit of a shared covenant, to which all submit. Hobbes goes so far as to make the state a 'person', an almost-anthropomorphic figure whose absolute and unchallengeable internal sovereignty corresponds to an external sovereignty, on which the sovereignty of other sovereign states puts a brake.[7] Thus, in a move that was destined to have profound and enduring effects, Hobbes projected the Leviathan – the animal of primitive chaos, chosen as an emblem of state power – beyond the borders. Though it has been contained domestically, this savage lawlessness, however, reproduces itself in international relations. If persons in flesh and bone find a peaceful way of living together, thanks to the contract that has bound them to sovereignty, outside this contract a permanent virtual war rages between the artificial persons – the sovereign Leviathans, the wolves – that are states.[8] It is thus hardly surprising that Hobbes dedicates only a few pages to the international arena, instead concentrating his attentions on the power that the state exercises within its own borders.

The dichotomy between internal and external, sovereignty and anarchy, cuts through all modern thought in different forms and through different conceptions. Continuing even today, it imposes a hierarchy of problems, prescribes solutions and justifies principles – first among them, the principle of obedience to state power. And this is a constitutive sovereignty, for it also delineates the limits of the political sovereignty that, most of the time, adapts itself to the presupposition of sovereign statehood.

This dichotomous vision more or less explicitly introduces the distinction between civilization (internal) and its absence (external). It draws the line between the norm and lawlessness, between order and chaos. It is not worth emphasizing the value judgement inherent within this: if the principle of sovereignty is positive, then anarchy must instead have a negative stamp.

The word 'anarchy' is of Greek provenance. It consists of the privative *an-* and *arché*, which means 'principle', 'beginning', but also 'command', 'authority', 'government'. It is assumed in its specific meaning as a political form that denies principles and command, or in the derivative and pejorative sense of an 'absence of government', meaning disorder. Or, rather, it is the dichotomy itself that pushes the word 'anarchy' towards this semantic usage. The intention is obvious: it legitimizes sovereignty as the only condition for order, the only alternative to the absence of government.[9] 'Anarchy' becomes another way of invoking that savage tumult which rages in the boundless 'outside' that lies beyond state sovereignty.

This separates out two counterposed spaces. On the one hand is the internal space – the one within which living well is a possible objective and where progress, with its bearers and its effects of justice, democracy and human rights, plays out. On the other hand is the external space, in which the very best outcome is mere survival, and in which there are, at most, vague cosmopolitan projects for a confederation of peoples, if not the reproposition of the state model in a global republic.

Globalization has, however, changed this landscape, deeply undermining the dichotomy between sovereignty and anarchy – even if simply because it forcefully expands the global outlook towards the unlimited. It thus brings out into the open all the limits of any politics anchored to traditional borders. The speed with which bytes travel through telecoms networks, cancelling out what were once insuperable distances, has become emblematic of the flows that cross borders, evade controls and untie spatial binds. This compromises the entire structure of things, which thus seems to tip chaotically into a 'new global disorder'. As a promoter of globalization, the nation-state is irreparably damaged by it, for it loses that control over territory and over the body politic of citizens from which it had drawn its strength, and with which it had governed for centuries. No longer is the sovereign he who commands territory, but whoever can cross it quickest. Speed is the new power.[10]

The deterritorialization of sovereignty represents the crisis of politics in its modern form. Moreover – especially from the post–1945 period onwards – the continuing applicability of the state model to international relations seems ever more open to challenge. Those who have studied or practised in this field have acquired a different perspective. It has become clearly apparent that the scenario outside and beyond the nation's borders is being populated by other protagonists, beyond states themselves – namely, international institutions, supranational organisms and humanitarian organizations. Power now appears multiform, divided, often shared-out and difficult to pin down.

The political landscape appears more complicated than ever before. For, while sovereign nation-states continue to play the main role, providing the normative context for whatever happens, they no longer constitute a homogeneous system, and there are ever-vaster spaces, both real and virtual, opening up across borders. This demands that the anachronistic dichotomy be put to one side, in favour of a better scrutiny of what is going on outside, to take up an external standpoint, and consider internal problems also from this perspective.

Entering into this unknown landscape would require new maps which do not yet exist. If the system of nation-states has not reached its conclusion, the new political forms barely emerging on the horizon are still difficult to distinguish.

Migration helps us to make them out, for it leads beyond sovereignty, into the open space that has always been delivered up to anarchy. Called into action here is that philosophy whose task is to deconstruct the obvious, to explode whatever purports to be normative and which can only take recourse to the force of the law in order to cloak itself in legitimacy. The philosophical question emerges outside of the borders and beyond the dominion of sovereignty. It asks: do states have the right to impede or limit entrance onto a given territory at their own discretion?

6 Philosophy and migration

There still does not exist any philosophy of migration. We lack either reflection on migrating, or thinking that revolves around migrants themselves. Migration does not yet make up part of the inventory of philosophy. In vain do we seek out traces of migration in the encyclopedias and philosophical dictionaries that ought to offer a historical-conceptual reconstruction of this phenomenon.[11] Out of either disinterest, disregard or amnesia, philosophy has not recognized citizenship rights for the migrant.

This fate is not so different from that of the alien, who is forever relegated to the margins, and confined to the slums of metaphysics. The migrant is *atopos* – without a place, out-of place – just as much as the alien, or rather more so. For the migrant is placed at the frontier, in the attempt to cross it. The migrant is neither citizen nor alien. Unwelcome everywhere, she is an intruder who blows up barriers, wipes out boundaries and provokes embarrassment.

Therein lies the difficulty in thinking about her. Unless, that is, the world's agreed boundaries are put back into discussion, and we revisit the centuries-long foundations of the city and citizenship, and alter the entrenched pillars of the state, sovereignty and the nation. The migrant is indefinable because, in her threatening, out-of-place position, she breaks apart boundaries: she remains an 'unthought' of philosophy, which has preferred to pass her over in silence, indulging the omissions in the official vision.

Philosophy has chosen the permanently settled, has legitimized it and assumed its perspective. It has thus propped up fences and strengthened barriers, every time underscoring the border between 'within' and 'outside' in its own search for alignment and its attempt to delineate a concentric order. Seen in this regard, the transversality of migration cannot but appear as something suspect and threatening. To defend its own conceptual system, philosophy has refused welcome and denied hospitality. Even when it has allowed itself the ambiguous privilege of the margin, it has done it only for gaining a panorama-view from the edge, for a never-sated desire for the esoteric, or with the aim of reconsidering its own metaphysical centre. But it has not made the jump from the margin to marginalization; it has not ventured into that cross-border zone inhabited by the migrant, which for philosophy remains a *terra incognita*.

It is not that 'migrate' and 'migration' are terms wholly absent from the philosophical lexicon. It suffices to recall its use in the texts of Cicero, in which the Latin *migrare* has a very great semantic breadth, and indicates different forms of movement: from a change of home (from the Greek *metoikesis*) to expatriation, and from crossing a boundary to the transgression of a rule – *communa iura migrare*.[12] Even up to the ultimate passage that is death – or, as Cicero writes, *migrare ex hac vita* ('he departed this life').[13]

These are, however, liminal occurrences which remain in the background and do not allow for the elaboration of migration as a concept. As the meaning of migration gradually becomes more precise, to the point that it finally designates the foreigner's relations with citizenship, i.e. her movement of exiting – *emigrating* – or entering – *immigrating* – this theme disappears from the horizon of philosophy. If philosophers at the threshold of modernity did take a stance, they do so in order to uphold the rights of property, to defend the appropriation of the earth and to legitimize the division of the world into nation-states. Only Kant concerns himself with guaranteeing at least some form of 'hospitality' in an ever-shrinking planet. His contribution remains a point of reference for the right to asylum. Yet, despite his cosmopolitanism, Kant, too, remained Eurocentric – i.e., within that philosophical centring

which excludes and stigmatizes *a priori* any migratory movement
and any nomadism. Certainly, Kant was far from benevolent or
tolerant towards the 'reason' for the 'gypsies living as vagabonds'.[14]

Only between the two world wars, when migration was already
a mass phenomenon, did an exceptional refugee, Hannah Arendt,
give voice to the stateless, the homeless, the Jews fleeing Nazism,
who no longer seemed to find a place in the world. Her short 1943
essay *We Refugees* marked a watershed in thinking on migration.
But her pioneering ideas, further developed in her later works, were
not in fact adopted and elaborated into any overall philosophy of
migration.

In the second half of the twentieth century, this theme was once
again overlooked. Philosophy did not anticipate the times. It arrived
only belatedly, when a public opinion had already developed in the
face of the urgent circumstances, and a certain morality was already
inspiring and guiding international accords. This morality, which
has often been uncritical and simplistic, the result of compromise,
the product of a state-centric vision, has long remained a tacit and
undiscussed set of assumptions. But philosophy has not pulled it
apart. Rather, having arrived on the scene only belatedly, philosophy
continued to push migration out of its own repertoire, whether
denying this theme a philosophical status or itself adapting to what
had become the widespread morality. It presumes to inquire into
the principles of social and political justice, and to hold forth on
human rights, without ever speaking about migrants' rights, and
without ever touching on the question of reception. This reticent
silence appears almost self-evident. John Rawls, considered the most
famous theorist of justice, only sporadically mentions this topic.
And he even goes so far as to theorize exclusion: for him, in a society
of liberal peoples, 'The problem of immigration is not, then, simply
left aside, but is eliminated as a serious problem.'[15] The migrant
is seen as the alien who might undermine, if not even dissolve, an
already-consolidated solidarity. That is why in the liberal idea of a
well-ordered universe of states, philosophy's task becomes, at most,
that of governing and disciplining migratory movements.

From the morality that had underlain the international treaties,
over the late twentieth and early twenty-first centuries there emerged
an ethics of migration in an Anglo-Saxon mould, with a practical
attitude and a strongly normative calling. Philosophers have thus
been put to the test. What should be done about immigrants?
Welcome them? Not welcome them? And how should they be
defined? How to distinguish between the migrant and the refugee?
Because of this development, the term 'immigration' did earn a place
in the *Stanford Encyclopedia of Philosophy* in 2010.[16] But the debate

remains limited to for-and-against arguments, within the terms of a democratic liberalism that tries to confront the uncomfortable problem of migrants as best it can, albeit not without evident contradictions. It is, indeed, possible to envisage the reception of migrants, but only according to the dictates of a supposed 'ethic' which is meant to mitigate or soften the harshness of a policy that is also prepared to put up walls.

As separate from its political import, migration asserted itself as an ethical question in the German public debate only after September 2015, when Germany opened its borders faced with the *Flüchtlingsdrama*, the great 'refugee crisis' that exploded with the war in Syria. Philosophers were consulted and questioned as part of the sharp polemics over that decision.[17] But the problem was limited to the 'moral' terms of how to fix the quantitative and qualitative criteria for either welcoming refugees in or turning them away. At the end of 2015, the Gesellschaft für analytische Philosophie launched an essay contest on the telling question: 'Which and how many refugees should we admit?'[18] In the discussion that this provoked – whose echoes have still not died out – the participants started out from the concern to identify criteria of selection and exclusion. What was demanded in this context was an 'applied ethics'. Meanwhile, an accusing finger has been pointed at theory and its abstract limitations.[19]

Elsewhere, in the various different currents of continental philosophy, from Derrida to Balibar and from Agamben to Esposito, the coordinates for a politics of hospitality have been outlined, in either sharper or more implicit fashion. However, even this has not meant that this theme has passed from the periphery to the centre of reflection. It is as if the presuppositions on which political philosophy has built itself over the centuries were put at risk by the reception of immigrants. A philosophy of migration would, then, be a philosophy that questions itself as well as its own long-incontestable foundations.

7 A shipwreck with an audience: on today's debate

Perhaps in no other context like migration does the interpretative perspective assumed play such a decisive role. Hence, this perspective needs to be made explicit right from the outset. To reflect on migration is to stand on the shore and see the migrants arriving. If reflection always demands stopping and taking a pause, there are many different ways to stand on the shore – and some of them even contradict one another.

One possible way of considering what is happening lies in identifying with the 'we' of those who have taken up a position on the shore for some time – years, decades, centuries – and claimed ownership over it. That is, to look out to sea from within a national community and its established borders. More or less proud of being within the city, the citadel, the fortress, and self-satisfied at belonging to it, one can react to this arrival by counting the migrants as they disembark, asking how many can legitimately be accepted, and, to that end, trying to introduce criteria to distinguish as impartially as possible who deserves to be admitted from who should instead be excluded. For this, it supposedly suffices to ascertain where they have come from and what causes have driven them to hazard this inadvisable voyage, ruinous for them as for others. Those on the shore shake their heads in disapproval and intolerance of the new arrivals. They do not feel the need to offer them any 'welcome' – for these new arrivals will bring problems to their community, which will be obliged to host them at least temporarily, and maybe even to integrate them.

Thus far, the philosophers who have openly confronted the question of migration have adopted this same perspective. Certainly, there is no lack of differences between those who do more to highlight the needs of the community and those who defend the individual's right to freedom of movement, between the so-called 'communitarians' and the supposed 'libertarians', between the neocontractualists and the utilitarians – to note just some of the many labels for the schools in which which the Anglo-Saxon mould of political philosophy presents itself. On closer inspection, however, the similarities are both deeper and more numerous than might be imagined. Everyone is watching from the riverbank, with a certain detachment. They quarrel over whether the borders should remain shut or if they could be opened – perhaps not exactly thrown wide open, but made to seem 'porous', at the least. They discuss whether, and in what measure, the political contract can be extended to newcomers without undermining the welfare state. They hypothesize more or less restrictive measures and provisions to regulate inclusion and safeguard security and public order.

This debate first unfolded in US universities, before more recently being taken up in the European academy, and especially in Germany. Surprising, here, is not only the way in which everything that ought to be put into question is instead assumed to be somehow obvious – from the state-centric order of the world to the concepts of citizenship, belonging and territory – but also the more or less nakedly normative character of the contributions themselves, in the search for a certain 'objectivity' in both analysis and conclusions.

On the one hand, philosophers seem to aggregate themselves to the social sciences, following its methods and investigations, and on the other hand, they end up voicing the good old common sense. As if philosophy's vocation were not precisely to deconstruct consolidated habits of thinking and critique that action which parades its own legitimacy.

So monotonous and dull does this debate appear that it does not even manage to break out of the academy walls. It is so sterile and ineffective that it sparks hardly any interest and has an extremely limited political impact. Discussions of governance and the management and regulation of migration flows may as well be entrusted to experts and professional politicians. What use are philosophers, then? Behind the intricate discourse, the meticulous observations and the subtle argumentation, in which the phenomenon of migrating itself seems to disappear from view, what becomes noticeable is the emotional indifference, the cold imperturbability, the impassive detachment, which so irritatingly contrast with the migrants' own drama. Who should be admitted? How, and why? Should the borders be opened or not? The impression is that the debate is nothing but a contained tiff, a temperate exchange of ideas between well-off *bien pensants* who have in common both their intent to resolve the problem and the wholly internal perspective they adopt in order to observe what is going on outside of them. It is as if the sedentary position that they have themselves acquired means that migration cannot affect them.

To illustrate this internal perspective more clearly, it is worth turning to the famous image with which Lucretius begins the second book of his *De rerum natura*: namely, the image of the spectator on dry land who contemplates the shipwreck suffered by others: 'Sweet it is … to gaze from the land on another's great struggles'.[20] Hans Blumenberg has charted the winding course of this metaphor, which has passed through Western thought in multiple variants.[21] Already, at the threshold of modernity, Pascal noted that the land no longer appeared firm or secure, but rather uncertain and vacillating, like the sea. In vain, then, could anyone set himself up as a spectator of the world's ills, seeking stable orders and privileged points of view.[22] The spectator is always-already implicated, because the waves in which he sees others drowning are a threat that has never been overcome forever, and they could abruptly submerge his own rock, too. It is better, then, to recognize the need to act. Perhaps just by holding out a hand.

To consider the migrant from the shore, even just to extol her liberal right to free movement, amounts to reinforcing the barrier between 'us' and 'them', the border between residents and foreigners. Above all, it means not taking the migrant's side, not putting on her shoes, not assuming her point of view. Hence the lack of human feeling in a philosophy that exhausts itself working through norms and definitions, without bringing out the existential nudity of whoever arrives after escaping the waves, after having experienced some extreme situation, on the limit of death. There could be no more strident contrast than the one between this limit and the bureaucratic frontier, in which the thinking that conforms to the internal perspective ends up becoming an authoritative form of surveillance.

It can be seen why, in a philosophy that sets out from migration and makes reception its first theme, what happens on the outside is decisive. To allow migration itself to become a starting point is to free oneself from the *arché*, the principle that founds sovereignty, and around which the body politic immunizes itself. This implies not only receiving the migrant who arrives unexpected – with her existential nudity and her baggage of suffering, desperation and distress – but also making her the protagonist of a new anarchic scenario. The migrant's point of view cannot but have effects on both politics and philosophy, and it cannot but enliven both.

8 Thinking from the shore

A philosophy of migration is, first and foremost, a *philosophy of the migrant*. The genitive, here, is eminently subjective. The reason for this has already been explained above: the migrant is the protagonist, the actor and the interpreter of this epochal drama. But who will recount this drama, who will grasp its historic importance, and who will be able to pass judgement on it?

The migrant needs someone else on land who not only extends her a hand but watches, considers, bears witness, from that edge. Before, that is, everything ends up in the vortices of the watery abyss or the oblivion of an unwritten story. In her drama, the migrant entrusts herself to a 'spectator'. But which? Certainly not the one who stands at the border to wave the flag of his own belonging, raise the standard of his own community, and vaunt the position of strength that he derives from being on the inside, within the limits that he consolidates by marking the within from the without. What must be put into question is the metaphysical dichotomy between the internal and the external – the foundation of political separation.

A philosophy of the migrant requires a spectator capable of moving from the internal to the external, and vice versa; able not only to recount and redeem the shipwreck, but also to pass judgement on it. Hannah Arendt offers important suggestions in terms of revisiting the figure of the spectator. Her ideas on this are contained in her posthumous, unfinished work *The Life of the Mind*. Arendt died before she could complete the first and second parts ('Thinking' and 'Wishing') with the third, concluding part, 'Judging'. She was denied that crowning moment. Nonetheless, she left some texts that indicate the direction of her research: a *Postscriptum* and the *Lectures* on Kant's political philosophy that she gave at the New School in 1970.

In her final years, an Arendt ever more concerned to emphasize philosophy's political vocation devoted her reflection to the nexus between thinking and acting. She had good reason, then, to echo Heidegger's great question: What does it mean to think? If common sense puts individuals at peace with the world – where they thus feel calmly at home – thought, on the contrary, provokes disorientation, which is to say: homelessness. Whoever thinks no longer feels at home in the place they inhabit. The bind of common sense weakens. To think is to 'withdraw from the world'.[23] Hence the solitude of the philosopher, and what to others appears as her oddness and uniqueness. And that is necessarily the case: to think whatever is unfamiliar makes us foreigners. Already in his *Politics*, Aristotle spoke of *bios xenikos* – the life that alienates itself, the life of the foreigner – with reference to the philosopher who dedicates himself only to thinking, at a distance from any active participation.[24] Even if it is never complete and definitive, the philosopher's taking-leave from the world certainly is radical: she abandons her kin, breaks away from their precarious opinions, and separates herself from the irritating common sense, which would be an impediment to her own ability to decentre, to estrange herself, to emigrate towards an outside from which she attempts to subvert the established order. Thus, Arendt says, thinking is always 'out of order'.[25]

But what about politics? And the nexus between philosophy and politics, one of the nodes that Heidegger had left unresolved? The answer lies in the 'judging', that political faculty *par excellence* that, although bearing some affinities with thinking – at least in the initial move, the retreat from the world – then heads down a different path, towards another end. What sticks out next in Arendt's pages is the figure of the spectator, a term that translates the Greek *theatés*, from which the word 'theory' was then derived. Witness and listener, the *theatés* watches a drama play out. Her role is different from that of the actor playing her part. For she is neither wholly absent, like someone who is simply elsewhere, nor wholly present, like someone involved in the action; the spectator in the stalls instead has that peculiar position of being distant enough from the stage to be able to have an overall view of it. This does not mean that she occupies a higher ground from which she can contemplate *the* truth which remains inaccessible to common sense. The spectator's seat is in the theatre of the world; what distinguishes her is the liminal condition from which, precisely because she does not act in the drama directly, she can seek to comprehend its meaning and pass judgement on it.

In short: the spectator stands in relation to the philosopher as judgment stands in relation to thinking. There are at least two differences: unlike the philosopher, the spectator withdraws from active involvement only temporarily, in order to assume a privileged position from which to consider the whole; for she is not solitary, but rather makes up part of an audience, a public. One need only think of the spectators in the rows of a theatre or a stadium. One can then understand why, in Arendt's reflection, the spectator becomes the figure key to shedding light on the relationship between philosophy and politics, and to delineating a new political philosophy. Then it is Kant's turn to speak; he 'was the first, and remained the last, of the great philosophers to deal with judgment'.[26] But, according to Arendt, Kant's merit is precisely the fact that he did not neglect to note the plurality of spectators.

If the spectator is extraneous, this is not true in the same profound, limitless way that it is for the philosopher. Rather, the spectator's is a horizontal extraneousness, that demands that she stop to watch the world as if from the outside even as she remains internal to it. Neither wholly outside nor wholly within, the spectator's viewpoint is marginal, like that of the foreigner, but does not exclude her and is not itself exclusive. Rather, it is shared. The catharsis of thinking opens the way to the faculty of judging. The stalls are the site from which the audience looks out, offering the perspective which the spectator – who has no illusion of grasping *the* truth that stands beyond appearances – can compare her own point of view with others', take on new perspectives, and formulate common judgements. And, in her *Lectures*, Arendt insists on the 'common' dimension, in which the public practice of thinking is articulated. This link with others ought not to be misunderstood, however, and interpreted as a 'broad empathy', as if one could know what was happening in the next person's head. Rather, it is a matter of extending thought in different directions, as when one travels, seeing other points of view at closer hand, also thanks to the imagination's ability to overcome limits and barriers. This already happens when, almost without noticing it, the spectator ends up considering what is happening from the viewpoint of the actor – of whoever is acting. Kant's *Weltbetrachter* is characterized precisely by this passage to other forms of presence in the world.[27] Each person is called on to be a 'spectator of the world', in both the senses that this figure seems to have taken on in Arendt's political philosophy. First and foremost, because only through the spectator's judgement do the world's events assume meaning, and does the world itself produce history. What would the French Revolution be if there had been only actors and not spectators? But the *Weltbetrachter* is also the person who accepts her disorientation, who allows herself to be guided by a political – or, better, cosmopolitical – calling and who, in assuming the perspectives of others, becomes able to articulate what are necessarily common judgements.

Here, the spectator is the citizen with the capacity to become a foreigner, the one who abandons her own fixedness and indulges the decentring that allows her to be where she really is not, in the passage from the inside to the outside (and back again). And its effect is that she no longer feels at home on this shore.

9 Migration and modernity

However much one might be tempted to sketch out the history of migration, without doubt the continuity of this phenomenon is profoundly marked by its caesuras; the differences are so great as to draw into question its very homogeneity. The mere existence of a generic ability to move around does not allow one to speak of 'migration'. Both statistical–quantitative parameters and socio-economic criteria are misleading, in this regard, for, while they both aim to be 'objective', they end up proving inadequate to dealing with the complexity of historical events. Conversely, taking a political–existential perspective better allows us to cut through the forest.

If migratory movements date back to the dawn of human history, what distinguishes the more recent era from earlier ones is not simply the intensity, frequency or multiplicity of this phenomenon. Considered in philosophical terms, migration – such as it is understood today – appears to all intents and purposes inscribed into modernity. It is legitimate, then, to distinguish between the migration of the ancients and that of the moderns, applying an already well-tested criterion (though here it will be necessary to run through further arguments and evidence).

In the past there were no lack of forms of movement, from nomadism to military conquests, from invasions to bold and adventurous journeys, up to and including the first real efforts to found colonies. All these forms of movement were dominated by the collectivity: it was the group that moved, as it sought to establish or widen its dominion over some territory. The individual participated in a collective (if not necessarily unanimous) action, in which she shared the same goal as others – or rather, the goal of some recognized political or military chief. The model *par excellence* of this is the Greek colony, conceived, according to the criteria advanced by Plato in the *Laws*, as a second-rank *pólis*. This latter resulted from an expulsion, from the distancing of outcasts and the unwanted, for whom, however, requirements of cohesion, organicity and compactness were also enforced, given their link with the homeland.[28]

How, then, is one to explain the great political exiles banished from the city, starting with Alcibiades? These extraordinary individuals – for instance, the exemplary case of Socrates – were already pointing towards modernity.[29] This is also true of the figure of the heroic traveller, which found its eminent expression in Ulysses. These were, then, aristocratic anticipations of the modern condition.

Ancient migration – which still knew nothing of nostalgia or duplication – restored the previous form of life somewhere else, without this change of place having effects on the self and its introspection. That is why its collective character asserted itself even when it was just an individual who moved. For this latter nonetheless remained protected, and was not exposed to the dizzying spatiality of modern migration.

In this sense, the ancient and the modern do not only constitute the criteria for a chronological scansion of migration, but also represent two different paradigms of this phenomenon, which can sometimes even appear in hybrid and mixed configurations.

10 Columbus and the image of the globe

Modern migration began from a new vision of space – from an unexpected image of the Earth. And we can date this shift very precisely, to 1492. This date immediately brings to mind – and rightly so – Christopher Columbus's first voyage, which set sail from the port of Palos de la Frontera that same year. But 1492 is also the date of the first world-map (a more or less fantastical portrayal), composed by the German navigator and cartographer Martin Behaim. What great discovery was arrived at with the circumnavigation of the globe? The discovery that the Earth is a round planet, and a far from hospitable one, both because it is not guarded by the reliable turning of the skies and because it no longer seemed to offer niches, cavities, internal spaces, within which life could find sanctuary. A globe mostly covered in water, in which large stretches of sea separate the so-called 'continents' far more than one might have imagined, no longer contained, received and protected. The inside was suddenly supplanted by the outside. This had immeasurable effects on the human self's efforts to locate itself. The catastrophe struck not only at the centre, but also at the world's peripheral regions. It became apparent that the farthest limits were not, in fact, limits at all, and that, beyond, there opened up a boundless, chilling space. As the abyss of the skies opened wide, there also opened up the endless atmospheric chasm of an absolute exteriority. The world was no longer a human abode. Exposed and without any safe haven, human beings realized that they would have to conduct their existence at the outer edges of the Earth's round surface, on some point of a wandering star lost in the universe, from which their gaze lost itself in the freezing, boundless outside.

This was the era of the 'image of the world' – as Heidegger would put it, in reference to modernity.[30] The world-map arose as an icon of the new era. It was impossible to preserve the immemorial interiority of native sites, of historic shelters, of remote refuges. Different forms of navigation, exploration and discovery gave rise to globalization. This also marked a new way of being in the world, for it coincided with the ruin of local ontologies. The imaginary casings of an indigenous life dissolved one after another. Globalization gradually directs the sense of space to the outside world; in this regard, it is the history of an externalization.[31] This seismic shock to humanity's traditional way of locating itself would have decisive side-effects for migration and migrating.

Another time and place: Seville in 1522. The eighteen sailors who had survived Magellan's voyage, begun in 1519, approached the city's port Sanlúcar de Barrameda. They were the first to have circumnavigated the globe, having passed via the extreme south-western tip of the Americas into the enormous expanse of ocean that they baptized the *pacific*, because 'not even one storm took place there'.[32] Their return was not like Ulysses' arrival back in Ithaca. The homeland of previous times had been transformed in the eyes of those who not only were returning from the opposite side of the Earth, but now had another sense of space – the one proper to the modern era. Seville was no longer Seville. It was no longer the centre around which the world was arranged – rather, it was a point on the surface of the globe, now observed from the outside. The circumnavigation of the Earth had prompted a disenchantment, destined to leave its mark on their way of seeing both place and their own selves. The returning sailors could not get their bearings again, for they now felt differently situated in the world.

Upon their return, these first eye-witnesses to the roundness of the planet brought both good and bad news. There did exist unknown regions and unexplored continents for them to occupy – but the Earth was also finite. The good news would drive conquerors, traders, missionaries, colonizers, gold-hunters and adventurers to follow in the circumnavigators' wake, opening up the great chapter of modern migration. But it was the bad news that had repercussions for not only the image of the world, but also the possibility of inhabiting it, if it truly was a globe – a circular and circumscribed extension of space. It was Kant who first raised the question. The paradoxical political–existential condition of the planet's inhabitants would be to be both ever more cramped and ever more isolated.

After the debunking of the myth of the Pillars of Hercules, which had previously stopped people looking beyond these magical obstacles, Columbus's voyages produced, and at the same time enshrined, Europe's dis-orientation. Such was the source of the New World, the second Europe in the Americas. Turning his back on the East, Columbus accidentally set off to the West, inaugurating what would be a Western modernity. Europe itself was Westernized. The legend of the far West would, for centuries, remain the horizon of a new ordering of the global space. While, even upon his fourth voyage, between 1502 and 1504, Columbus did not want to admit that he had found by mistake something he had never been looking for, he was certain that he had been entrusted with an eschatological task. He explicitly acknowledged this in his *Book of Prophesies*, displaying himself ever more convinced of the quasi-messianic value of his leap into the oceanic abyss.

Once studied and examined, the world-map offered each person the possibility of identifying her own geographical location. And it would become the instrument of an epoch-defining expansion. The homelands of ancient times were definitively set aside – even for those who did not set off travelling. The outside everywhere exploded whatever remained of the 'inside' space. There was no point on the globe that was not linked together with the rest.

The path towards the outside world thus also became a form of alienation, of decentring. Unless they insisted on keeping their eyes shut at all costs, no one could still feel that they were at the centre of the world. But alienation is also a kind of liberation. The leap into the ocean opened up a new and previously unthought path to salvation. For the desperate, the frustrated, the disappointed, the mad, the vagabonds, outcasts and persecuted, the sea became the alternative to death. The dream of a better life was projected onto the world beyond the seas, a 'world beyond' that was not heavenly but earthly. But it was also the site of another Earth.

Hence the utopian character of migration, which from the onset of its modern variant has been synonymous with emancipation.

Socialism-on-sea. The agitated and the unsatisfied embarked in the hope of breaking their own chains and finally accessing possibilities that were otherwise precluded for them. And also embarking were all those not ready to change course.

11 'We refugees': the scum of the Earth

Hannah Arendt was the first to reflect on migration as a global phenomenon. She identified the refugee as an exceptional figure, out of place in the territorial order based on nation-states, and even able – in her irreducible atopia – to point to a future global order, a new community to come. Adopting an external perspective – a view from that margin in which the refugee confronts state sovereignty – Arendt raised the question of the rights of the stateless and indicated that statelessness would be the great political theme of the twentieth century. Her prophecy came true above all in the last century.

It must, then, be a surprise that, in today's debate on the 'ethic of migration', Arendt is in fact absent, and that her ideas have not been re-elaborated such as to develop a political philosophy of reception, as they ought to have been. Even where, as in Seyla Benhabib's book, a reference to her does seem necessary, Arendt's thinking – accused of not providing solutions – is judged through a normative lens, very far from the critical aspiration that Arendt herself set for philosophy.[33] Different – or rather, opposite – is the case of Giorgio Agamben. He adopted the figure of the refugee in his *Homo sacer*, a further, overall reflection on 'bare life' in the presence of sovereign power. But, here, the motive for migrating is diluted and goes missing.[34] What has not found a following is not so much Arendt's key ideas, the foresight of her intuitions, which are indeed revived here and there, so much as her political–existential framework.

The short, explicitly autobiographical essay 'We Refugees', published in the English-language Jewish review *The Menorah Journal*, dates to January 1943. This essay marked a turning point in the philosophy of migration. Having only recently reached the United States – after fleeing Germany in 1933 and spending a long exile in, first, Prague and Geneva, and then several years in Paris – Arendt spoke about herself in the first person, also in the plural. She included herself in an uncomfortable 'we', the 'we' of those who were called – despite themselves – 'refugees'.[35] The phenomenology of this unprecedented figure, often delineated in narrative tones, has at least three distinctive traits. Right from the outset, in recognizing herself as a refugee, Arendt looked at the question from the side of the refugees, from outside of the state, from the outer limits of the law. Herself emotionally involved, she avoided the snares of self-compassion and separated herself from this 'we' so that she could then reflect on this shared existential condition, which she inspected by using the built-up experience of European philosophy. After all, the writer was a pupil of Heidegger who did not forget the uprootedness which is always-already at the foundation of human existence in the age of planetary technology.

Ultimately, a bitter and pungent irony marks the political summit of the essay, when in inserting herself back into the narrative 'we', Arendt connects herself to the 'hidden' Hebrew tradition – from Rahel Varnhagen to Heinrich Heine, Bernard Lazare and Franz Kafka – in which there prominently features the figure of the 'conscious pariah'. This latter is the refugee who does not reject her exile, her atopia, her marginality, but rather embraces them and takes them on her shoulders, as she openly lays claim to the status of the stateless, the outlaw, the person without a homeland. It is worth emphasizing that, also because of her Central-European and Ashkenazi outlook, Arendt strangely did not see the *marranos* – perhaps considering them only in the same way as religious refugees – as the beginning of this 'hidden tradition', the first of the proscribed able to subvert the very meaning of banishment and expulsion. It was a 'few refugees', Arendt writes, 'driven from country to country' who could represent the vanguard, not only of the Jewish people but of all people. Arendt felt that she belonged to this vanguard, and even spoke in its name. Hence the accusing notes and strongly political stamp of this short essay.

To be a refugee is to be in a condition of disgrace. The European Jews who found refuge on the other side of the Atlantic recognized this. They preferred simply to be called 'immigrants'. But what explains the discomfort with the label 'refugee'? 'With us', Arendt observed, the term had changed meaning. Before, it designated those who had been forced to flee and request asylum because of some action of theirs, or because they had upheld certain political ideas. This does not apply to the Jews, who could not say – either to others or themselves – what guilt they supposedly had to answer for. They could not explain why they had suddenly lost all they had – their homes, their occupations, their languages – or indeed why they had had to leave friends and relatives behind in the ghettoes or the internment camps. Of course, they had been saved. They thus began living again, hurrying to forget the past, imagining that their whole previous existence had been nothing more than a long exile, convincing themselves that only in their new country had they finally felt at home. But there was something not quite right about these 'odd optimists' who 'turn on the gas or make use of a skyscraper in quite an unexpected way'.[36] It is bizarre that among the saved there was such a high number of suicides, not only in Berlin or Vienna but also in New York, Los Angeles, Montevideo and Buenos Aires. These European Jews, who had committed no crime, nor dreamt – for the large majority, at least – of having any radical political view, did not manage to get their heads around their condition of exclusion, rendering them strangers and suspects even in the 'communities of native-born Jews' they ended up heading towards as they fled from Nazi Germany. Arendt refers to their condition as 'outlawing'. They were expelled because they were not wanted; they were not wanted because they were Jews. They sought refuge without being able to explain it. For many, the shame of feeling themselves excluded from any ties, of no longer having a place in the world, was unbearable.

Arendt points an accusing finger against assimilation, the incessant process of adaptation depicted in exemplary fashion by Mr Cohn, the Berlin Jew, the 'German super-patriot' after 1933 prepared to rapidly become a super-Czech or super-Austrian, and ultimately a real Frenchman.[37] Mr Cohn is the 'ideal immigrant' who, wherever fate may have taken him, 'promptly sees and loves the native mountains'.[38] Despite all his efforts to scrub away his Jewishness, in others' eyes he remains a Jew. The portrait of Mr Cohn sums up the tragic history of the assimilation that ended up destroying the German Jews. Mr Cohn creates an illusion for himself – that he can find a way out all by himself – and he is thus ready to present himself with a new national identity wherever he may be. He grotesquely thrashes around between the optimism that he can assimilate, and a confused, suicidal desperation. Like other immigrants, he is convinced that political developments have nothing to do with his fate.

The story of the Jewish refugees took on sharper contours in the light of the Holocaust, as Arendt wrote in perhaps the most widely read and discussed pages of her 1951 work *The Origins of Totalitarianism* – namely, the ones devoted to refugees all over the world. Seeking to portray these latter, Arendt turns to an unforgettable image. Ever since nation-states have carved up the planet, a 'scum of the Earth' has taken form between one border and another. It can be trampled on with impunity, yet never ceases its back-and-forth and its growth.[39] The scum is what remains of the carved-up Earth: the stateless, those without citizenship, the refugees, caught between national borders, who appear as oversized waste, foreign bodies, undesirable beings. No place is set out for them in the global order. Here emerges a new human race: the 'superfluous'.

Arendt was the first to identify, in its proper complexity, the appearance of refugees as a mass phenomenon. She reconstructed the historical coordinates, demonstrated the core philosophical questions, and raised the decisive political questions. It is in the scenario outlined by Arendt's text that it is possible today to reflect on the epoch-defining theme of migration, at a moment in which the decline of the nation-state has still not been consummated.

Everything started with the First World War, when the great empires that had held together many different nations – from the Austro-Hungarian Empire to its Russian and Ottoman counterparts – broke up. This overturned the previous demographic and territorial ordering of Central-Eastern Europe; a new order emerged from the peace treaties, which was now made up of nation-states that lacked homogeneity and thus had all the greater need to consolidate themselves. Enormous masses of people now moved, in just a short period of time: 1,500,000 White Russians; 1,000,000 Greeks; 700,000 Armenians; 500,000 Bulgarians; and hundreds of thousands of Hungarians, Romanians and Germans. But the unforeseen complication was the so-called 'national minorities' who could not find any place for themselves in this new order. The 'Minority Treaties', which were supposed to protect them, proved ineffective. This was a warning sign for a problem that would intensify over the subsequent years and decades, especially in the period between the two world wars, when Nazism in Germany and the Civil War in Spain helped swell the ranks of refugees.

The attempt to make the European states' borders conform to nations brought out a profound contradiction: the impossibility of guaranteeing the rights of whoever was not a citizen of a given nation. This was paradoxical, given that, if anything, it was those who were condemned to statelessness and denied the rights guaranteed by citizenship that most needed to be defended and protected.

Caused and simultaneously penalized by the nation-state, statelessness in Arendt's view became the great political question of modernity. If we look at the provenance of the Italian term for statelessness, *apolidia*, we see that it is made up of the negative alpha, *a-*, and *pólis*, city; and, as this suggests, the term designates whoever lacks citizenship. Nor does this imply that the stateless person is a new figure. Rather, it was a figure already known at least as far back as the Greek tragedians. We could note countless illustrious examples of this. But these were also individual cases that concerned elite figures, and once they were in exile the problem was resolved through their entrance into some other *pólis* – indeed, in a world that still seemed open and boundless. Arendt instead spoke of the mass statelessness which, in a world subdivided into nation-states, risked not being a temporary phase, but instead mutating into a final, irredeemable condition. Even more so, given that every war, every revolution, every political development added fresh waves of stateless people, which thus prevented this phenomenon ever being definitively resolved.

If before, in the imperial context, the *Heimatlosen*, the stateless, could still be tolerated, subsequently, with the organization of humanity into families of nations, this figure – still suffused with a romantic aura – stepped aside in favour of the stateless, who are also right-less. The stateless person is not *national* and is not *native* to the nation – two words that each refer to the other, given their common etymology. The nation corresponds to *birth*.[40]

When national states do consolidate themselves, playing on the homogeneity of the population and their rootedness in the territory – two static and restrictive criteria – the nation gets the upper hand over rights and makes the state its own tool. In this fiction, through which birth becomes the foundation of sovereignty, Arendt aptly identifies the ineluctable decline of the nation-state. What destabilizes it are precisely the anomalies that take form from the outset: minorities and the stateless. In truth only half-stateless – for, legally speaking, they do belong to the state organism – minorities remain dependent on governments' indulgence and consigned to the hatred coming from the majority. And, so long as the treaties that ought to protect them remain a dead letter, the minorities are not absorbed, but instead become a permanent institution.

But the problem of the stateless is even more acute than this. The height of anomaly and the embodiment of deviance – caught in the middle, in the web of nation-states that are woven around the Earth – the stateless person discovers that, not having state protection, she has also lost what had been considered inalienable human rights. Out of place in the political order, she is tolerated only so long as her condition appears temporary: either repatriation or naturalization lies in wait. But when it becomes clear that getting rid of her is much more difficult than imagined, then the stateless person – she who seeks refuge without finding it, bare human life not wrapped in any national flag – seems like a challenge to the criteria and state norms which are no longer able to 'normalize' her. Her position deteriorates, becomes worse than that of the enemy-foreigner who is at least defended and aided by his own government. It is discovered that the stateless person is 'un-exileable', for no one will take her in, no one will accord her leave to remain.[41] She is the undesireable *par excellence,* even to the point of jeopardizing her right to asylum, the only residue of human rights left in international relations.

Anything but temporary, the condition of the stateless proves to be an enduring one, and it continues ever further. Statelessness spreads its reach. The scum seems to spring from an inexhaustible reservoir that ends up diluting any clear distinctions between naturalized citizens, the displaced and stateless, refugees and migrants. Those 'expelled from' the 'old trinity of state-people-territory' give rise to a growing movement.[42]

> What is unprecedented is not the loss of a home but the impossibility of finding a new one. Suddenly, there was no place on earth where migrants could go without the severest restrictions, no country where they would be assimilated, no territory where they could found a new community of their own. This, moreover, had next to nothing to do with any material problem of overpopulation; it was a problem not of space but of political organization. Nobody had been aware that mankind, for so long a time considered under the image of a family of nations, had reached the stage where whoever was thrown out of one of these tightly organized closed communities found himself thrown out of the family of nations altogether.[43]

The novelty was not the fact of being expelled, but that of no longer finding any refuge in the world. Arendt shed a spotlight on this nudity of the refugee, who required further protection yet instead provided the grounds for an intolerable scandal. The state exercises its sovereignty also over the refugee – and its sovereignty is never as absolute as in matters of emigration and expulsion. This is most obvious when it is the totalitarian state making interventions, preferring the politics of de-nationalization and deportation to repatriation and naturalization. But Arendt cautions that, between the totalitarian state and the democratic state, there is a difference only of degree. The production and rejection of undesirables is a particular trait not of totalitarianism, but of the nation-state itself, as it seeks to normalize this deviance and, where it does not manage this, consigns these pariahs of humanity to the transit areas and internment camps, the only 'substitute ... homeland' the world yet has to offer to refugees.[44]

The stateless, relegated to the sites of banishment, the *banlieues* of the great states and the metropoles, are, then, by definition 'outlaws' – illegals. To reside in some territory without authorization becomes a crime. This is but further proof that the state's law is deeper-rooted than human rights. When politics comes into contact with statelessness, with the illegality that is nothing other than a lack of protections, it reaches its own outer limit. The state consigns refugees to a policing operation empowered with an exceptional sovereignty.

Arendt raises the question of migrant reception: how to make room and give rights to those who are left at the edges of an ever more globalized global humanity – to those who are denied the possibility of participating in a shared world.

12 What rights for the stateless?

It is precisely by assuming the viewpoint of the stateless, of the displaced, of refugees, that Arendt can point to the paradox that the French Revolution bequeathed to subsequent centuries: the Rights of Man and the Citizen. While these rights ought to allow for migrant reception, they are in fact exactly what prevents it. For Arendt, they also mark the limits of politics. The revolutionaries who formulated them considered themselves citizens. Thus, the rights accorded to Man are but the privileges of the citizen. Those who do not have citizenship, or who cannot show papers proving that they do, do not enjoy the protection of the law or belong to any community. In short, those who have nothing but their own bare humanity cannot enjoy those rights. 'Man' presupposes the citizen. These inalienable and irreducible rights, not deriving from any authority, are natural only by way of the naturalization entailed in citizenship. Indeed, whoever becomes a citizen is 'naturalized'. Still at work, here, is the fatal connection between birth and nation. Once again, it is the sovereign state that dictates the law, and recognizes only the members of the nation – citizens – as having civil rights.

When, in the course of the twentieth century, the masses of 'foreigners' deprived of citizenship and legal protection burst onto the stage of history, the paradox emerged in all its gravity. Indeed, the question exploded. Nation-states looked on at these masses with apprehension, convinced, nonetheless, that they could assimilate them. Everything would be absorbed back into the state-centric order. But historical events belied this expectation. The masses of 'foreigners' would become ever more numerous.

Arendt had a direct experience, to which she gave voice in her thinking. She saw a naked humanity shipwrecked – one that could assert nothing other than its humanity itself. No longer having any nation of origin, these foreigners found no other nation to offer them refuge. Thus, precisely the human beings who were most defenceless, were left without any defence. It is, in fact, the law that protects, not the fact of humanity. But the law stops at national borders. Outside that? There is no cosmopolitan law that guarantees human rights. Arendt writes in one of her most famous passages:

> We became aware of the existence of a right to have rights (and that means to live in a framework where one is judged by one's actions and opinions) and a right to belong to some kind of organized community, only when millions of people emerged who had lost and could not regain these rights because of the new global political situation. The trouble is that this calamity arose not from any lack of civilization, backwardness, or mere tyranny, but, on the contrary, that it could not be repaired, because there was no longer any 'uncivilized' spot on earth, because whether we like it or not we have really started to live in One World. Only with a completely organized humanity could the loss of home and political status become identical with expulsion from humanity altogether.[45]

For want of any 'right to have rights', those who most ought to be protected are instead marked with the stigma of superfluity. They are then consigned to the world's police, to be knocked back, deported and interned. Their condition is even worse than that of someone who has committed a crime. For this later enjoys a certain juridical status, and no one can deny her a trial. On the contrary, the foreigner can be arbitrarily arrested and imprisoned, sent to a concentration camp, without her legitimately being able to appeal to any law.[46] Sometimes, it can even be enough just for her to have set foot inside a sovereign state's territory – as if even this could be a crime.

Arendt attacks the irritating *naïveté* of those liberals who believed, and still do believe, in the rights of the individual and proclaim her abstract freedom in highfalutin' tones. The misfortune of the stateless, the foreigners, the displaced is not their lack of freedom or of equality before the law, but rather the lack of a community. Those who have been pushed back towards the perilous outside edges, to the fearsome banishment zones – the very areas where sub-humanity is produced – ask to be accommodated, to have a place in a community. But, for Arendt, community does not mean the nation. Rather, the implicit question is whether there exist political communities that are not delimited by national borders, and whether it is possible to find a place for the foreigner in a reception policy in which the common is not reduced to a nation's own self-immunization.

The 'right to have rights' – or, if you will, the right to belonging – is the dilemma bequeathed by Arendt, who was sceptical over the possibility of guaranteeing this right within the world's state-centric order. And the dilemma has endured, while the paradox of human rights has proven to be the paradox of democracy itself.

13 The frontier of democracy

Despite the consensus that seems to envelop it, democracy is a highly problematic, debated and contested concept. Its contours are fluid, its very essence is elusive, and its foundation vacuous. Its definition is itself the subject of unending controversy. What is democracy? One can answer this question only by confronting logical contradictions and working through political antinomies and ethical dilemmas. Chantal Mouffe has aptly spoken of the 'democratic paradox'.[47] Beyond its semi-mythical origins in the Greek *agora*, democracy draws legitimacy from two different philosophical sources.[48]

Hence the tension inscribed in the heart of liberal democracy, which violently rebounds on the question of the border. It is migration that brings this tension to light. Or, rather, we could say that the border is the very site of the democratic paradox: on the one hand, it delimits the territory over which democratic sovereignty is exercised, and on the other, it separates the citizens – members of the community – from the foreigners who try to enter; on the one hand, it protects the *demos* and its power, and on the other hand, it discriminates and excludes, violating any principle of equality. As Étienne Balibar has observed, the border is the 'absolutely non-democratic condition' of democracy.[49] A line of partition, which decisively contributes to constituting the body politic, it seems to be the necessary – and nonetheless troubling – condition of the democratic sovereignty that is not able to justify the discriminatory act of closure theoretically, either to itself or to the excluded themselves. Still, this embarrassing silence is extremely telling. Almost euphemistically, this blind spot of democratic theory is called the 'boundary problem'.[50] On closer inspection, it becomes apparent that the paradox is in fact a genuine vicious circle, for every decision on the border presupposes a circumscribed community whose existence is made possible through a demarcation which in every sense resembles a border. That is to say, this decision starts out from a presupposition that still has to be tested. In more concrete terms: the *de facto* situation precedes the *de jure* situation. In the citizens' eyes, the migrants who reach the unbreachable threshold of the border have committed not only the original crime of having moved there, but the impardonable wrong of bringing to light the democratic paradox, which is to say the constitutive dilemma between the assertion of sovereignty and the recognition of human rights. The frontier of democracy is not, then, only its inevitable outer edge, but also –and above all – its ruinous internal limit.

The two different – in certain aspects, opposed – philosophical sources from which democracy originates have over time mixed their waters, to the point of almost totally confusing them. So, it is worth briefly reviewing the course they have taken. Surrounding these sources is the landscape of the French Revolution. The first source, which had begun to flow already before then, thanks to its eminent precursor Jean-Jacques Rousseau, is self-legislation, popular sovereignty or – according to his famous formulation – 'the general will'. The people is elevated to the rank of legislator: this is democracy. Following in the wake of Rousseau, Kant, too, understood the problem in analogous terms: popular sovereignty is the transformation of power, which now becomes self-legislating. Contrary to what is generally imagined, for neither of them did this mean the overthrow of royal sovereignty or the result of a partition, a pact, an accord. The 'social contract' – however misleading this expression may be – is, rather, the model of a political power that legitimizes itself through democratic self-legislation. Kant does much to clarify this when he writes that 'Thus only the united and consenting will of all, when each decides for all precisely the same as all decide for each, can legislate, therefore only the general, united will of the people can legislate.'[51] 'All rights' emanate from this sovereign power of the people. When a political decision that concerns others is taken, the risk of injustice – Kant argues – is always lurking; this risk decreases if the decision directly concerns whoever is making it. Self-legislation means that the people is both subject and object of its laws.

In Kant's words, one can already see an alarm sign, a warning of a concern. What is to become of individual rights? Can they be reconciled with the collective will? This question is all the more starkly posed when this latter has to disregard particular interests if it wants to apply universal laws. The very exercise of popular sovereignty, which itself provides rights, could end up trampling on them. For his part, Rousseau worked around the problem by identifying the self-constitution of the sovereign people as something close to a political–existential act through which atomized individuals turned themselves into solidary citizens, thus giving rise to a collective body, a *moi commun*, a 'common me', a new subject prepared for an unprecedented legislative praxis, empowered by a permeating moral virtue and free of any private ties. The collective will would, then, enjoy an absolute sovereignty. Conscious of the threats weighing down on this will – exposed to corrosive forces and unhealthy influences – Rousseau suggested possible defence mechanisms, most importantly including a rigorously egalitarian political participation.

But there soon came to light the fatal slippery slope that would, in the twentieth century, become the majority's authoritarian turn – thus showing all the defects of a democracy thus conceived. The general will: a fiction that asserts itself by repressing the heterogeneous individual wills. And a supposed autonomy allows evident traces of heteronomy to emerge.

The second source is liberalism, in its multiple streams. It places the accent on individual rights, while it interprets popular sovereignty as a principle that requires restrictions. In such a context, it is worth delving into the image of the contract. Considered as a field of contractual dispute in which each person asserts their own rights and defends their private interests, democracy is hollowed out to the point that it becomes an instrument that appears all the more legitimate the more it demonstrates its own neutrality. This to the point that it is reduced to nothing but the conditions that render possible the peaceable coexistence of a plurality of different life projects, with a view to a consensus that can be reached by way of reason. In the free contractual exchange – no less a fiction than the general will – it is difficult for the weaker or for minorities to prevail. In this declension of the concept of democracy, individual rights which ought to have been defended from universal rationality precisely because they constitute a deterrent, an antinomic potential, are pushed outside of politics, in an aleatory morality.[52]

Liberal democracy does not eliminate the paradox but intensifies it. The discourse on human rights ends up looking like a paroxysmal contradiction, since what is first and foremost being denied is that freedom of movement which has always been held to be a primordial right. Freedom is protected within, not outside. The same can be said of equality.[53] There is no universal idea that extends beyond the borders – unless this can be democratically justified.

Be it radical or liberal, democracy breaks against the border and turns back on itself, like a wave. It denies itself precisely in order to affirm itself.[54] Democratic inclusion simultaneously reveals itself to be an undemocratic exclusion. The borders that separate citizens from foreigners can be changed only by the citizens, while the foreigners have to respect them. So it seems difficult to legitimize in democratic terms a political praxis that oppresses these same individuals, excluding them and discriminating against them as non-citizens. The unilateral control of the border is the exercise of a coercive power in the hands of the democratic sovereign, which avails itself of this power in order to territorially circumscribe the system of representation. Rather than take the limit-case of the

border as a permanent injunction to critically reflect on democracy
and its limits, all the attempts at accounting for and justifying the
closing of the borders more or less ingenuously and intentionally
assume and reproduce the democratic paradox. For this reason,
from the outset, they are null and void.

14 The sovereigntism of closed borders

Michael Walzer was the first to clearly spell out the need – and,
indeed, duty – for the community to defend itself from immigration,
pushing back whoever comes from the outside and drawing a clear
line between citizens and foreigners. An exponent of the heterogeneous current perhaps mistakenly called 'communitarianism'
(for it reacts against theories centred on the individual and her
freedoms), Walzer himself moved within the terms of a normative
and liberal politics. The difference was that he chose the kaleidoscope of the community in order to consider the various questions
of justice, equality and democracy. The pages he dedicated to the
theme of immigration appeared in his well-received 1983 book
Spheres of Justice.[55] While this text is dated – it was published in the
period of incipient globalization, when migratory movements had
not yet taken on their present dimensions – it nonetheless constitutes an unmissable reference point, both theoretically – offering
a well-argued and complete sovereigntist perspective – and in
practical terms, given that it indicates, often tacitly, the guidelines
of the current politics of exclusion. After that point, Walzer would
repeatedly return to this theme in order to reassert his initial theses.[56]
    Striking in Walzer's reflection is the inexplicable lack of any
mention of Arendt. This is all the more noticeable given that Walzer
seems to adopt her critique of an abstract and simplistic concept
of equality that overlooks concrete historical conditions. Arendt
had raised caution over those human rights that were destined
to remain mere waste paper if they were asserted by an isolated
individual, outside of any community. What sense would it make
to invoke the right to move, or to flee, without first having asserted
one's belonging? The knotty question at the centre of immigration
is the question of belonging to the community. But, in unravelling
this, Walzer took a path opposite to the one suggested by Arendt.
    His starting point is the political community, understood as that
shared world of language, history and culture from which there also
spring analogous ways of feeling and thinking. The community is
not, however, a mere context: rather, it is a good – indeed, the most
important good. Belonging to the community is the foundation

of life itself, for it is the condition of any other good that may be distributed. Who remains outside of the community is condemned to have nothing, whereas whoever is within it, who is a member of the community, can take part in the distributive justice. Walzer describes a landscape pockmarked with communities, beyond which there opens up the political void. Here looms the spectre of a global government, which, insofar as it is the result of an artificial universal accord, would centralize power and end up proving a bureaucratic tyranny.

'Within' and 'outside' sanction an irreparable political–ontological separation. Walzer would never step back from this, even in subsequent texts. A constitutive pillar of the community, belonging – membership – is a valuable good whose attribution cannot be entrusted to some external authority. This must, instead, result from the considered verdict of an internal decision. In fact, the future of the community, its ability to endure, depends on this decision. How, then, can this good be equitably distributed? This is the decisive question that Walzer raises. The theme of immigration is thus properly inserted within the wider framework of distributive justice.

But this further move already marks a disappointing closedness: for the idea of distributive justice presupposes a delimited world. Whoever is within benefits from this justice; whoever is outside can take part in exchange, above all on the market, but in her vulnerable position she remains excluded from all the goods that the community distributes. Those who do not have a 'reserved place', who are external, are the stateless. As Walzer himself deigns to comment, 'Statelessness is a condition of infinite danger.'[57]

This does not in fact drive him to pose the problem of the stateless, who are banished to a planet-wide beyond. On the contrary, he raises the question of migrants, those who move from poor and authoritarian countries to freer and more prosperous ones, in the attempt to change their residence and citizenship. This phenomenon is taken for understandable but it is also implicitly condemned – without this disparity itself raising question marks. For Walzer, the ordinary and necessary action is the absolute action of sovereignty, against which Arendt had pointed an accusing finger.

The political community is called on to decide. Walzer sets himself up as a spokesman of the elite countries to which everyone would like to move; he speaks as a citizen of the American community to which everyone would like to be admitted; he passes into the first-person plural, defending the choice that 'we' have made. And he states that: 'we who are already members do the choosing, in accordance with our own understanding of what membership means in our community and of what sort of a community we want to have'.[58] Only the sovereign 'we' of the citizens can decide whom to admit or whom to exclude, according to its own criteria. The others, the 'extraneous', those who are 'like us, but not our own kind', have no right to intervene and no influence, if not to champion their own admission. The troubling term 'candidates' recurs frequently. Migrants are like candidates who want to get into some elite university where, as they know, the admissions process is governed by the limited number of places. This disconcerting and inopportune comparison is bound to have major repercussions. It conveys the idea that immigration involves a sort of exam, which allows one either to 'pass' or else be rejected. But it also presents as merely obvious other presuppositions, which, on closer inspection, are far from self-evident. Namely, that citizens ought to exercise the sovereign power of choice; that the make-up of the community itself can be constituted by a summary decision; and, ultimately, that it is possible to decide with whom to cohabit. The internal perspective, the sovereigntist outlook, are thus affirmed. After Walzer, democracy becomes compatible with the politics of exclusion.

15 Philosophers against Samaritans

The boundary between citizens and foreigners cannot be overcome. Or it can only be overcome by citizens themselves in the exceptional case of 'mutual aid', which hospitality is limited to, and conditional on. Taking due caution, Walzer evokes the parable of the Good Samaritan and the chance encounter – at sea, in the desert, by the wayside – with a stranger in need of assistance. Aid is, indeed, necessary, so long as it does not involve risks. And it is 'our morality' that imposes the obligation to save the stranger who has been wounded or whose life is in danger. This is not only an individual obligation; it also applies to a group. In this case, however, the aid is well defined – also because it takes on a political colouration. And this means that hospitality and care are temporary. It is unnecessary to get tied up with the injured guest; one cannot let one's own life be determined by chance encounters. With a slippage from the individual to the community, and vice versa, the pretension to set the terms of cohabitation is advanced once more.

In the backdrop here, it is not difficult to make out the classic argument on the right to asylum as formulated by Kant. For him, whereas hospitality is indeed legitimate – this being understood as a temporary visit – permanent residency is not, however, to be granted. Aid does not, then, amount to a welcome. To interpret the question like that would be to explode the border between internal and external. The encounter with the foreigner in need of assistance takes place at the margins, at the edge of the planetary void. Hence, one should immediately step back from this encounter, if one does not want to jeopardize the community, which must, after all, have some admissions policy if it is indeed to remain a community. Membership of the community cannot just be distributed willy-nilly.

Who knows? Perhaps one day everyone could be part of a planetary state, which Walzer imagines as a socialist totalitarianism, or else – and this would be the inverse, libertarian hypothesis – the world would be a place for uprooted strangers to wander. In the one case, membership of the community would be more 'equitably' granted, and in the other there would be nothing to distribute. But, so long as the world is subdivided into political communities, immigration must be regulated.

Walzer openly defends the sovereign state, whose walls preserve the 'cohesion' of the community, and indeed its very existence. To knock down these walls would mean creating so many little fortresses. Able to guarantee the proper fit between *demos* and *éthnos*, and to ensure that democratic sovereignty is at one with the 'political community of fate' – formed according to an outright 'ecological' protection of the nation – the state has the authority to control the admissions policy and to 'restrain the flow of immigrants'.[59] It is no surprise that in this state-centric vision Walzer indulges and reproduces the paradox inscribed in international law, through which, while emigration has to be free, immigration is instead limited or prohibited. The right to leave and the right to enter are supposedly 'morally' asymmetrical, for while the former is purely individual, the other clashes with the community's unchallengeable right to self-determination.

In this perspective, community is not just the fact of living in the same vicinity – a space indifferent to who comes and goes, and above all to who decides to reside there. It would instead be more like a club whose founding associates can 'select' aspiring new members. The bizarre comparison suggested even by the very term 'member' – as if the status of the citizen could be equated with that of a partner or adherent – serves to emphasize not so much the need for closeness as the requirement to be 'admitted'. Walzer is conscious of the danger lurking within his position: namely, the danger of racism. How can anyone forget Ellis Island? And the laws introduced to guarantee the homogeneity of a country intended to be white and Anglo-Saxon? But he makes this only a question of the necessary criteria, while also holding on to the idea that it is, indeed, legitimate to select incomers. The state has a sovereign right which it exercises in its political – perhaps one ought to say, 'biopolitical'

– choice of new arrivals, who are admitted if they respond to the conditions and characteristics of the host country.

If this is right 'in legal terms', it may not be so at a moral level. It often happens that citizens feel 'morally obliged' to open their own countries' doors to some 'national or ethnic "relatives"'.[60] Here, the state less resembles a tight-knit circle than a family whose members feel themselves linked not to those who have been *chosen*, so much as to those who may live far away but are nonetheless relatives. Here, the bind of 'consanguinuity' prevails. Walzer underlines how useful and well founded this is, both in terms of so-called 'family reuunion' – the recognition of a worker's right to have her relatives back with her again – and also in the sense that the state becomes a refuge for the members of the nation who, having remained outside its juridical boundaries for historical reasons, now turn to the 'motherland' with legitimate expectations. The political expression of a community life that extends beyond its territorial limits, the nation-state is like a big family that welcomes back its own children, whether according to the criteria of birth, blood or descent.

The example given is one dating back to the early twentieth century, namely the example of the Greeks hunted out of Turkey, and the Turks hunted out of Greece, who were granted the right to return to their respective national families. The treaty they signed at Lausanne in 1923, with which the Greek and Turkish governments committed to exchange their respective minorities, was referred to in Carl Schmitt's *Constitutional Theory*; the German jurist saw this instrument as the opportunity to restore territories' cultural integrity. In controlling immigration, it is necessary to take recourse to 'modern methods' such as expatriation and denaturalization and to take measures to reject 'undesirable elements', even to the point of eliminating 'foreign bodies'. Thinking about the effects that these theories of Schmitt's produced for the Jewish population of Nazi Germany, one can detect the danger of parallels like the one Walzer makes between the state and the family, a rash comparison that forgets even the recent past.

Yet not only blood, but also soil, finds a new legitimacy in his pages, where it is forcefully asserted that the nation-state is grounded in territory. Belonging is a stable and static relationship. The 'we' of the community is rooted, established. Walzer defends the state's territorial jurisdiction by adopting Hobbes's classic argument, according to which each person has the individual right to a 'place to live'. This right is conserved even after the social contract and can even be advanced against the state. But it is precisely in order to protect the place in which each individual lives that the state asserts its own jurisdiction over the soil. Thus, territorial law has both an individual and a collective form, even if this latter is derived – and thus legitimate – only as a protection. Even conceding that the place in which one lives cannot be determinate – it could be any place on Earth – Walzer does not hesitate in indicating where it is: it is the place where the inhabitants have always lived. And for those who have changed place? The norm is a sedentary existence, whereas movement is rather more of a stretch – and is not foreseen in advance. Moreover, Walzer claims, 'the link between people and land is a crucial feature of national identity'. He sharply criticizes political projects – such as that of the Austrian socialist Otto Bauer – that seek to deterritorialize political communities.[61] Giving up on the territorial state would mean giving up on any real self-determination.

This is the crucial point for confronting the theme of immigrant foreigners. Who decides the admissions policy? There is no room for doubt: it is 'those who are already there' who should decide. This would mean sanctioning the primacy of the first-comers, if it were not for the fact that, precisely in the case of the USA, the native Americans have to be considered the 'original inhabitants' on that land. But for Walzer this problem is easily resolved, for it is sufficient to govern them peacefully. In between the lines, in what is not said, one can make out the old adage according to which a people that has not given itself state form cannot do anything.

It is the 'we' of the community that manages immigration policy, through what is clearly a political choice. Can the destitute, the stateless, the famished, the needy be admitted simply because they are foreigners? Of course not. The democratic sovereign people can push back at the border whoever wants to enter its own territory – even if that means the displaced and victims of persecution. Never mind if they are only few in number. For if the numbers did increase, then the people would risk being drowned. One cannot assert the right to live in some place, against the host state itself. So the only ones who can be admitted are the few who demonstrate their affinity with the 'we' of the community, who do not prejudice its cohesion and do not damage its ethno-cultural homogeneity. It is, then, necessary to wish the displaced good luck in their entrance exam. This is liberal democracy, with all its humanitarian limits, which has no obligation to deal with other people's misery. Emma Lazarus's words were noble, generous: 'Give me your tired, your poor, Your huddled masses yearning to breathe free ...' Walzer cites them only in order to emphasize how far they stand from any realistic immigration policy, and to caution that the Samaritans of each era are, if not a danger, at least a great nuisance. Hence, mutual aid should not in any way upset sovereign self-determination.

The members of a community have the right to 'shape the resident population'. The criterion of homogeneity stipulates that the stranger be gradually naturalized. In this sense, Walzer distinguishes between admission and welcome. To be admitted does not yet mean to belong – that is, to be recognized as a citizen. The condition of the 'resident foreigner' can only be a temporary one. Residence brings with it citizenship. This should avoid the formation, within the community, of a layer of people without political rights – like the metics in ancient Athens – or a mass of guest workers exposed to all manner of exploitation.

These proposals of social-democratic fairness, which have had great influence and are still today successfully proclaimed, are based on a belonging that cannot be exported, and a territorial justice that defends only the interests of those who have the privilege of being within. And this consigns whoever is on the outside, facing the planet's most adverse conditions, to isolation and penury.

16 The primacy of citizens and the dogma of self-determination

Walzer's pioneering pages contain *in nuce* arguments, considerations and themes that would later be adopted in justification of closing down the borders. The hinge that his thesis pivots around is the right to self-determination, which allows a community settled in a given state-territory to reject migrants. This does not mean systematic closedness and exclusion, but rather the power to control new arrivals and regulate residency.

There is a wide range of positions in this regard, running from more 'humanitarian' ones, disposed to introducing elastic criteria from time to time, to, on the other hand, the extremely rigid ones that seek to defend fellow citizens alone, excluding foreigners in all circumstances. Communitarians, nationalists, liberals and modern cosmopolitans wield different lines of argument, but they agree on the sovereigntism invoked already by Walzer: 'At some level of political organization, something like the sovereign state must take shape and claim the authority to make its own admissions policy.'[62] Despite their different emphases and distinct ideological hues, in the positions of those who support rejecting people, we can identify three main shared arguments: self-determination, the integrity of an identity, and the ownership of territory. These arguments are closely connected and each corresponds to the others. One can demand self-determination insofar as one can boast of a territory and exhibit some identity that ought to be defended. Without overlooking the connections between these themes, it is useful to consider each of them individually.

Self-determination is but the most modern and pragmatic version of the 'self-legislation' supported by Rousseau and Kant, which is based on the principle of sovereignty. The state asserts the right to defend its borders, even by force, appealing to its own unchallengeable sovereignty. This, even if it means impairing the freedom of movement clearly granted by the French Constitution of 1791, itself a co-originator of the general will. Even if self-determination has multiple different inflections, the sovereigntist argument is very fragile theoretically, and, notwithstanding all its rhetorical acrobatics, it is unable to hide a tautological shift, in which the response appears as a repetition of the premises. Indeed, in no way does it succeed in justifying why on Earth the rights of those who belong to a state-community should prevail over the universal rights recognized by the Jacobins' policy.[63] In this sense, the pretension to self-determination is rather more the sovereign performative act with which the state-centric order delimits, or rather, re-delimits and again marks out its arbitrary historical confines, held up as somehow natural. This discriminatory act can be summarized as 'Silence delimits itself!'

Depending on how it is interpreted, self-determination means either autonomous determination, freedom of choice, a deliberative autonomy – i.e. in its liberal sense – or else a collective determination of the self, the possibility of defining, moulding and preserving the identitarian self in the present and future – i.e. in its communitarian sense. Often the two senses of the term mix together and get confused. It is hardly worth mentioning that, especially in the latter case, self-determination becomes a prop to integrity.

Adopting the same themes as Walzer, and even writing in more conservative tones, the liberal nationalist David Miller explains in his recently published book (with the emblematic title *Strangers in Our Midst*) that self-determination is the control that the political community exercises in order to avoid its 'self' changing over time, and the presence of immigrants influencing the 'composition of the civic body'. Self-determination implies the existence of a group crystallized in a self, 'cohesive enough' to share values and have common objectives, to the point that the members of this harmonious and unitary whole 'can feel that they are in control of their own destiny'.[64] The more cohesive the self is, the better it is able to self-determine; through its democratic sovereignty it imposes a migration regime that, unconcerned with human rights and all other ethical-political considerations, limits entry onto the territory as

befits the nation's identity, history, culture, interests and the intentions of the 'natives'.[65]

Proposed anew over the last decade, albeit in different forms, the
thesis that links self-determination to community of fate – decreeing
citizens' uncontested priority over immigrants – has enjoyed
enormous success and become the dogma of recent migration
policies. The closing of the borders should, in large part, be traced
back to this thesis, which sanctions the exclusion of the non-citizen.
The attempt to vest the discriminatory act in moral trappings,
denouncing the recourse to selective criteria such as sex, skin colour
and religion, does not stand up. This is, at all events, an ethnocentric
exclusion process incompatible with the principles of a democracy.
No one knows and no one can say why *raison d'état* should override
the rights of the stateless, or why the settledness of citizens should
prevail over migrants' mobility.

With the same strategic goal of reinforcing barriers and closing
borders, liberals interpret self-determination in terms of 'deliberative autonomy'. Again, Walzer is the point of reference, with
his comparison between a state and a private club: freedom of
association legitimizes the power to include or exclude. If, after
introducing this comparison with some caution, Walzer nonetheless
drops it, looking rather more to the analogy with the family, others
repropose this same comparison, but in a narrower sense. The state
is like a club – or, better, it is a club – which can autonomously
accept members for itself or reject them. Here, the pretext of a
harmonious, identitarian self is not even needed in order to justify
rejection. Nor, indeed, is any specific justification needed; there is
nothing secret, mysterious or complicated in the right to choose.
According to the classical liberal model, sovereignty is exercised
through the contract. It can even parade a certain universal
rationality and boast of moderately cosmopolitical applications.
But this demonstrates that, contrary to what is generally believed,
the liberal principles of universalism do not in any way prevent
discrimination.

17 If the state were a club: liberalism based on exclusion

All this becomes sharply self-evident when pure contractualism is
taken to its extreme conclusions, as in the arguments of Christopher
H. Wellman. Accepting that a state functions like a club, citizens
can accept or reject the immigrants who request entry, just as a
club can do with new members. In both cases, freedom of association is the principle that applies.[66] The members of a club are not

compelled to justify their choice, to clarify why aspiring members seemed too extraneous and culturally different. It is *their* club – and this gives them their right to self-determination. 'Legitimate states may choose not to associate with foreigners, including potential immigrants, as they see fit.'[67] If this were not the case, that would mean violating a right that also pertains to individuals. The example given is marriage: each woman should be free to refuse a suitor's proposal, if she does not want to share her life with him. Conjugal freedom is part of self-determination, too. The same can be said of religious freedom. For Wellman, these are self-regarding affairs, in which each person should be able to enjoy freedom of choice. This also implies freedom of rejection. And this argument is then projected from the individual to the collective: 'just as any person can decide who to marry (and if to marry), likewise a group of conationals can decide who to welcome into their own political community (and if to welcome them)'.[68] The fact that Wellman then distances himself from the classical doctrine of sovereignty, as he restricts this prerogative to legitimate states alone, does not change the substance of his discourse.[69] In short, the right to exclude new arrivals is legitimate because citizens, in their autonomy, are free to determine and control their own 'self', free to choose with whom they will cohabit, without necessarily referring to any cultural premises.

This line of argument is absurd – indeed in countless ways; the unjustified oscillation between individual and community, the equivalence drawn between the intimacy of a married couple and denial of residence, and indeed the ridiculous analogy between the state and a club, which reduces migrant reception policy to nothing more than the possibility of participating in a game of golf. Such images clash sharply with those of the people knocked back by force at the border, those who are fleeing political persecution, those escaping disastrous economic conditions. This is not a matter of the free choice of the marital suitor or the aspiring club member, but a request for aid made by those who are forced to risk their lives. It is hardly worth underlining, either, that the analogy between state and club does not hold up, even if simply because citizens do not join and leave by signing up for a card; and if it is legitimate to deny membership to members' children, citizens' newborns are not themselves denied citizenship. The list of inconsistencies could go on. And all by way of this heightened insistence on individual freedom, which does not however apply to foreigners, given that the state discharges its own obligations also by refusing access to refugees and the persecuted; humanitarian assistance in their places of origins is sufficient.[70]

Beyond noting these absurdities, it is worth bringing out the kernel of the argument, which, moreover, stands in line with the liberal tradition – namely, the fiction of the contract. It is suggested that people are free to associate and disassociate, to admit or to reject, as in the sealing of a pact or the signing of an accord. The very pretension to self-determination, to the autonomous choice of the self, is based on this fiction. When one is born, in general one does not choose a state to which to belong, and nor is one asked to do so. In promoting the autonomy of the self – this proud legislator ready to dictate laws for himself – this pathetic liberalism conceives society as an agglomerate of so many autarchic selves. These latter are like wolves who sniff each other out and delimit their own space, circumscribing their own range of action, so that the war of all against all might turn into exchange and trade. Here, free assent rules – even with regard to one's own responsibilities, as if the obligation towards the other did not come prior to any contract. And deadly consequences derive from this powerful political fiction, this vicious circle of ethics: first and foremost, the idea that it is legitimate to choose with whom we will cohabit.

18 The defence of national integrity

The next pretext that is adopted in order to justify the right to exclusion is the integrity of identity. In the communitarians' discourse, this second argument takes on a preponderant role. Self-determination is invoked in the name of preserving the community, its traditions and its culture. This is supposed to legitimize a selection of immigrants at the border, if not closing the borders down entirely. But, despite their different approaches, the normative prescriptions advanced by the communitarians, liberals and nationalists end up largely coinciding.

This second argument enjoys great popularity and exercises a both pervasive and harmful influence. Above all, it feeds the conviction that the migrant represents a threat to a people's identity, and to its democratic principles themselves. From this stem all the metaphors linked to 'contamination', preconceptions about incompatible values, and the supposed need to defend national culture, even at the cost of denying to migrants escaping from war, conflicts, abuses and injustice access to the national territory. Citizens are called on to put up walls to defend their supposed ethnic-cultural homogeneity. In fact, this derives from the supposed 'historical community of fate', whose continuity ought to be protected in order to allow citizens to recognize themselves in this stable, unitary and easily identified collective Self. But there is but a brief step from the defence of the borders to the expulsion of contaminating, impure, extraneous elements. One need only think of the demands advanced by Schmitt in his call for the restoration of territories' cultural integrity – for example, swapping different minorities. His next suggestion was the elimination of 'foreign bodies' – and, as we know, it was welcomed by Nazi policy.

The strong point of this argument, which arrogantly asserts the primacy of citizens, lies in the overlap between *démos* and éthnos. The borders of the community of the people are national ones. With the irruption of the nation onto the stage of sovereignty, no longer is it simply citizens who are deciding on the reception policy, but rather the members of the nation. Habermas has given a clear explanation of this slippage from political citizenship to national identity, which took place from the French Revolution onwards. A pre-political context distinguished by ethnic – or at least linguistic, historical and cultural – identity, the nation offers a solid basis for democracy, from which, in return, it receives the legitimation of a state sovereignty. The nation, capable of creating a bind of solidarity between individuals who would otherwise be strangers, ends up representing political identity, to the point that national belonging becomes synonymous with citizenship.[71] The critique that Habermas addresses against Walzer and Miller can be directed against all of those who defend the identity of their own culture and the integrity of their own form of life. Political citizenship can and should be uncoupled from national identity – which is to say, from assignation at birth, from the laws of blood and soil. The aspiring citizen ought not, therefore, to be held to become a member of a national community – which is, moreover, a largely fictitious and sacralized community, constructed around myths. This is because cultural identity is nothing but a pretext. The new immigrant-citizen ought not to be forced to integrate by embracing the national culture of the host country, giving up her own form of life. Rather, maintaining this latter would be enriching for all – the possibility of widening and multiplying their perspectives, regenerating their own culture in dialogue with others'. Moreover, culture is not monolithic or lacking in discordance and rifts, and nor is it a rigid and inert inheritance. What should be asked of the new citizen is that she share in democratic *political culture*. Safeguarding this latter does not imply imposing one's own form of life.[72] The state is no longer a homogeneous ethno-national community. Nor can culture be understood as an identitarian property.

19 Owning the land: a baseless myth

'This is our land.' Thus rings out the ultimate, decisive argument, the one that can still sustain the vacillating border, protect it and defend it from the immigrant who is readying to enter. 'This is our land. We inherited it from our mothers and fathers who lived here. And that place over there, which we did not inherit, ended up becoming our possession, because we watered it with the sweat off our brows, we cultivated it, shared its fruits, and through our work made it what it is today.' Concealed in the very basis of this argument is the idea that pushing back the foreigner at the gates is not only legal, but also legitimate, because citizens, as such, are proprietors – they own the soil delimited by the state's borders. In short: the state's territory would then be the private property of the citizens who reside there, as if a part of this collective possession belonged to each of them. Considered together, these different parts constitute the territorial assets, the foundations, that justify the state's right to exclude anyone coming from the outside. So this right to self-determination belongs not only to a nation, but to the state.

The close connection that needs grasping is the one that links state sovereignty to private property. And land ownership is the private property *par excellence*. This connection pervades modernity's entire liberal tradition. On closer inspection, however, it is necessary to go yet further, and look back to the paradigmatic case of ancient Athens.[73] In the recent debate on migration, the appeal to private property has emerged in more or less explicit forms. Ryan Pevnick has reasserted it in order to combat arguments in favour of open borders. Behind him stands a long series of philosophers and political scientists (especially in the US context) who have each in turn reinforced and reaffirmed this connection.[74] It is telling that Pevnick directly invokes Locke, who can be considered the progenitor and founding father of this liberal tradition.[75]

It is worth pulling apart one myth right away: namely, the myth of private property over land. No matter how many efforts have been made to justify and explain it, no argument is able to stand up. Private ownership over land has no foundation. It follows that state sovereignty is also groundless, having built itself and legitimized itself on the basis of that property over the centuries. If things are so – that is, it cannot be demonstrated that there exists an exclusive right to own the land – then any right to exclude the other is discredited, belied, demolished. Since I cannot prove, on the basis of my citizenship, that the place within the state's territory on which I stand is my own, my property, belonging to me, then nor can I purport to banish whoever would like to live there instead of me.

'[O]riginally no one has more of a right to be at a given place on earth than anyone else'.[76] Thus wrote Kant in the third article of his famous 1795 work *Perpetual Peace*. Importantly, Kant uses the terms *Ort* ('place') and *Recht* ('right'). No one has any more right to a place than another person does.

This is a decisive observation, and it does something to interrupt a dense series of attempts, from Bodin to Rousseau, firmly to establish in political thought the insuperable connection between sovereignty and possession. In this perspective, the sovereign is the proprietor, and, in turn, the proprietor is sovereign. Given that the state's sovereignty is based on property, the supreme goal of the state would, then, be to defend private property. By definition, the citizen is a proprietor, even to the point that whoever proves unable to own a property is excluded from civil society. The principal motive that drove human beings to break with natural law and stipulate a contract – uniting themselves in a state order – would, then, be the preservation of property. And, thus, this would also be the purpose of any political government. Rousseau goes as far as to say that the right to property is the most sacred of all civil rights.[77] In different forms, and with more or less pragmatic accents, the philosophers of modern liberalism try to demonstrate not only that it was possible to take possession of the land, but that this possession is sanctioned by a contractual agreement, and that the history of these beginnings must necessarily have been deeply coloured by struggles over appropriation.

It is sovereign power that imposes what is mine, yours, hers, which assigns land to each person. And, as it constitutes property, it in turn also constitutes itself. This is summarized in Hobbes's argument in a classic passage of *Leviathan* in which the state of nature – when each person can assert his right to each thing – is painted in the dark hues of war. 'Propriety' thus proves to be 'sovereign power, is the act of that power, in order to the public peace'.[78] Locke follows a different course, for he instead seeks to justify individual rights. He pushes Hobbes's sovereign – who exercises his power to divide up property – and, opposed to this, the Biblical image of the non-appropriable sharing of the land, extolled by the Psalm of David, into a mythical background.[79] Thus, Locke asks how private property was arrived at – not to abrogate it, but rather to back it up with philosophical arguments. Not by chance, these arguments remain the point of reference for those who defend the state's right to reject migrants precisely by invoking property.

In the second of his *Two Treatises of Government*, first published anonymously in 1690, Locke even writes that God gave the world to all in common, but in order that they make best use of it. Nature offers up many fruits and products spontaneously. Each is free to take them. But there must be some means of individually appropriating them. And, for Locke, labour provides this means. Work is accomplished by one's own body, with one's own hands, property which no one can question – and it is thanks to labour that each human being acquires things, by taking them away from the common condition in which nature leaves them. It is thanks to work that they can be appropriated. Decisive is the act with which fruit is picked and water is tapped at source. There is no theft here! Even if it lacks others' consent, this is not a predatory act. Anything but. Whoever does it makes a contribution, precisely through the fact of working. This legitimizes the act through which, in removing things from the common state of nature, a person will give rise to private property. The product removed from nature with this addition of work – and which thus become hers – receives the seal of property. No one can take it from her. If anything, *that* is what would be unjust. In short: Locke justifies the right to appropriation, even if within certain limits – that is, the limits of consumption. Locke believed it necessary to avoid appropriation degenerating into accumulation and hoarding. And what goes for the fruits of the land also goes for land itself, which is the object of property *par excellence.* Certainly, it is legitimate to appropriate it for oneself through work. Whoever ploughs, sows or drains, 'encloses' the land, substituting private property for common ownership.[80] When God gave the world in common, did he not perhaps also command the working of the land? *Cultivated* land is also *appropriated* land. It is almost superfluous to add that this equivalence served Locke in two senses. First of all, to complete the passage from the private property of the individual to the private property of a country, for example England, and from individual enclosures to state ones. If, in this latter case, the area concerned was much vaster, and included many individual enclosures, there persisted the same political and ethical principle revolving around cultivation. This, secondly, authorized the appropriation of uncultivated and abandoned land, for instance in America.[81]

Perhaps it is no coincidence that the Latin word *colonia* comes from the verb *colere* ('cultivate') or that 'culture' and 'colonization' have the same etymology. Following Locke's argument, consent is irrelevant and agreement is pointless. Appropriation and settlement are legitimate within the terms of cultivation and acculturation. The territories across the oceans were held to be unpopulated and in large part desolate. It did not matter that there were, indeed, others living there. Those who arrived, the future colonists, were authorized by their labour – which would supposedly bring wellbeing and profits – to appropriate this soil for themselves. Moreover, the ideology of colonization had precedents. In the second book of his *Utopia*, published in 1516, Thomas More had paid tribute to the foundation of the 'colony'. For it is a 'very just cause of war for a nation to hinder others from possessing a part of that soil of which they make no use, but which is suffered to lie idle and uncultivated'.[82] Very few voices were raised against this 'law of conquest'.[83]

Kant did not share Locke's theses. His reflection started out from the fact that the Earth is a sphere. This theme recurred through both his *Perpetual Peace* and the doctrine of law contained in his famous *Groundwork of the Metaphysic of Morals*. Each person originally has legal possession of the soil on which she finds herself. This, through the common ownership of the land, which Kant also recognizes. Then everyone could spread out without any risk of encountering each other, or – better – of coming to blows. But the Earth is a sphere. And since this space is limited, it is necessary to put up with one another.[84] From this springs the need for cosmopolitan right, which is called on both to govern the relations between peoples – which nature has despotically closed down within the limits of the globe – and to regulate mutual 'commerce', i.e. the need for a continual exchange between strangers, which must not end in a war among enemies.[85]

Even in his time, therefore, Kant glimpsed the problems of globalization. In such a context, in which transgressing a right in one part of the world has repercussions everywhere, it is illegitimate to take possession of the land. Unless, that is, those who already live there declare themselves in agreement. Kant was gravely troubled to see the actions of Europe's masters of colonization, who abused the right to visit in order to subject other peoples, to pillage and enslave them. He could not, therefore, follow Locke's argument: property is not legitimized by the working of the land. This is but an old idea based on the illusion that 'bare justice as a transcendent principle, and cogitated to an invisible subject, defines the right of this personified Being'.[86] There also exist other ways of stamping the seal of possession. Kant did not in fact renounce property and the attempt to justify it. What is property, then? What is *mine* is that 'with which I am so connected that another's use of it without my consent would wrong me'.[87] Legitimate property is, so to speak, that property that is legitimized by an agreement.

For Kant, the 'primeval' common holding of the land was a 'legend'. Perhaps even a dangerous one, because it would sanction a sort of communism. Such a community could be instituted if everyone transferred their own private property into the common property. Kant was speaking in the conditional. And he added – not without a certain sarcasm – 'history would have to give us proof of such a contract'.[88] Different is the case of the 'original' community of land, which can be summarized as the right of each to have some place in the world. This right to a place, however, also extends into outright appropriation. Kant admits an original taking-into-possession: the appropriation of part of the soil that had still been free. This takes place only thanks to the advantage of 'temporal *priority*'. This is the justification of whoever arrives first. Thus, Kant can say 'blessed are the proprietors'. This choice is an arbitrary one, but also one with which a legitimate, even if still temporary, possession is defined; to become 'peremptory', certain and unchallengeable, it has to be ratified by the free accord of all, expressed in a judicial deed. What was then a simple appropriation became, to all intents and purposes, an occupation. This contract operated the passage from the state of nature to civil status. And the 'juridical' community of possession was established.

If civil society can guarantee each his own, that is because it already presupposes 'his own', which implies a splitting up of 'mine' and 'yours'.[89] Kant, therefore, had nothing against the division of the land, which, once regulated, allowed for that particular possession which could avert conflicts. But in this irenic, rational landscape, there remains a big question mark over the original acquisition, of which there cannot be any proof. Who acquired it, and from whom? More than an original 'acquisition', one would properly speak of an original 'appropriation', an act which – Kant confesses – cannot easily be understood. Every acquisition is thus undermined by its temporary character, which, unless the contract extends across the whole human race, is destined to remain temporary, like all possession.[90] In the last analysis, this argument also applies to the territory of a state.

Not even Kant managed to justify the exclusive right to property over land. The attempt, proposed by Locke, to substitute in the pragmatic criterion of labour, marked the beginning of a liberal vision – in part, a welcoming one. The accord of a juridical community of possession would allow the closing of the door, and yet this accord rests on shaky foundations and is undermined by the fact that the land was originally held in common, which would instead demand an open door. If an exclusive right is groundless, then it is illegitimate to purport to exclude others from a territory. Even after Kant, no matter how many efforts have been made, the exclusive right to the land has not been given philosophical foundation.

20 Freedom of movement and birthright privileges

It would be impossible to find a natural justification for state borders, fenced-off nations and arbitrary enclosures. But these do stop people from freely circulating across the Earth's surface. And yet freedom of movement is a fundamental individual right. Who would deny it? In a certain sense, it could be said that it is a right even more fundamental than all other human rights. There is no one who does not want to move. This is, therefore, a constitutive right that concerns the individual liberty of the body itself. Even before any philosopher, even the little prince well knew that no one is the owner of the whole planet, and that everyone – like wild birds in their migratory movements – must be free to leave, to move around, to return.[91]

It is difficult to understand, then, why this right should be placed at the mercy of state sovereignty, which can condition, limit and deny it. This is problematic, above all, for liberal political thought, which ultimately runs into utter impasse. Individual freedom has, indeed, always been at the heart of liberalism, which cannot allow this freedom to be oppressed by the community or, least of all, subject it to the self-determination of the sovereign state. The impasse brings out an internal dividing line that separates the sovereigntist liberals, more preoccupied with maintaining the state-centric order and safeguarding the borders, from cosmopolitan liberals ready to highlight the risk of universal reason bowing down to national feelings.[92] It is these latter who call for the abolition of borders.

The champion of closed borders has a name, just as does the promoter of open borders. Only four years after the publication of Michael Walzer's book *Spheres of Justice*, in 1987 Joseph Carens intervened to criticize the sovereigntist argument, with his essay 'Aliens and citizens: the case for open borders'.[93] Carens pointed an accusing finger at those restrictions that prejudice the freedom and equality of all human beings – values that a liberal democracy cannot do without. The label 'liberal', which in the English-speaking world designates a truly vast range of ideas and perspectives, here exhibits all its ambiguity, for it could be applied to both Walzer and Carens. And, moreover, Carens is driven to speak by a liberal profession of faith, moved as he is by the need to defend the freedom of the individual against the state. If anything, his position is not so much opposite to Walzer's, as it is its mirror-image. For he asserts the other side of liberal thinking – this Janus face – which risks succumbing under the oppressions and restrictions that come from sovereigntism.

Those who call for the closing of the borders uphold three main arguments, albeit with different emphases. These are self-determination, national and cultural integrity, and ownership over the territory. There are likewise three arguments to which the opposed assumptions of those who defend the cause of open borders ultimately correspond. These are freedom of movement, the egalitarian redistribution of goods and the sharing of the Earth. Here, too, there is no lack of differentiations. Carens is father of the first two arguments, while the third one remains at a lower level. And it is symptomatic that he does not deal with it at any length.

'Borders have guards and the guards have guns.'[94] This denunciation begins Carens's discourse, whose aim is to spark critical reflection on what is instead taken for given. First of all, armed borders. And yet the need for the opposite – which is to say, free movement – should be self-evident. What gives anyone the right to point their weapons at those who want to cross the border? Such a violence could be legitimate, if this were a matter of criminals, armed invaders or enemies of the state. But why is a Mexican who seeks work in California, in the search to provide a decent life for her family, instead arrested or perhaps even forced out? For Carens, the pretext of state sovereignty – the theme of self-determination – does not stand up, for it manifestly violates an inalienable individual freedom. That is to say, the freedom to leave and enter, to emigrate and immigrate. Indeed, he highlights the apparent asymmetry between the right to *emigrate* and the right to *immigrate*. For Carens, any person must be able to abandon the place where they live in order to find some residence elsewhere. And this is all the more true for those migrants who leave the Third World and make their way to the First. '[C]itizenship in Western democracies is the modern equivalent of feudal class privilege – an inherited status that greatly enhances one's life chances.'[95] This line was destined to have important consequences, and rightly so: for the first time, citizenship was defined as a privilege, akin to the old class privileges.

Carens is to be credited for clearly linking his two arguments. For he invoked, in support of the freedom to immigrate – the more widely contested freedom – the continuing disparity between one citizenship and another. After all, one's place of birth, which no one chooses, can influence one's existence no less than other arbitrary factors, from inheritance to skin colour and from family to gender.[96] This residency-disadvantage is reflected in the global injustice that no perspective able to see beyond the borders can overlook. In the conflict between sovereignty and rights, Carens thus seems to take sides with these latter, in the name of a moral equality of individuals that must be defended against any prevarication and any iniquity. His egalitarianism, which protects the individual from the community, fits perfectly into the liberal tradition. Moreover, Carens himself draws on three of this tradition's normative theories: Robert Nozik's libertarian thought, John Rawls's idea of justice, and utilitarianism.

There are many ways of being libertarian. This current is not always on the Left, as is often believed. On the contrary, it is important to distinguish between left-libertarians, whose position is mitigated by a certain requirement for equality, and the right-libertarians of whom Nozik is the most emblematic exponent.[97] Perhaps the very title of his best-known book *Anarchy, State and Utopia* has contributed to creating misunderstandings. For this right-wing 'libertarian', an inflexible advocate of private property who looks to the state of nature described by Locke and aspires to a return to an 'original liberalism', state action must be limited. In this vein, Nozik speaks of a 'minimal' or even 'ultra-minimal' state, to which each person has entrusted, through contract, individual rights over her own body and goods.[98] The best state is that which remains in the wings, allowing individuals to interact without hindrance. Otherwise, it would end up contravening its own task. Such a state cannot, therefore, violate the right to free movement, precisely in the name of its own sovereignty – for in this case, even more than in others, the priority of the individual must be affirmed. Even if Nozik is not explicit in this regard, in his world there should not exist any constraints on immigration. It should be supposed that whoever reaches a territory wants to enter into society together with those who are already its members – whom Nozik, not by chance, even calls its 'customers'. The success of this exchange, interaction and integration is up to individuals, to citizens, and above all to the foreigner, her interest and her capacities. The state can establish the criteria for citizenship, but it must never close off society and forbid entry to it. Unless, that is, individual property rights are to be wronged – but this applies to citizens no less than for foreigners.

More important is Carens's recourse to Rawls's theory of justice. Beyond the author's own intentions, Carens in fact re-interprets one of Rawls's most powerful conceptual tools: the 'veil of ignorance'.[99] This is the thought experiment through which it is possible to give a fresh start to justice. The veil deprives the participants of any previously accumulated information and produces a sort of – artificial, improvised – amnesia, which forces them to assume the viewpoint of the most disadvantaged. This is not out of altruism, but simply for the sake of rationally pursuing their own interests. It is like becoming blind, in order to see better; not knowing, in order to understand more clearly. This veil of ignorance, which projects us into a hypothetical original state, should drive us to choose the egalitarian principles of justice that would forbid any form of arbitrary power or discrimination. For Rawls, the participants will necessarily agree on two principles of justice: the principle of fundamental freedoms, and the principle of distributive justice. Carens, in turn – thinking with and against Rawls – redeploys this experiment on a global scale. If each person behind the veil of ignorance had to consider the question of migration, without knowing her own place of birth, she would come to see residency as an arbitrary disparity, and citizenship as an inadmissible privilege. She would thus add free movement and the right to enter any country to the list of fundamental freedoms.[100]

Perhaps Rawls would not have agreed with this extension of his experiment. Besides, it is telling that he consistently evaded the border question. As Charles Beitz has observed, the original sin of Rawls's reasoning lies precisely in the fact that he circumscribed justice within the borders of the nation-state.[101] Yet globalization has fractured the state-centric order, thus radically changing the international landscape.

The aim of Carens and others after him was to extend the veil of ignorance across the globe, thus overthrowing the sovereigntist liberals' schema, in order to bring egalitarian concerns into the foreground. If they are to be consistent, liberal democracies cannot block by law the arrival of foreigners – all the more so, where they employ the utilitarian calculation of the 'maximum benefit'. It is thus incumbent on them to open the borders. This does not mean that a limit cannot be placed on freedom of immigration in some circumstances. For Rawls, too, fundamental freedoms can be limited in the name of freedom. And similarly for Carens, it is legitimate to reduce entries or temporarily to close the borders when there exists some real threat to public order, when there looms some danger to national security, or when some destabilizing impact on democratic institutions is foreseen.

The criteria advanced by Carens are striking for their abstract simplicity. Everything is reduced to the attempt to recover, from the foundations of liberal thought, a now-vanished cosmopolitanism that would allow human beings freely to circulate around the Earth's surface and to recognize one another as equals, beyond any national ramparts and overbearing state sovereignties. The maximum openness, freedoms extended to all. This egalitarianism sounds all the more strident in a world that every day belies the ideal of independence, distributive justice and individual freedom. It is as if every political, economic and social problem, from exploitation to violence and from corruption to poverty, always and only owed to a lack of freedoms. In short, rather than interrogate the asymmetries that exist, this reading starts out from an ideal symmetry between free and equal individuals. This thus takes for granted what should, instead, itself be a theme of critical reflection.

Carens is no exceptional case. And here comes to light his position, which is not contrary to that of those, also identifying with liberalism, who promote closing the borders, but rather mirrors it. It is just that Carens wants to limit the reach of the community and make the state a sort of agency in service of citizens, which should not interfere in their exchanges. However, on closer inspection, it is the points they have in common that count for most. Carens, too, reduces the social relation to the model of the contract stipulated between two free individuals, unbound from any community, untied from any responsibility, projected against the backdrop of a neutral and ascetic symmetry in which they can voluntarily reach an accord based on their interests. Each relation is a transaction. It is as if the arriving migrant were a new partner, able to negotiate her entry on equal terms, as if she already had everything that she in fact does not, starting precisely with the freedom to negotiate. But, beyond contractualism, Carens also shares a certain way of depoliticizing the question, in which one speaks always and only of 'moral rights' and, indeed, the internal and normative approach that drives him, too, to consider the phenomenon of migration only from citizens' point of view.

To call for freedom of movement in this abstract form – like Carens and all those who followed in his wake – means not only to reduce migration, in all its complexity, to the pedestrian flatness of individuals moving back and forth, but also completely to overlook the decisive theme of reception. In this perspective, it would suffice to eliminate the barriers so that each person would be free to move around a planet conceived as a simple space of exchange, an immense market of choices and opportunities accessible to all.

21 Migrants against the poor? Welfare chauvinism and global justice

The defence of an abstract freedom of movement not only left itself open to more than one critique, but paradoxically ended up opening the lid on all those arguments that attack migration as a threat to economic stability. All the populists who railed against the migrant influx and cried 'invasion', instigating hatred and whipping up fear, thus found an excellent pretext, an unexpected alibi. Their eminently small-minded reasoning is the following: if it is the Market – a hidden power of which politics is but the long arm – that wants global mobility; if it is Capital that is imposing free movement; then one can only be against migration, against migrants, and for borders and for the nation ... and so on and so forth, in a patriotic drift that often sinks into a sovereigntism underpinned by racism.

What makes this question even more troubling is that some of these themes have even been redeployed on the Left. And this has created confusion and disorientation. An old social democracy, which already before the great global conflicts made a nod to aggressive nationalism, has been combined with a newly minted sovereigntist Left – on closer inspection, a miserable chorus for the reactionary Right. One would more correctly use the term 'sovereigntism' to indicate the political front that defends the nation's sovereignty to the death. This front is not a transversal one – as some have asserted – for the simple reason that whoever takes sides with the state against migrants is not on the Left.

The main lines of the problem were traced out already in Walzer's text, where he underlined the danger represented by guestworkers, the latest version of the metics. They can be tolerated temporarily but cannot be taken in permanently, for, as they joined the domestic workforce, they would enter into competition with local workers – taking their jobs – and would also benefit from welfare programmes. Justice has borders – and they are the borders of the nation. What goes on outside these borders is no concern either for citizens or for the state.

Arguments such as these have been elaborated in recent years. More than employment – and variations in job numbers make this argument more than shaky – it is welfare that constitutes the hinge of this discourse. Economic immigration should be drastically cut, or rather stopped entirely, because it takes work off locals, lowers wages, reduces productivity incentives, damages state budgets, and offers subsidies and healthcare to foreigners who can benefit from it without having themselves made any contribution. In short, all this would amount to so many handouts dispensed at the expense of the poor, who are forced despite themselves to pay. This supposedly risks the maintenance of the welfare state itself. It is no chance thing that the European countries where welfare is strongest – the ones where not only individual living standards, but also the standards of collective life, are considered sacred – that have proven harshest and most intransigent in this regard. One can't ignore the bill passed by the Danish parliament on 26 January 2016, which stipulated the confiscation of jewellery and money from migrants in order to provide for their upkeep. Similar measures are already in place in Switzerland and in some German *Länder* – indeed, the very richest ones, Bavaria and Baden-Württemberg. Jewellery in exchange for welfare.

Since 2016, many authoritative German philosophers have taken a stance in favour of closing the borders, specifically invoking economic questions. Thus, in his recent book, Julian Nida-Rümelin forcefully insists on the impossibility of a welfare state whose remit is not limited by national borders. In this view, immigration risks bringing the public sector to collapse, causing serious damage to the citizens for whom the government ought to be responsible, and without this actually helping the foreigners. Nida-Rümelin also takes recourse to the controversial theme of 'brain drain', the flight of so-called 'human capital', which supposedly leads to the impoverishment of the countries of departure. All the more so, given that the ones who move are those who have the most means, the youngest, the best able to resist, while the rest are consigned to penury. It would, then, be better to help them back home with specific, targeted programmes.[102]

This argument invoking welfare has many champions, even if they are distributed across a wide array of political positions, running from social democracy to the far Right via moderate liberalism. It is not difficult to understand why this is: here congeals the whole self-immunizing logic of the nation, the economy of 'us first' that may seem not only pragmatic, but also an approach rooted in responsibility and solidarity. What counts, as Paul Collier argues, is 'the economic wellbeing of indigenous households'.[103] So it is important to be careful to avoid contaminating the social and economic system of the democratic countries, and not to spoil, pollute and disfigure it with immigrants. This is music to the ears of the citizens, future voters, able with their vote to punish the politicians who may hazard backing different arguments. And, indeed, even if the data in many cases show the opposite – that is, that immigrants do not take work off locals, because they do different jobs; that, more than being necessary, they increase GDP; that they increase tax revenue in their own countries and thus help alleviate poverty – all these 'utilitarian' arguments are doomed to come to nothing.[104]

Those like Carens who defend freedom of movement, but nonetheless remain within the state-centric perspective, seem to be wielding blunt weapons. The discussion descends into a war of numbers, a dispute over statistics, in which those who argue that migration is not an effective antidote and does not assuage the living conditions in Third World countries end up getting the better of the dispute. To what end this charity? Citizens are impoverished and subjected to further sacrifices, without this helping those who live in conditions of extreme destitution. Nor is it possible to imagine shouldering responsibility for all the world's misery! In its dry accounting, in observing the panorama of pros and cons, in drawing up a list of probable consequences, a debate elaborated by moral philosophers of the analytic school, reasoning in their classrooms on the bases of 'as ifs', winds in on itself and gets knotted up, to the point of pushing ethics itself into the abyss.

Peter Singer's bestseller *Practical Ethics* has proven to be a definitive work. In its chapter entitled 'Rich and poor', Singer introduces a disconcerting analogy. Those in the rich countries who could provide money to save those threatened by famines, diseases and poverty are like the teacher who, crossing the park from the library to a classroom, sees a child about to drown in the pond, even though the water is only shallow. Obviously, he should save the child, even if this would mean 'getting my clothes muddy, ruining my shoes and either cancelling my lecture or delaying it'.[105] Beside the discomfort that this example provokes, in all its elements, it is hard to see what the analogy would be with this case, which among other things plays out entirely in the singular. Yet these pages of Singer's work continue to exercise many. As if this allowed us to find the solution to the problem. But Singer's strategy is all too clear: poverty is passed off as a natural disaster which no one has to answer for, and so long as everything seems decontextualized and lacking in historical content, the theme of immigration will be reduced to a single, accidental matter of saving someone in the park. In short, it is possible to provide assistance every now and then, but certainly not to offer welcome. Situated along this slippery slope in more recent times have been not only the interventions of those who point to immigration as a factor for further imbalance, but also the interpretative hypotheses that call into question certain key concepts, starting with that of poverty itself. Such is the case of Thomas Pogge, who, sceptical towards the antidote represented by immigration, believes that poverty should be seen not as an injustice for which it would be possible to define specific blame, but rather as the result of systemic factors inscribed in the global economic order; it would, then, be necessary to spread awareness of this latter's unsustainability.[106]

In a discussion of globalization, there is no getting around the theme of 'global responsibility', which is, indeed, also on philosophy's agenda today. However one seeks to confront it, with normative aims or critical objectives, in revisiting the concept of responsibility or rethinking the globalization process as a whole, it is no longer possible to imagine a justice confined within national borders. The fragmentation of responsibility, a diffuse and disconcerting phenomenon which many have already highlighted, can no longer be an alibi. Not to see the effects of one's own actions does not mean one is innocent. Thus, it is no longer legitimate to light-mindedly profit from the low-price goods that have come at the cost of the inhumane exploitation, or even the lives, of other people. Nor is it legitimate to close one's eyes to arms sales and all the trafficking conducted by one's own country more or less under the counter. But the theme also has a wider import and, moreover, concerns the historical responsibilities of the Western countries. Thus, whoever discusses global justice is also posing the question of hunger. In 2015, the number of people worldwide suffering undernutrition hit 795 million. Beyond the numbers and the attempts to define and classify the different levels of poverty, the problem is the incomprehension among the citizens living in rich countries.[107] Those who have not lived through hunger, experienced it, have difficulty imagining it. As Martín Caparrós has written:

We know hunger: we're used to it. We are hungry two, three, times a day. But there is a world of difference between the repeated, daily hunger that we experience, which is daily and repeatedly sated, and the desperate hunger of those unable to sate it. Hunger has always been a motor of social change, technological progress, revolutions and counter-revolutions. Nothing has had greater influence on the history of humanity. No disease, no war has killed more people. Still today no plague is so lethal and, at the same time, so avoidable as hunger.[108]

It is precisely the possibility of averting hunger that makes it all the more unbearable. If globalization has allowed many of the planet's inhabitants to avail themselves of a wider variety of goods at lower cost, if it has given hundreds of millions of poor people the opportunity to reach a higher standard of living, and if it has drastically reduced 'extreme poverty', almost by half, it has not, however, defeated hunger. In many parts of the globe, there are still chasms of inequality. And one cannot understand what is happening today if one does not recognize that these inequalities have been aggravated by the global media networks that everywhere broadcast, even in the remotest villages, the seductive, intoxicating images of advertising. If, in the Western countries where it is produced, this advertising is deciphered in terms of its performative signals – however unreal – in the Second and Third Worlds it appears as the faithful, reliable description of the legendary comforts of the First World, of the Western lifestyle that everyone would like to share. It is pointless to proclaim that this is not how things really are, that poverty reigns also in the peripheries of the Western cities. The saga of the New World, the myth of El Dorado, now works the opposite way around, and drives more dreams than it did before; it drives masses of poor people to try and conquer that happiness for themselves. And what right has anyone to stop them?

In a short footnote in his imposing volume *Faktizität und Geltung*, Jürgen Habermas made a brief intervention on the question of immigration, a theme that he has in general avoided (indeed, he has been criticized for this). Declaring himself in favour of 'political asylum' in given conditions, he argues that 'the individual has no subjective right to immigration', even if 'Western societies are, for many reasons, morally obliged to adopt a liberal policy on immigration.'[109] He thus refers to the essay he had earlier published in response to Charles Taylor as part of a debate on multiculturalism. Indeed, if Habermas's position is ambivalent and, in many regards, almost comes close to a liberal one, this short 1993 text contains decisive arguments formulated with great clarity. Already back then, Habermas could make out a looming 'policy of closedness toward migrants', judged favourably by the citizens of the European Community, where xenophobia was spreading. The various states would, in this perspective, seek to block the 'tide'. But this would translate not into a total shutdown, but rather into a restrictive and selective entrance policy.

Habermas leaves open the question over the self-determination which the receiver society may wish to assert. However, he emphasizes that it is impossible to consider the problem only from the viewpoint of wealthy societies. This is forbidden for 'moral' reasons. It is necessary to assume the migrants' own viewpoint – not only that of displaced persons who seek asylum, but also the mass fleeing poverty, which moves in search of 'a life worth living'. There have always been migrants in search of work. Europe knows them well. And it has always taken advantage of this, in both senses. For this reason, too, it has further responsibilities added to the obligation to provide help, 'which emerges from the ever-closer interdependencies of global society'. That is not to mention the First World's debts 'deriving from the history of colonisation'.[110] This is why it is specious to draw any rigid dividing line between refugees and migrants.

Whoever artificially separates the questions of political exile from questions of immigration-through-poverty is implicitly declaring that they want to rid themselves of Europe's moral obligation toward the refugees who come from the world's poor regions. In exchange, they declare themselves disposed to tacitly tolerating an illegal and uncontrolled immigration which could at any moment – for the purposes of domestic politics – instrumentally be attacked as an 'abuse' of the right to asylum.[111]

Habermas points an accusing finger at what he calls Europe's 'welfare chauvinism'.[112] Though he cannot concede that there exists an 'individual right to immigration', he emphasizes the moral obligation that ought to drive states to practise a 'liberal policy' that does not limit quotas in terms of the economic needs of the receiver country, but, moreover, follows criteria that are acceptable to migrants themselves.

Recognizable, here, is Habermas's conciliatory stamp, the wish that both sides' rights be respected. Even if one cannot agree with his overall philosophical-juridical framework, it is, however, worth underlining his attack on a welfare chauvinism that has, over time, even come to assume more aggravated tones. Also important is the fact that Habermas notes the existence of a certain entrance policy that simply folds to the demands of the market. Thus, in a given situation, the barriers will be lifted in order to let through those who dispose of specific qualities that capitalism particularly cherishes. So, this is not a matter of being for or against open borders, as Žižek also seems to believe.[113] Rather, the mechanism (*dispositif*) of immigration ought to be read within the terms of the neoliberal market logic that has engulfed society and sees in the human being nothing other than a *Homo oeconomicus*. This does not justify an economistic reading of immigration that seeks to transform citizen-workers into useful human resources. Any reductionist reading is doomed to crash up against the real complexity of this phenomenon. Certainly, mobility does play capital's game. The mechanism of immigration is built on this; if, on the one hand, it attracts migrants, on the other, it pushes them away – two sides of one same political strategy directed at neutralizing and exploiting migration flows. The agreements that suit 'the demand for a foreign workforce' can thus be combined with repressive measures directed towards 'the fight against illegal immigration'. Immigration is, at the same time, exclusion. The migrant is always wanted but not welcome – required as a worker, but unwanted as a foreigner. Without taking on any responsibility for people's lives, migration policy filters, chooses, selects.

This explains the forms of neo-slavery, the ethnic segmentation of the labour market, and the material and existential precaritization of migrants, who are constrained to follow the paths and rhythms they have been assigned. Power is exercised over docile, temporarily admitted bodies, which are later expelled. The immigration mechanism appears, then, as a form of the wider flexibilization mechanism imposed by the market. On the one hand, evoking an economic ideal passed off as freedom, no more obstacles are put up to the 'free movement' of the workforce than to the free movement of goods; on the other hand, the freedom of those who emigrate (what Sandro Mezzadra has called the 'right to flee') is expropriated, tamed, translated into mobility, made a simple matter of adaptability.[114] Hence the reason why the immigration mechanism, contributing to a merciless competition, ultimately proves functional to flexibilization.

Even to speak of 'the market', understood as a homogeneous entity, is misleading in this context. As Balibar has made clear, the much-heralded unification of the market has not been completed. The nation, in which conflicts are more easily resolved, remains a protagonist in the 'world-economy'. Hence the development of the 'social nation-state', a provider (or providential) state within which the classes that ought to be in conflict consider themselves different sides, but all part of one crew embarked on the same galley.[115] And the migrant body is to be found at the convergence of two discriminations which are today combined in unprecedented fashion – the discriminations of both 'race' and 'class'.

22 Neither exodus, nor 'deportation', nor 'human trafficking'

In referencing the act of migrating, or migration, as a phenomenon, recourse is often made to terms or circumlocutions that ought to work as synonyms, but in fact already contain some interpretative thrust of their own. Before asking about the significance of 'migrating' and its political potential, it is first of all worth making clear that it would be reductive to draw an equals sign between migration and flight, or exodus.

Fleeing is a further element of migrating, and it recalls the act of the exile, the dissident, indeed the fugitive, who acts in this way in reaction to abuse, injustice and persecution. Flight here becomes a manifest form of struggle. And the emphasis falls on a freedom – the freedom to move, to leave – while reception remains wholly in the background. But even if flight is only apparently spontaneous, there is also the risk of making the migrant who passively suffers her condition into a political exile.[116] This applies all the more so to the analogy between exodus and migrations, perhaps suggested by its

'Biblical proportions'. Hence the bizarre syntagma 'mass exodus'. Migration today takes place under the banner of individualism. It is not a community that migrates, and nor is it by crossing the sea that a people constitutes itself. This does not mean that it is not worth grasping certain important similarities, albeit without abstracting from the differences.[117]

In a clear attempt to stigmatize migrants, they are sometimes discussed in terms of 'deportation' – in many regards an unfortunate expression. First of all because, now that it has such strong connotations, it brings to mind the deportations carried out by the Nazis. And it is hard to see in what sense migration can be understood as a forced transfer of the condemned. The interpretative hypothesis at work here is the opposite of flight or exodus. But, just as migrants do not act in absolute freedom with no restrictions, nor are they merely passive. Even in the extreme cases in which they accept conditions bordering on blackmail, if not outright deceit, one ought nonetheless to recognize a certain margin of choice among those who emigrate and among those who run risks in order to escape a condition with no future, exposing themselves to a period of 'voluntary servitude' in the certainty that there exist no other ways out.[118]

Graver still is the use of the despicable formula 'human trafficking'. This is a comfortable alibi for evading or denying any responsibility. It instead makes a clutch of unscrupulous 'smugglers', 'slavedrivers' and 'traffickers' shoulder the blame, laying all the fault on them and, indeed, pointing to them as the one true cause of migration. This makes it possible to pass off an exclusionary policy as a 'war on the traffickers', and to peddle rejections and repatriations as a 'fight against illegal immigration'. The hypocrisy even reaches the point that some set themselves up as liberators of migrants, while on the one hand criminalizing them and, on the other hand, considering them individuals afflicted with the status of children.

23 *Ius migrandi*: for the right to migrate

The intransitive verb 'to migrate' is not – as is often thought – a synonym of 'to move'. Present in the Romance languages – *migrar, migrer, migrare* – and spread thanks to loan words, it comes from the Latin *migrare*. It is thought that the Latin root *mig-*, which means moving from a place, in the sense of leaving, comes from the Sanskrit root *miv-*. This is seemingly attested in the noun or adjective *migros*, made up of the suffix *-ro* and the Indo-European root *h2mei-gw*. Even though there was no specific Indo-European word for 'to migrate', this root, in its basic form *h2mei-, has come to make up part of the languages that have derived from it. What does this root mean? In all its combinations it means 'to move', 'to change place', 'exchange place', like how offerings are exchanged, such that the foreigner is welcomed as a guest rather than an enemy. In Latin, this root produced, among other things, *mutare, mutuus, munus*. In short: right from the beginning 'migrating' has never been a simple movement; rather, it corresponds to a complex exchange – an exchange of places. It thus materializes within the landscape in which one encounters the foreigner, where the ethical-political praxis of hospitality begins.

There is no migration without a change – or, better, exchange – of place, without the other, and without the encounter that could, depending on the place, descend into a confrontation. To migrate is not, therefore, only a biological process. Migration does not equate to evolution.[119] To defend a general mobility, it is not enough just to note that humans – starting with *Homo sapiens* – have always been migrating, from their origins in the African continent. The evolutionist hypothesis wholly misses the significance of migrating, because it abstracts from history, the other, and the complications of the encounter with the other. To migrate is a political act.

This explains why *ius migrandi*, the right to migrate, is anything but self-evident and, over the centuries, has sparked bitter conflicts. Still today, it is only recognized in part, as the right to emigrate, to leave a state's territory, but not as a right to immigrate, to enter within another state's borders. If the former is now universal, though it was denied up until a few decades ago, the latter still depends on states' sovereignty – and it seems they are very reluctant to grant this right. In this sense, *ius migrandi* represents one of the great challenges of the twenty-first century. Since 2007, the Global Forum on Migration and Development, headquartered at the UN, has tried to elaborate a project for a global governance of migration. But it has encountered many obstacles, for the most part put up by questions of state sovereignty. Nonetheless, the goal is to invert the current logic, dictated by power relations, and give priority to the migrant, not the state – thus calling for a right for the individual, which cannot be limited, or still less denied, by states' own economic requirements or demographic needs.[120] *Ius migrandi* is the human right for the twenty-first century that –backed by the work of activist associations, international movements and an ever better-informed and more alert public opinion – will require a struggle at the level of the fight for the abolition of slavery.

Was *ius migrandi* ever discussed in the past? And when? This discussion came right after Columbus's voyages, when the need to legitimize the conquest of the Americas, in some manner, began to become apparent. This was the context in which international law first began to take outline form. *Ius migrandi* was advanced by the European colonizers in order to justify their violent usurpation – that is, by the same people who, after having crossed the world and devastated it with their pillage and then their promises, today wail about the migrant 'invasion'.

As is well known, the conquest of the other was far from painless. The impact with the 'barbarians' of the West Indies, the clash with that dizzyingly distant otherness, had effects that defined an era. The greatest genocide to exist in the historical memory remains enigmatic, in terms of both its dimensions and the means by which it took place. The number of people living in those territories at the end of the fifteenth century is unknown. But there was an immense demographic catastrophe, brought about by a combination of different causes: not only the immediate violence of the *conquistadores*, the killing, the cruel abuses, but also the people reduced to slavery, the unknown illnesses, the breaking of both environmental equilibriums and balances in communities.

The subjection of bodies came in tandem with cultural devastation. The *indios* gave in very rapidly. It is still difficult to understand how a few hundred Europeans could have won so quickly. According to Tzvetan Todorov's renowned thesis, all this happened because the Mayas and Aztecs did not understand the events, having 'lost control of communication'.[121] Conversely, both Columbus and, even more so, Cortés not only enjoyed supremacy in terms of the military technology they could deploy, but also pursued a coherent political–communicative strategy that aimed not at the recognition of the other, but at its systematic destruction.

Already in 1493, Pope Alexander VI, Rodrigo Borgia, defined the first global hyperfrontier with his bull *Inter coetera divinae*; it 'donated, conceded, destined' to the king of Castile 'all the islands and lands, explored or to be explored, discovered or to be discovered, to the West and to the South' of the meridian to the West of the Azores. This owed to the 'fullness of apostolic power'. But the legitimacy of this move sparked not a little doubt. The Catholic sovereigns themselves raised questions about the *indios* reduced to slavery. Was it legitimate to treat them like this? Were they not, perhaps, also human beings? The *conquistadores* had painted them in a very contradictory light: sometimes as bloody savages, other times as tame people ready to receive the word of God. Upon his third voyage, Columbus moved on to the *encomiendas* system, with which land was distributed, and the *repartimientos*, where work – no longer slave labour – was compensated with wages. But the effects were disastrous: everywhere the population was dying out. The Dominicans were the first to point out what was happening. The friar Antonio de Montesinos, who preached the Gospels on the island of Hispaniola, launched a very sharp attack against the *conquista* on 12 December 1511. Called back to Spain by the king, he recounted the crimes he had witnessed, before a *junta* of theologians and philosophers called to meet in Burgos on 27 January 1512. Thus began a lasting dispute.

How was it possible to reconcile the Christian morality of equality with reducing people to slavery? There were no lack of extremist voices like the Scottish philosopher John Mair, a professor at the Sorbonne, who invoked Aristotle's theory of natural slavery in order to argue that the peoples of the West Indies, who lived under the Equator, were *ferini*, given that they lived *bestialiter*, and thus they had to be considered *natura servi*, 'by nature slaves'.[122] Others also associated themselves with his evaluation. The Latin term *servus* helped to decide the question, given that its meaning had expanded so that it designated not only slavery but also many forms of forced labour. Thus could the king decree the Leyes de Burgos – the laws in which the *indios* were defined 'free subjects of the crown'. The year 1513 saw the writing of the *requerimiento* – the document read out upon each fresh 'discovery' in order to attest to the legitimate legal authority over the land.

As heated arguments continued apace, Francisco de Vitoria, a Dominican priest considered the greatest theologian of the time, made his own intervention. During a lecture he gave at the University of Salamanca in the first half of 1539, Vitoria outlined two *Relictiones de Indis*, in which he set the question of the *conquista* and the even thornier matter of colonization within the wider context of international law, which he thus helped to found. For the first time, Vitoria formulated a duty of hospitality sanctioned by what he called *ius migrandi*, the 'right to migrate'.

Dominium was founded on *humanitas*, 'humanity'. Each human being is a *dominum*, master, in that he is created in the image of God. Neither deadly sins nor *infidelitas* were an obstacle. Thus Vitoria turned the discourse around. And, to make things clear, he added that it is a *dominus* who can suffer an *injuria* – damage, violation. Even children are *domini*. This was the turning point: the *indios* were *domini*. Indeed, they had cities, they had arranged laws, and they led an ordered life. So they could not be denied their property, despoiled of their assets. In short, no one could purport to justify the *conquista* by invoking the supremacy of civilization over barbarism.

Rather, if the *indios* were *veri domini*, masters of their lands, then it was necessary to find convincing reasons why they should be hospitable. Given that the human being is a social animal, as Aristotle teaches, she, by her very nature, requires a *ius communicationis ac societatis*, a 'right to communication and sociality' that is articulated in a series of rights that derive from it, as corollaries. And these are: the possibility of commercial exchanges, *ius commercii*; the right to preach and herald the Gospel; the right to travel, *ius peregrinandi in illas provincias*, and even to reside, *ius degendi*, or even to make one's home, *accipere domicilum in aliqua civitate illorum*; and, finally, the right to migrate to the New World, *ius migrandi*.[123] The *indios* would have committed a grave *injuria*, if they did not accord these rights to the Spanish, who would, then, have been able to assert a *ius belli*, and take recourse to war. All the more so given that, in the *communitas orbis* – the world made common and united by communication – these rights were natural and should be recognized for all human beings.

This theological-political legitimation of *conquista* was ambivalent: it recognized the sovereignty and dignity of the *indios* in the very same moment as it obliged them to accept the Spanish presence, thus endorsing their expropriation. Incapable of governing themselves with autonomous political forms, the *indios* would thus need 'oversight'. Without entirely betraying the Christian legacy of hospitality, by which it is 'humane and right' to treat strangers well, Vitoria was attracted by the idea of promoting an international law, even though he was keenly aware of its paradoxes, if the desire for sociality did, indeed, have to impose itself through force.[124]

24 *Mare liberum* and the sovereign's word

In seeking to give a theological foundation to his right to communication, Vitoria had picked up on a narrative that was destined to become a *topos* of natural right. The world was originally held in common by all; there had existed no borders or property that impeded free passage; only subsequently were nations established and was property accepted. Communication partly restored the original stage. But what had this to do with the sea? Well, the seas were set aside from the division of the globe.

Some time later, in 1604, it so happened that the *Santa Catarina*, a Portuguese ship crossing the Malacca Strait, was boarded and assaulted by Dutch sailors who seized from it a booty equivalent to 3 million florins. What law could have stopped them? Heated arguments raged.

In defending their cause, the Dutch called on Hugo Grotius, a philosopher and brilliant lawyer who worked for the Dutch East

India Company, the Vereenigde Oost-Indische Compagnie. And there could be no doubt: for Grotius, it was the Dutch who were in the right, as they had opposed the Spanish and Portuguese monopoly over the seas. As for the booty, it was the result of a privateer war through which the Portuguese were punished for having transgressed natural law.

In Leiden, in spring 1609, Grotius published his anonymous pamphlet *Mare liberum*. It was fated to have many echoes among his contemporaries, and to produce profound repercussions on how geopolitics were seen – starting, indeed, with the contrast between land and sea.[125] Natural law determined that the sea is free. No regime of sovereignty over it could be acceptable. Unlike the land, the air and water escape appropriation. Nonetheless, sources and rivers, which are public property, could be ceded or leased. Conversely, the sea, which 'cannot be accounted in the nature of goods', is among 'those things which at all cannot be possessed nor as it were possessed and whose alienation is prohibited'.[126] Grotius thought of the immense ocean, which 'can not be enclosed, does not cease except in the case of a diverticulum alone; and a diverticulum of the sea is very like the air shut up in a building, which it is absurd for anyone to say becomes property'.[127] One cannot prevent innocent peaceful navigation, nor passage – in case of pressing need – through places that are contiguous with the sea, such as beaches and shorelines, or adjacent to appropriable lands. Hospitality is a duty and refuge cannot be denied. 'It is barbarous to reject foreigners ... One cannot approve of those who forbid foreigners entrance into the city.'[128] Although Grotius sought to develop commerce, in the widest sense, responding to Vitoria's communication, he outlined an open hospitality in which the sea remained, despite everything, the space standing outside of sovereignty.

But it would be Pufendorf, who took over the chair at Heidelberg University from Grotius, who shifted the goalposts. Hospitality was pushed out of the political sphere, as it now acquired an ethical value only. The Europeans reversed the steps that they had taken, admitting that they had erroneously used it as an alibi in order to subject the *indios*.[129] Following in the same furrow as Hobbes's *Leviathan*, Pufendorf thus opposed both Vitoria and Grotius. Of course, one ought not to reject the refugee or refuse passage to a voyager. But hospitality, which had been sacred and inviolable for the ancients, could not be granted to just anyone, without conditions. Rather, it was necessary to sift, to choose and control; some yardstick had to be imposed. Hospitality was not, then, a right, but a favour conferred by the sovereign.

25 Kant, the right to visit and residency denied

It is no exaggeration to say that the manner in which the theme of migration is dealt with in the third millennium had already been outlined in the ambivalent compromise that Kant proposed in his essay *Perpetual Peace* in 1795: a compromise between appropriation of the soil and the possibility of passage, between sovereignty and hospitality. Tellingly, the 1951 Geneva Convention on the status of refugees, which declared the principle of *non-refoulement*, adopted almost to the letter the words in which Kant had argued that the foreigner must not be denied first entry if this could cause him damage, *Untergang* – if this could put his life in jeopardy.

It is in the *Third Definitive Article for Perpetual Piece* that Kant speaks of a 'cosmopolitan right' and 'universal hospitality': *Weltbürgerrecht* and *allgemeine Hospitalität*.[130] These most famous few pages were destined, through their visionary depth, to exercise an enormous influence. For Kant, it was necessary to reconcile opposing requirements: on the one hand, the requirements of states, ready to defend their territorial sovereignty at all costs; and, on the other hand, the requirements of foreigners – that is, of those who, relocating from one place to another, would prefer not to run up against barriers, fences and enclosures. What solution could be found?

Kant pushed further, into that complex space still exclusively given over to the law of war. This is a space in which states not only face and confront each other but also decide on whether they should admit foreigners, and according to what procedures. This was the space for a new *ius cosmopoliticum*, in which it would finally be possible to look forward to peace, if only the necessary conditions were set in place. In this context, Kant proclaimed the 'right of a foreigner', *das Recht eines Fremdlings*, meaning the right to hospitality. This was a matter of an individual – universally valid – right, that ought to be understood in its political sense. It was not, in short, a question of 'philanthropy'. And it could be summarized as follows: the foreigner who arrives on others' soil cannot be treated *feindselig*, 'in a hostile way'. It is as if Kant wanted to issue a warning, in order to highlight that old etymological and political confusion between *hospes* and *hostis* – which had already caused so many conflicts and misfortunes, as it led the foreign guest to be considered, at first sight, as an enemy.[131]

The cosmopolitan right to universal hospitality is the condition of perpetual peace. Any person, wherever fate may steer them, has the right to enter the territory without being taken for an enemy. This is a natural right, since each person has a right to a place on the globe, which is spherical and finite. It echoes in secularized form the theological principle of the primeval commonality of the Earth. But Kant elevates hospitality to a juridical and political category. This right has nothing to do with morals. Even a devilish people would be able to take part in the cosmopolitan space, acquiring a juridical-political architecture on which basis they could offer and reciprocate hospitality. You don't have to be good to be just.

What interests Kant is *Verkehr, commercium*, both in its narrower sense and in the wider sense of exchange, communication, the reciprocal relations between strangers that will ultimately end up encountering each other ever more often in a world that has set off along the course of globalization. How, otherwise, could distant peoples have peaceful relations? Commerce, almost a metonym of cosmopolitanism, becomes not only a means but also an end, a fact that itself demands the realization of a community.

It seems that the reconciliation has succeeded: a cosmopolitan sense of right recognizes states' territorial property and persons' individual freedoms. Up till this point, one can only applaud Kant. All the more so given that, if the previous state of war set its targets on the enemy, the right to perpetual peace starts out from the foreigner. Her entry must be seen as an inclination to enter into society, as a declaration of sociability. A new political path opens up that goes beyond love for one's neighbour and beyond the disastrous practice of war. It is necessary neither to love nor to hate the foreigner, but simply to respect her. Remembering the wrongdoing committed by colonial expansion, and the injustices perpetrated by Europeans who in '*visiting* foreign countries and peoples' took no account of the inhabitants and made the 'visit' into a 'conquest', Kant wanted both to avoid this being repeated and to leave open all the paths of commerce. Hospitality did not, therefore, authorize the foreigner to rob, exploit and enslave. The condemnation of imperialism was accompanied by the defence and promotion of the incipient capitalism that was advancing across land and sea. Kant thus celebrated the ship and the camel – defined as the 'desert ship' – which cut distances and make it possible to intensify exchanges with the indigenous and peoples who remain isolated. Conscious of how far-reaching his own perspective was, Kant called Grotius and Pufendorf 'miserable comforters' because they still thought in warlike terms and supported the interests of individual states.[132] The right that he instead outlined, within the cosmopolitan space, simplifies the encounter under the banner of mutual respect.

But what happens to the foreigner once she has been granted permission to enter? Can she stay? Even for a little while? Or, perhaps, decide to establish herself there forever? Kant makes a very sharp distinction between the 'right to visit', *Besuchsrecht*, and the 'right to welcome', *Gastrecht*. What is conceded is only the former, not the latter. So long as she is 'peacefully in her place', the foreigner can visit others' countries, as a tourist, a trader, a pilgrim, an explorer and so on. But she cannot assert a right to be welcomed as a guest for a protracted time – that is, to reside there. If that were the case, Kant writes – between brackets, as if to minimize and distance such a possibility – this would demand a 'contract', a *Vertrag*, or rather a 'benevolent contract', such as to allow her to be a *Hausgenosse*, a 'housemate' living in the same house, 'for a certain period', if not forever. The conditions of such a stay are not really clear.[133] What is certain is that the foreigner can never become a resident. Her right is limited to visiting. As Derrida observes, it seems that here the foreigner is the citizen of another state and that hospitality is bestowed within the confines of citizenship.[134]

In the Kantian universe, the foreigner would not be taken in. There is no right to residency. And there is no human right outside of the confines of property, which moreover slide dangerously from public to private limits. This has given rise to many misunderstandings – as if the foreigner were entering a house and not a state territory. Kant was concerned to prevent any possible form of subversion of property, and thus to ensure individual freedoms within these confines. Hence the foreigner's fate is decided by the sovereign. Thus, hospitality is simultaneously both the accomplishment and outer limit of public law in the sense in which Kant conceived it, and in the sense in which he handed it down to modernity.

2

THE END OF HOSPITALITY?

We are the countless, doubling at every chessboard house
We pave your sea with skeletons so we can walk on it
You cannot count us, if counted we become more,
the children of the horizon, which draws in on us like a
drawstring ...
We carry Homer and Dante, the blind and the pilgrim,
The smell that you lost, the equality that you have beaten down

Erri de Luca, *Solo andata*

1 The continent of migrants

The migration issue is again on the agenda. It has emerged as one of
the main points on the political agenda; it attracts media attention
and sparks daily anxieties among public opinion. The debate often
assumes emotional tones and extreme accents, polarizing into a for
and an against, while the complexity of the phenomenon ends up
relegated to the background. Generalizations abound, common-
places make headway, words are used out of place, concepts become
indistinct and obfuscated, and statistics are more often invoked to
frighten than to inform. Thus results a *partial* picture of global
migration, in both senses of the word: on the one hand, limited and
incomplete; on the other, one-sided and unfair.

The migrant is cast as a threat that looms over the sovereign state.
Here takes shape a conflict. Faced with the migrant who seeks entry,
the state cannot but exercise its sovereign right to control its borders.
If the migrant tries to cross these borders nonetheless, not only does

she evade the barrier or violate the law, but most importantly she undermines the state's sovereignty. That is why the conflict becomes so acute. Its supremacy challenged and its foundations jeopardized, the state puts the brakes on 'irregular immigration', reasserting its own power of self-determination as it excludes, rejects and expels. To this end, the state rallies the nation together, it points to the need to defend the borders and it sounds the alarm over security. The sovereigntists – the adepts of state sovereignty – respond to this call, but so, too, do frightened citizens, or even just those who are worried about remaining protected within borders. Conversely, those who hold more to the duty to support migrants' human rights do not respond to this call. This polarization agitates the public debate and inflames protests in the squares. Hence the two opposed perspectives: the state-centric or nationalist one that looks on migration with dismay, as an extraneous event, an external factor for disturbance; and the extra-state or inter-national one that instead assumes the migrant's perspective. But it would be mistaken not to detect, behind and beyond this polarization, the deeper, decisive clash between the state and the migrant.

Even if, historically speaking, migration is hardly a new phenomenon, the global events of the twenty-first century have radically changed its significance and dimensions. There is no part of the planet exempt from it. The effects are so widespread that it is difficult to imagine that there are those who still have no experience of it.[1]

But what do the numbers say? Who are the migrants? Where do they come from and where are they going? Which routes, which areas are most afffected? Which aspects of this are unprecedented? Contrary to what is generally believed, the numbers are not 'objective' and they never tell a clear story. The war of statistics is, in this context, even tougher, both because the countries of provenance often do not keep a tally of the co-nationals who emigrate, and because 'irregular' migrants, who are not in the minority, evade the official statistics.

The UN defines as a 'migrant' whoever finds themselves outside of their country of residence for at least a year. According to the *International Migration Report* for 2015, that year the number of migrants in the world reached 244 million.[2] This amounts to around 3 per cent of the globe's overall population. But this is higher than the number of people living in Indonesia. One could speak of an outright continent of migrants. The weakness of the numbers is that they fall short, not that they overcount, for it is virtually impossible to calculate the number of irregular migrants. This pushes us to estimate that the numbers are even higher.

If one considers the enormous disparity between the great closed sphere of the Western and Westernized world – where the system of capital, of technology, of comfort, has been built up over time – and the boundless hinterland of misery, the planetary suburbs of hardship and desolation, one may rightly ask: how come, even now, so few have emigrated? Moreover, if a quarter of humanity disposes of riches and resources that are withheld from the other three-quarters, and if inequalities are sharpening, there is also a growing awareness – thanks to the media and new media – that a better life is possible, at the same time as the access routes seem more rapid and speedy. So, it is highly surprising that the number of migrants is not much higher. And it is not difficult to hypothesize that the numbers will go on increasing exponentially. The losers whom globalization has left at the margins are likewise potential migrants. Those who do not move – the greater share – are simply the poorest, the most marginalized, the ultimate victims of the imbalance. Those who have the least economic opportunities stay where they are. Migration is also an investment.

Over the last forty years, the number of migrants has tripled, risimg from 77 million in 1975 to 244 million in 2015. The directions in which they are heading have also changed. Migrants move from poor countries to rich ones. But that does not mean that the route is always, as is widely believed, from the South to the North. The novelty is that the South has also become a pole of attraction: 110 million have moved towards the South of the world, whereas around 130 million have moved towards the North. If America is no longer the El Dorado it once was, there are ever more frequent South-to-South movements – also on account of the attractive power of emerging countries such as Brazil, South Africa, China and India. Nonetheless, in 2015, Europe continued to play host to the highest number of immigrants – around 76 million – followed by Asia, which played host to 75 million, and then the other continents. Looking instead at individual countries, the classification seems more eccentric and varied: 47 million migrants reside in the United States, 12 million in Germany, a similar number in Russia, and 10 million in Saudi Arabia. If these numbers clearly indicate the destinations migrants are heading towards, rather more opaque is the question of where they are coming from, given that the countries of origin do not always register expatriations. Finally, one should mention two unprecedented developments: the growing rate of internal migration, which especially takes place in Africa; and temporary migration, i.e. relocations for limited periods, often for work reasons.

But the geopolitical landscape of migratory movements has particularly changed on account of the accelerated consequences of

globalization. It is no longer possible to make any clear and definitive distinction between place of departure and place of arrival.
Suddenly, one same country can be simultaneously the place of
immigration, of transit and of emigration. This is what especially
happens in Italy and, more generally, in the whole Mediterranean
area, which illustrates this dynamic circulatory movement better
than any other part of the world.

After the 'Arab Spring', the war in Syria and the emergence of
ISIS, the world's total number of refugees has increased. According
to UNHCR (United Nations High Commission for Refugees) data,
in 2015 the numbers surpassed 20 million. This is the highest figure
reached since the Second World War. The greater part of them
come from Syria, Afghanistan and Somalia. Tens of thousands
have met their deaths in the attempt to cross the Mediterranean.
This displaced population is temporarily 'received' in camps that
sometimes stretch to the size of cities. They are concentrated in
Turkey, the single country that plays host to most refugees, followed
by Pakistan, Lebanon and Iran.[3] To the refugees one should add,
following the figures supplied by the UNHCR, almost 40 million
internally displaced persons (IDPs) and 2 million asylum-seekers,
together with 10 million stateless people.

The continent of migrants, dispersed everywhere across the globe,
is an enormous and varied people in movement that challenges the
frontiers of the global order. Against this people stands the state,
the ultimate bastion of the old order, of the obsolete *nomos* of the
Earth. From this stems the acute conflict between state sovereignty
and the right to migrate, between a citizenship restricted at the
borders and a new, deterritorialized citizenship.

2 'Us' and 'them': the grammar of hatred

Hundreds, thousands – hanging on to the sinking dinghies, massed
on the ships that have rescued them, lined up in endless queues
upon disembarking, assembled in the 'reception centres' after their
arrival. Not to mention those stuck in the Libyan *lagers* or the
crowds parked in the camps for the displaced. The images are
always the same: they show anonymous crowds, indistinct and dark
masses. Rarely do the TV cameras focus on a face. Nor do the
terrified eyes, or the tears, appear on the screen. The TV viewers'
everyday existence remains immune to all this, or rather immunizes
itself against it. Contributing to this are the words that accompany
these images, in the media, on the web and in political discourse:
'immigration emergency', 'humanitarian crisis', 'Biblical exodus',

'new waves', 'human tide', 'invasion of clandestine migrants' and so on.

This wandering humanity is an anomalous wave, a tsunami, a catastrophe, crashing against 'us'. Alarm, danger, emergency – multitude, exodus, invasion. 'We' who 'can't take them all in!'. 'We' who 'are at the limit of our capacities!' 'They' who 'are a challenge for our institutions'. 'They' who 'are a threat to our workers, to the young and unemployed'. 'They' who 'put our identity at risk'. For 'they' are 'different' to us in every way. Suddenly, the human tide no longer has anything human about it. It is a knot of bodies; a confused, crawling mass; a sinister and dark swarm. 'No, we don't want them.' Doors and hearts close. 'What do they want here?' 'They should go back where they came from!' Fear gets the upper hand. 'We' are few, defenceless, impotent, faced with 'them', who are a hostile, imposing, inhuman mass. The fear of the other has had its effect. The gap cannot be bridged.

'We' – 'them'. Pronouns are not indifferent. They situate individuals and groups when they speak, they delimit their roles, and they direct their discourse. They are the first decisive borders – linguistic ones. Strangely, no philosophy of pronouns has yet been written.[4]

What, then, does 'us' mean? Its meaning is ambivalent. 'We' is the first grammatical form of the community. It ought, therefore, to include. The 'I' and the 'you' seem to melt into the unison of 'we'. It cannot be denied. And yet 'we' has always also had a bitter tonality. For even as it includes, at the same time it excludes. 'We' implicitly also refers to some 'you' (plural) which is not only the result of a split, but already has an almost warlike accent. And all the more so 'them' – or, worse, 'that lot'. What 'we' distinguishes from itself becomes the 'you' (plural), which still has the dignity of being personal, even if it is marked by hostility; what the 'we' cannot, instead, reach, which it cannot notice, once it is expelled from its ambit of sound and light, falls into the dark and mute 'them'.

Even in just pronouncing itself, the word 'we' continually runs up against its own borders, in the 'you' (plural) in front of us and the 'them' that remain in the background. It can aim at inclusion. Or it can lock itself down in an identitarian spasm, to the point of intoning 'Us First!' In this case, the 'we' reveals itself so minuscule and vacuous that, in order to feel stronger, it nonetheless needs some 'not-we'. And what's better, for winning this 'we' better visibility, for bringing it into relief than 'clandestine immigrants'?

Much could be said about the recent declensions of 'we' in its systematic attempt to exclude the other. Even to the point that some have proposed the formula 'we-ism' in order to describe this decline.[5] But the pronouns themselves are not guilty. The problem is how the 'we' entrenches, armours, fortifies itself,; how it hardens its own borders, erecting them as uncrossable barriers; how it belligerently confronts the 'you' (plural); and how, rather than welcome these others, these excluded third parties, granting them a place 'among-us', rejects them as an impersonal plurality, to the point of reifying them, making them into an anonymous and indistinct mass.

This is not only, then, a matter of an uncrossable gap that persists, despite everything, between the 'we' and the 'you' (plural). What deepens the hiatus, what makes the fracture more acute, is the indecipherable mass of the 'not-we' to which the 'they' is condemned. To envisage the other is no small enterprise. It is already difficult to envisage relatives, friends and acquaintances. And the same is true for strangers, and all the more so for foreigners. The pain of others – even when it is patent, flagrant, undeniable – can be ignored with indifference. One can go so far as to inflict this pain – as the case of torture shows. The long and complex phenomenological-hermeneutical tradition which has had the merit of reflecting on the 'other' has demonstrated its own limit by the very fact of assuming this other to be a single individual.[6] Attention is focused on sym-pathy, com-passion, 'putting oneself in her shoes', and too often this latter is considered an immediate and instinctive process. We never do manage to put on someone else's shoes; and the pretence of being able to do so itself appears suspect, for it takes the path of appropriation. It is dazzling, an illusion, that has recently found new credibility in the magic word 'empathy', given a new lease of life by the cognitive sciences.

If it is not possible to put oneself in another's place, it is, however, possible to imagine the pain of others, their suffering, anguish and torment. The work of the imagination is not, however, aided by images, when they do not allow the capturing of individual contours, the features and the peculiarities of the individual. The imagination is blocked, held back by the numbers, inhibited by the mass. For a moment, the gaze fixes on a woman wavering as she disembarks from a ship. But how is it possible to feel something without having an understanding of her history, without knowing anything about her? The opposite example is that of the literature that transports one beyond one's own self and towards the other, even if this other – for instance, Anna Karenina – is fictitious. A diffuse enculturation, distant from the world of letters, accompanies the daily usage of images capable only of blocking the imagination. And its political and ethical effects are devastating. The more that this block repeats itself, the more the viewer is driven to identify with the great 'we', distancing the mass of the multiple 'theys' from her own self. In this universe, reduced to the monotony of black and white, hatred prospers.

This is not a natural and spontaneous hatred. Rather, it is cultivated, nourished, fed. It follows models; it requires schemas and paths to follow: the discriminatory act, the mortifying concepts, the words of scorn. The rancour of the individual, finally free to hate, is channelled into the collective rancour. But free hatred has little to do with freedom. To be free to hate is a sad sentence indeed. And it indicates an existential frustration, an identitarian fanaticism, a political impotence. On the one hand is the 'us'; on the other, the dark and monstrous 'not-us', repugnant and detestable, guilty for 'our' malaise – no matter how, or why. But guilty.

In a piece of reportage written before the dismantling of Europe's biggest *bidonville*, Emmanuel Carrère described the rage, the ill will and resentment of the citizens of Calais, of the old and now fallen labour aristocracy and the new lumpenproletariat that has found, in immigrants, someone even lowlier to hate.[7]

3 Europe 2015

Hostility has caught Europe in its grip. The history books of the future that do not indulge the hegemonic narrative – the ones that want to give voice not only to those who were within, protected and sheltered – will have to tell of how the homeland of human rights, which ought to have offered welcome to those without a homeland, to those fleeing from civil war in Syria, from persecution in Eritrea, from oppression in Sudan, from the bombs in Afghanistan, and to those who tried to escape hunger, desolation and death, instead denied asylum and refused to host them. Rather, the potential guest was stigmatized *a priori* as an enemy. Fear won out; the cynicism of security prevailed.

At the borders, the use of radar, ultrasound and videocameras has multiplied. In the gloomy recent past, barbed wire has made its overbearing return – not just a few yards of it, which were always there, but rather miles'-worth of it. The two barriers at Ceuta and Melilla were already there, between Spain and Morocco, to impede the passage across the Strait of Gibraltar: a network of electronic sensors, high-intensity lighting, alternating surveillance posts, and special pathways for security vehicles. It is, therefore, impossible to cross. Yet, with the agreement of Europe's FRONTEX agency, the barriers have been raised up to a height of 6½ yards. This, in order to underline the desert of hostility in which refuge is a mirage and welcome an illusion. Suddenly, barbed wire began to ring the hills of Macedonia, tore its way through the meadows of Bulgaria, proudly left its trace across the plains of Hungary, and has even reached Serbia, Croatia and Slovenia – the countries that only recently emerged from fratricidal conflicts. Thus, the so-called 'Balkan route' has been closed – or almost. Enormous queues of refugees, whose top and tail disappear across the horizon, have followed the rails, passed through the cities, poured onto the motorways. Children, women, the elderly, men of all ages, bearing the marks of terror on their faces, on their bodies the traces of torture and the wounds of war, who have lost relatives or friends, who were lost, famished, frozen, exhausted, have been arrested, hunted out, violently pushed back.

The often crude and brutal images taken and broadcast by the media have moved very few people. No, there has been no pity. Compassion has been shelved, stripped of sense. The rationality of the First World cannot tolerate being ransacked by this repugnant chaos. Forgetful of its own history, Europe has turned its back, closed its eyes, hardened its heart. It has organized to protect itself according to the criteria of a policing logic: drones, helicopters, warships, soldiers, the forces of order, agents, intelligence, elite units. Ports and airports under surveillance, access forbidden, systematic controls – the fortress has walled itself in. Thus, in summer 2015, Europe sealed the end of hospitality. This is the history that needs telling.

The closing of the Balkan route has had immediate effects that are hardly difficult to imagine. Those trapped in the East sought an exit route; for those who were still outside Europe's borders, all that remained was the sea route. Many Syrians and Kurds gathered on the coasts of Turkey in the hope of finding some passage via the nearby Greek islands, whose coastlines can be seen from the Turkish shore. The traffickers have been both assiduous and zealous in providing the crossings, using small boats that can easily be hidden away. Seeking to film the arrivals, the lenses of the TV cameras sometimes even went there, to the places where tourists' holidays were disturbed by the irruption of voyagers arriving from the incomprehensible universe of Oriental wars.

But one photo on 3 September 2015 seemed to mark a turning point. It depicted Alan, a 3-year-old Kurdish boy born in Kobane, Syria. Even the sea had rejected him. His corpse was discovered early in the morning, together with those of other drowned people, on the beach in Bodrum. In his blue shorts and red T-shirt, Alan Kurdi lay dumped on the water's edge. He looked almost as if he were sleeping, waiting to be waken up. It was him, simply a little boy, who woke up public opinion. A Turkish policeman picked up his body – a photograph immortalized him in images that, once the first embarrassment had passed, travelled around the world. The shock was enormous. 'Alan, our son!' The indignation, mixed with compassion, could not conceal the sense of guilt. All the more so, given that Alan's story also included horrifying surprises that forced the West to account for its own responsibilities.

The family had tried to escape ISIS's violence by moving from Syria to Turkey – indeed, several times, and with various setbacks. The family hoped to move to Canada, thanks to some relatives who had already emigrated there. If at first it was the Turkish authorities who did not give them the expatriation permit, subsequently it was the Canadian authorities who turned down the asylum request, on account of bureaucratic technicalities. Thus, it was the power of bureaucracy that determined the family's fate. The father, Abdullah Kurdi, then decided to try his luck and cross that short stretch of sea that separates the Turkish coast from the Greek island of Kos – only 3 nautical miles, a thirty-minute crossing. He entrusted his fate to the local traffickers. After three failed attempts, he organized a fourth. On 2 September, before dawn, they set off on a dinghy that managed to evade the coast-guard. But twenty people were squeezed into a boat that could have taken eight people at a push. The mother, Rehana, reticent about this voyage, had acquiesced despite herself; she did not want to head out into open sea.

Many parts of the story are unclear. Perhaps the 'captain', accused of steering the dinghy so badly that he ultimately caused it to capsize, was Abdullah Kurdi himself. That, at least, is what the testimonies of the few survivors tell us. This should make us reflect on the hypocrisy that envelops the category of 'trafficker', on whom all the blame is offloaded. The tragedy played out in a few minutes: the life-jackets did not work and the sea engulfed almost all the refugees. Including Alan's mother and his 5-year-old brother, Galib. Only the father managed to save himself.

It is impossible to reconstruct, here, the effects that the photo of this little boy lying on his side on the beach produced everywhere, as he became the scandalous symbol of help denied. In this image, Europe had to recognize that it had itself been shipwrecked. Two German artists, Oguz Sen and Justis Becker, reproduced it in an immense, 130-yard long mural that stands over Frankfurt, on the bank of the Main, facing the European Central Bank. They put it there as a reminder, they said, of all the children who had died seeking a route to safety in Europe. But this *graffito* also portrayed in concrete terms the collapse of human rights when even rescue operations are denied.

Two days after the image of Alan was broadcast, the German Chancellor Angela Merkel decided to open the borders to the refugees stuck on the Balkan route, especially in Hungary. This fed the creation of humanitarian corridors from northern Greece to southern Bavaria. Thus, almost as if to mitigate the shame, there followed the images of Germans welcoming the Syrian refugees in rail stations, with cards saying *Willkommen*. This opening to hospitality did not fall from the sky, but most looked at it with some enthusiasm.

But the compassion soon ran out.[8] There have always been sporadic cases, initiatives by humanitarian associations or religious refugees, or even small acts by citizens – often remaining anonymous – who have spontaneously come forth with assistance. We see this from Lampedusa to Calais, and from Ventimiglia to Greece, where refugees blocked at the Macedonian border in their long journey to the north have recounted having received clothes and food precisely from the very poorest Greeks. The defeat of hospitality from the political authorities has prompted an ethical response, almost by way of reparation. This could lead to a misunderstanding, if this response were read as the definitive reduction of hospitality to a private act, to the moral supplement of a practice whose value is eminently political. Indeed, the personalization of hospitality risks emptying out its institutional significance. Certainly, this gesture of openness, attesting to the conviction that no one can be discarded, excluded and marginalized, is the existential test of an individual. But it does not represent a solitary act – it is inscribed in a community. In the impulse of those citizens who have not given in to the diktats of natural sovereignty and its exclusionary laws, in the exemplary ethics of their action, it is instead important to make out the call for another politics.

This call has not been satisfied in any way. Signed on the wave of emotion on 22 September 2015, the EU accord directed at sharing out the migrants concentrated in Greece and Italy among all EU countries remained a dead letter. Europe abdicated any common reception policy. Everywhere, the most mean-spirited sovereigntism prevailed. Taking in migrants has become a taboo. Migration has increasingly been stigmatized as a pathology to be removed in the name of the reality of the nation. It is imagined that it is possible to stop the 'flows of migrants' by extending the controls and strengthening the barriers.

The closing of the Balkan route has had disastrous consequences for refugees. They have no alternative but to try to cross the watery wall of the strait of Sicily, in fragile boats and perilous dinghies. Syrians, Kurds, Eritreans, Sudanese, Afghans and Iraqis have trusted the waves to take them from the coasts of Africa to the outposts of Europe. Their hoped-for destination: Lampedusa. For many, the long journey has ended at the bottom of the sea. Unreported, unrecounted, uncommemorated. The same scenes have played out repeatedly: migrants who struggle in the water, desperately thrashing around until they finally disappear. But no, these scenes have not made a great impact. Over time, force of habit has instead prevailed. The very people who were moved by the image of Alan, who expressed all their indignation on Facebook, have fallen silent faced with the hundreds of children drowned. With their silence, they have given their approval to the defence-of-Europe-at-all-costs – its fight against migrants.

Many have become wedded to the logic of the nation. Even those who earlier had a cosmopolitan air have rediscovered their patriotism, reneging on these old ideals and disowning them. Why on earth should Italian, English, French and German workers have to take others' misery on their shoulders? Few have dared to raise their voices to speak of hospitality. Populist discourses have had the better of things, fomenting hatred, cultivating fear and slyly associating immigration with terrorism. The new phobocracy has established itself.[9] Where the state of emergency existed already, it has been extended; special laws have been enacted; and, faced with the so-called 'migration crisis', many European states, especially ones in the East, have barricaded the doors. Racist incidents have multiplied; reception centres have been set alight and honest citizens have staged protests against refugees, women and children, arriving in their communities. Walls have been put up that ought to have been unimaginable, after the Berlin Wall. The biggest is one in France – a wall demanded and financed by Britain – next to the port of Calais, in order to block Channel crossings.

Germany soon regretted this generous hospitality towards the Syrian refugees. The borders are borders and must be respected: this is the almost unanimous chorus not only of German citizens, but also of journalists, intellectuals and philosophers.[10]

Both the holding camps for identification, rebranded 'hotspots', and the refugee camps outside of Europe's borders have multiplied. On 18 March 2016, Europe concluded an agreement with Turkey, whose only purpose was to contain the flow of migrants and repatriate Syrian refugees who had managed to reach the shores of Greece. The signing of this accord definitively sealed the forgetting of Alan and his image.

4 Hegel, the Mediterranean and the cemetery of the sea

The sea does not separate; rather, it 'connects'. It is the mountains that divide peoples and keep them at a distance from one another. The sea, which is boundless, and does not tolerate boundaries, invites a form of life consecrated to openness. Thus wrote Hegel, without forgetting, however, to underline its ambivalent, almost dialectical character. For it can suddenly turn into its opposite. The apparently soft, almost submissive watery surface, can suddenly become choppy, allowing perilous waves to rise up from the depths. Precisely because it does not resist any pressure, the sea does not afford anyone a grip. The fact that the water is so yielding can also prove dangerous. Curiosity rises up, courage reawakens, and it drives people to go beyond the limits, to the point of exposing themselves to shipwreck. Unlimited space, free from any restrictions, the sea encourages movement, promotes exchange, indulges progress. When it touches a piece of land, it does not leave the life there unchanged.

It is no surprise that, in this perspective, which looks from the water to the coasts, Hegel recognizes in the Mediterranean 'the axis of world history'.[11] It is impossible to imagine history without this sea, which, with its inlets, its bays, its gulfs, its recesses, has linked one land to another, abetting their mutual relations. The Mediterranean is the 'centre' of ancient civilizations, the meeting place of peoples, the route of commerce, the mirror of the Western shore as of the Eastern one. With a paradoxical inversion, Hegel went as far as to say that the Mediterranean is the 'centre of the world'.

After the discovery of the New World, history's centre of gravity shifted towards the Ocean; but this did not mark the twilight of the Mediterranean. Carl Schmitt's prophecy, which hypothesized an irreversible change owing to the consolidation of US power, has not been wholly confirmed.[12] The Mediterranean has not been abandoned to the past. On the contrary, it is perhaps the sea we talk about most. But, as a source of threat, it causes harm and calamity; it is from there that there come the new 'invasions', the never-banished spectre of the ones of ancient times. The jargon of 'rejections', which betrays centuries of hospitality, is echoed by the nostalgic rhetoric of the olive tree and the cypress, light breezes and sundrenched beaches, symbols of a lost splendour, a past that slips into myths and can arouse only an antiquarian passion. With the aggravating factor that the model of coexistence, a resource and challenge for the future, regresses to the point of becoming an unreachable dream, a form of paradise at most suited for oil-painted idylls.

The Mediterranean thus remains a protagonist in news reports, in a near-schizophrenic polarity; on the one hand, the legendary sea of infinite odysseys, the landscape of Greek myths, the cradle of civilizations, and, on the other hand, the sea of migrants, of unstoppable misery, of the revolt which takes on the waves, which threatens to disembark, which asks for hospitality, and which ends up shipwrecked.

The tourist and the refugee – or even one next to the other, on the same beach – are the emblematic figures between which the Mediterranean is divided. The contrast could not be more strident. Yet, while the surface of the water preserves no trace of this, and does not allow for billboards or commercial adaptations, the routes of globalization have crossed the length and breadth of the oceans. Even the Mediterranean has been caught in its net. Banished the adventure, quenched the desire for discovery, and exhausted the thirst for knowledge that had detained Ulysses in his countless landings during his return journey – very little remains of the epic feats of former times. Every day, imposing cruise ships offload tourists animated by the compulsive need to consume, while perilous dinghies and 'old tubs' lose part of their cargo in the abyss. Banality and disaster chase each other across the waves, leaving trails of refuse, drifting wreckage: on the one hand, plastic and cans; on the other, discarded humans.

The bottom of the sea no longer only preserves incredible finds from the past, and nor is it only a mysterious underground archaeological site. For some time, now, the Mediterranean has also become a watery cemetery.

> marble trembles over many shades
> and there, upon my tombs, the sleeping, faithful sea!

Thus wrote Paul Valéry in a long metaphysical poem on time, death and immortality.[13] The sea has always been a metaphor for a void from which there is no return, an enigmatic grave. Now the metaphor has lost its aura, instead collapsing into a gloomy reality.

Migrants have found their asylum in the sea depths just off Lampedusa, only a few miles from the destination to which they had aspired. The 'clandestine', the hidden, sunk in that secret, mute, solitary space, have never resurfaced into the light of day. The bottom of the sea has become their final abode, the tomb of their dreams, the cemetery of their hopes. Their eyes are lost in the abyss. Their bodies, stiff, delicate – and dressed in their best clothes, ready to disembark – have dissolved amidst the seaweed.

They will bear witness. They will tell those who come of their errant ways, which finished in the void; they will tell of their error, Europe. They will denounce the wrongdoing, they will unveil the scandal. Never again will the Mediterranean be the same as it was before. No one will be able wipe away the tombs of the clandestine migrants whom *mare nostrum* has welcomed into its depths.

5 Fadoul's story

Gathered in a small black backpack, made of second-rate nylon, is the fragmented story of Fadoul. The birth certificate, an ID document, a pair of letters – and no certificate of residency. Every now and then he opens it to check that everything is there, and then carefully closes it again. This backpack is the remainder of his identity, the home he is waiting for. He always carries it with him.

Fadoul is a son of exile. He no longer remembers very well the place where he was born: a refugee camp in Cameroon, on the border with Chad, whence his family fled during the civil war that lasted for more than a decade, from 1965 to 1979. One of those wars, that is, that the world preferred to ignore and which have never entered into the collective memory. Twenty years have passed. His mother and father are no more. Fadoul has learned a trade and married. But he has always remained in exile. Passing from one place to another, with his wife Kaltuma, he reached Libya. They made their home there, on the outskirts of Tripoli. Fadoul worked in an office. A first child – a daughter, Mouna – was born. And at the very moment that he discovered that Kaltuma was expecting a second, the 'revolution' broke out in Libya. It was 2011. They had spent four years in a small apartment, contenting themselves with what they had. But they abruptly found themselves in the middle of the violence, in the crossfire of rival tribal groups.

Fadoul set off on his way again, with his family. Together with hundreds and thousands of other displaced people, they took the road to the East and managed to enter Tunisia. Exhausted, worn down, with nothing left, they were received in the camps set up by the UNHCR in Choucha. In the first few days, they could catch their breath. Then began an uncertain wait. There, in the tent, weeks were followed by months, and then months by years. At first, they thought that they would be able to go back. Then they understood that such a return was foreclosed. Remain in Tunisia, or flee? They tried to start over again. The family, now including the newborn Hissène, thus moved into the city of Medenina, on the third floor of a crumbling building, inhabited by other migrants. Fadoul found a job. But things were not going well. Of course, it was better than living in a tent. But there was little food. And the Tunisians looked on them unfavourably; a couple of times, they had attacked them. The exclusion made itself felt – they could not continue for long like this.

'Survivors of the sea' – Somalis, Senegalese, Nigerians – often arrived in this block of flats. These were people who had already tried the crossing. The shipwreck had not defeated them to the point that they threw in the towel. The sea had taken them back to shore and they would resume their journey from that inhospitable resort, where they had no mooring. There was no other path to deliverance except the sea. And yet all of them had an atavistic, unconfessed fear of the sea. Perhaps also for this reason, on the eve of every departure, violent brawls broke out, vent was given to old grudges, and pointless disputes opened up unbridgeable chasms of hatred. Tension and worry were fed by rumours about the crossing but also by the outward ban, the almost sacral prohibition against talking about it. It was as if these accounts touched on episodes, acts, events, that ought to have remained wrapped in a sorry and appalled silence. Fadoul had known some of those who had died of thirst, because of a fight breaking out on board, or simply because of a lack of space, suffocated by the other bodies. They had also warned him that during the last crossing, when the boat moved too slowly because of the weight of its cargo, two Nigerians seized by an outburst of rage started to throw the other migrants – even women and children – into the sea. He had heard all this but had not changed his mind.

The decision had been taken. Fadoul had set something aside for it. He managed to muster up the rest by selling the little they had. It was 800 euros for the whole family. The departure was planned for night-time. They had to cross over 3 miles of salt desert to reach the Libyan border. It was a wearisome journey; and yet 6-year-old Mouna walked across these sands without complaining. The self-interested complicity of the Tunisians and the darkness of a moonless sky protected their march. On the other side, the 'traffickers' were waiting for them. They organize the voyage; they check the weather, they ascertain the sea conditions, they calculate the measurements of the vessel, the number of passengers and their weight. And, it should be understood, there are a lot of them. Fadoul did not think badly of them. Ultimately, they had given him proper recompense for the money he had given.

The migrants remained hidden between the sand dunes for a few days. Then came the departure. It was late evening when they met up in the agreed place on the shore. There were seventy of them, perhaps more. Offshore – more than 50 yards from the beach – could be made out a dinghy. The sea did not seem so deep at that point. Fadoul, his wife by his side, picked up the two little children and held Mouna by the hand. Almost none of them knew how to swim. A few did, however, manage to climb aboard. Among these, Fadoul recognized a young Somali woman; she lived in the same block in Medenina. He handed her the two little ones, almost with a jolt, digging his feet into a sand bank that was no longer able to support him. He had water up to his neck. Suddenly he realized that he no longer had Mouna beside him. He desperately searched for her. From the throng around the craft, his gaze turned bewildered to that black and slimy surface that hid a bitter void, the night of the abyss. He thought he had lost everything. It would be senseless to make the voyage without Mouna. But in the clamour, through the shouting, behind him, he thought he could make out more familiar tones. It was her, Mouna. Two women were lifting her onto the dinghy.

To believe in the sea, and trust its waves, one must still have hope on land. Fadoul did. And so, too, did the Sudanese, Somalis and Pakistanis crowded into the dinghy. For them, this was the last chance. 'Better to die than remain in Libya.' They repeated this, to themselves and to the others. A push. They were on their way. Fadoul could not calculate how long it would take, how many miles separated them from the other shore. He knew only that they had to cross that measureless darkness, and that their hope was called Europe.

It was a warm night, the air still, without even a breath of wind. A calm sea – something sailors fear almost even more than the storm. But the motor was running. The dinghy is no great vessel; it does not cut through the waves tracing agile and elegant movements, and above all it does not offer any firm bottom such as would cushion the striking waves. They were at the mercy of this only apparently remitting, yielding mass of water. Despite the lack of space and the nauseating smell of the petrol cast out into the depths, some did manage to get to sleep. Including Kaltuma and the children. Fadoul was awake. The black of the sea joined with the black of the sky in an indistinct whole. The anguish was overwhelming. He regretted this choice.

Over the course of the night, the tension rose. The drinking water had run out. Space started to become ever more contested. Insults and hints of commotion upset the dinghy. Better to wait till sunrise to see each other more clearly, thought Fadoul. Finally, he started to recite a prayer out loud. For now, only God could bring them to Europe safe and sound. A bird approached the dinghy. A sign. But the hours passed, one after another, and the expanse of water seemed to spread out infinitely. A while before, they had sent a text message asking for help, following the smugglers' instructions. But there was total silence. Even the mobile phone had run out of battery, forever. They were drifting. Perhaps the current was even dragging them back towards Libyan waters.

The passengers' eyes slowly began to close, through hunger, fatigue, resignation. Fadoul kept inspecting the horizon every now and then. Suddenly a colour – red – cut through the spectral hues of blue. It had to be a flag, an ensign. There were other colours, white and green. It was the Italian navy. Fadoul waved a T-shirt in the wind. The Italians came towards them. They must have seen them already.

Three dinghies were pulled together. The men were separated from the women and children. When he got onto the ship, Fadoul glimpsed Kaltuma and the children, sat next to the kitchen. He did not know Italian – he understood just a few words, the ones that are a bit like French. They told him that they would be landing in Sicily. But was it true? They weren't going to take them back? Below deck, in his seat, he opened the backpack to check that no water had got in. He prepared the documents for the landing, not without apprehension. Here was the coast. They had said Sicily. But, for them, this was Europe.

Perhaps because they are a family, Fadoul and his loved ones were luckier than most. They were taken to a reception centre run by Catholics. Everything was new: the centre had just been opened. A bed for each, a table to eat at. The worst was behind them. They stayed there for twelve days, comforted by a humanity that they had forgotten. But they had to continue the journey towards France. The Catholics tried to dissuade them. They would have an easier time of being recognized as 'refugees' in Italy. But nothing was to be done. He would struggle to explain the reason, but Fadoul was convinced that France was the end goal. Of course, they had told him about the rampant racism in the land of the Rights of Man. But he imagined that this would be true all over Europe.

They passed through Nice and the dream became reality: they finally walked on French soil. They reached Marseilles. Everything had been easier than expected. But at the train station, as he looked for water, three police officers stopped Fadoul and hauled him into the police station for identification. He explained that he was here with his family and that he could not leave them by themselves. They held him for a long while. Then, finally, they gave him a metro ticket to go back to the station where his loved ones were, on condition that he came back the next morning. Fadoul was worn down, despondent. Better get away from here as quickly as possible.

He found Kaltuma and the children again. They got on the first train – destination, Montpellier. They now set off, roaming like vagrants, spending days on end searching in vain for somewhere to sleep. Finally, someone pointed them to a CADA, a centre for asylum-seekers. They followed the bureaucratic procedures and they were allotted to a village in the slopes of the Pyrenees where other exiles coming from the most varied parts of the world – from Syria to Chechnya and Albania – had been living for some time. Here, Fadoul found everything profoundly alien. It was not what he had expected. The village was nothing but a refugee camp. But they had a little lodging and they received vouchers – little more than €6 a head – for food and everyday expenses. The children rapidly got used to it; Mouna even went to school. Fadoul searched, in vain, for a little work in the local carpentry firms. As had also happened in the past, Kaltuma let herself go, sinking into a torpor that could help her look past the passing of time.

The waiting threatened to engulf their existence anew. But this time, Fadoul was confident. The social workers had told him that if the verdict was taking a long time, this was because their application had a chance of being accepted. Higher up, the first snow fell on the mountains. And it gradually covered their memories. Far from the African landscape and far from the European territory that they had chosen as their ultimate destination, they found themselves in a cold and muddy limbo, as they waited to start living again. Fadoul underestimated the power of bureaucracy. He did not know that his files passed from one desk to another for months, without anyone wanting to face the trouble, the nuisance and the responsibility of making a decision. Finally, a courier came to the village. After examining his application, the OFPRA (Office français de protection des réfugiés et apatrides) had established that Fadoul had been born in Cameroon, not in Chad. A question of a few miles, of course. But a decisive few miles. His application did not satisfy the criteria set down in the Geneva Convention for the right to asylum. He, his wife and children had a month to leave French soil, never to return. Their roaming would begin again. It would begin, again, from some part of Africa, from a refugee camp like Choucha, to head once more towards Europe.

6 'Refugees' and 'migrants': impossible classifications

The 'migrant crisis' of 2015 brought out at least two new phenomena: on the one hand, the – tacit, albeit no less effective – violation of the right to asylum; and, on the other hand, the elaboration of labels up to the task of arresting – or at least reducing – the 'flows of migrants'. Words are not irrelevant or indifferent. They decide policy. Even to speak of 'crisis' has a meaning: it insinuates the idea of being 'too full' and invokes the need to find 'realistic solutions'.

In the name of this necessity, and the imperative to drastically reduce the 'numbers of landings', a requirement has gradually asserted itself in the public discourse to distinguish between those who fled for political reasons (and thus ought to be welcomed), and those who have left their countries because they were driven by 'economic goals' or the 'ambition to improve their lives' (and thus can 'legitimately be rejected'). The former are labelled 'refugees' and the latter 'migrants'.

If the term 'refugee' almost corresponds to a form of redemption, 'migrant' is a border-label, which is raised in order to immobilize whoever purports freely to make use of her freedom of movement. These names assuage the conscience of a humanitarian governance which, in resorting to an apparently 'neutral' selection principle, exercises a biopolitical power. On the one hand are the 'good', on the other the 'bad'; on the one hand, the 'real' ones, on the other, the 'false' ones. Thus, Western states have come to agree on rejecting the migrants, these 'false refugees'.

As so often happens, by force of repetition this anything-but-obvious distinction has ended up imposing itself in the media and in public opinion, in studies on this subject and in a political strategy which is in search of institutional classifications. A philosophy of analytic stamp and normative tendency has also rushed to the aid of this strategy. Indeed, peddling itself as *Verantwortungsethik*, a 'morality of responsibility' – that is, a morality that purports to take account of the risks and consequences of immigration – it has dedicated itself to establishing the criteria suitable for detecting the *Asylant*, the 'false' or 'negative' asylum-seeker. In short, it has dedicated itself to defining certain classifications. The main question is the 'what', even more than the 'who' – what is the refugee? How is it possible to grasp its essence? The essentialist definition has the dual scope of guiding the law and making things easier for politics in its selective practice. And this is proof of the dangerousness of such philosophical definitions.[14] It seems that what counts, here, is the possibility of using 'objective' norms and methods to decide 'how many, and which, refugees' ought to be welcomed.[15] This analytical morality, which was already always at home in Anglo-American circles, has established a foothold in the German context, with the sometimes explicitly declared goal of combating the Neue Linke, the Italian–French philosophical New Left. Beyond weakly founded, almost embarrassing conceptual divisions – for instance, the one between flight and migration, *Flucht* and *Migration*, starting out from the more general concept of *Wanderung*, understood as the simple movement of walking – this patriotic casuistry ultimately puts itself forward to give moral legitimation to political discrimination against migrants.[16]

Rather than harden the divisions and consolidate the frontiers by handing greater power to dubious definitional labels, what is instead necessary is to deconstruct the logic of selection, questioning the semantic logic of terms that are anything but neutral, and whose different interpretations ought to be read in light of their historical pedigree. Disparate names spring out from the archives – exiles, the stateless, the proscribed, migrants. These names followed one after the other as early as the nineteenth century; with the aid of these terms, those who crossed the incipient nation-states' borders could be identified on the basis of the motives that had pushed them to get moving, from political resistance to economic need. In those years, the refugee, the product of a permanent tension between the protection of human rights and national sovereignty, did not yet have a universal status. Even subsequently, the 'refugee' remained a problematic concept, a controversial definition. The point is that the 'refugee as such' does not exist. The term has assumed different hues and connotations depending on the historical era in which it is applied and its different political uses; indeed, it ends up saying more about those who use it than those to whom it is applied.

A category in constant transformation, the term 'refugee' demands an – albeit brief – dive into history in order to bring its fluctuating character into relief. On closer inspection, the term made its appearance only in the mid fifteenth century, in English and French. It was reserved for the Huguenots who fled France after the repeal of the Edict of Nantes. It is worth noting that only Christians were 'refugees', and not the Jews, the *conversos* and the *marranos* hunted out of Spain. Later, the term would become increasingly decoupled from the religious context to indicate – riding on the wave of political events – the foreigner who sought protection in the state in which she arrived after leaving her own country. But it was during the two world wars, with the break-up of the Great Empires, that the figure took on more precise contours, even though whole groups were securing welcome. First were the Russians, from 1921 onwards. To be a refugee, it is necessary to belong to an ethnic group.

The Russian exile is in many regards emblematic. The sentimental, nostalgic, aristocratic anti-Bolshevik described by Joseph Roth in such masterly fashion had been left stateless after the October Revolution, and had decided not to return to his homeland.[17] The Norwegian explorer Fridtjof Nansen, at that time director of the

High Commission, created a new document in 1922 with him in mind, the 'Nansen passport'. A prelude to the right to asylum, it accorded residency to Russian refugees – not without causing controversy. These exiles, the victims of communism, were destined to leave a deep and lasting mark on the collective imagination. Things went very differently for other groups – for instance, the Italians who fled from Benito Mussolini's regime. The same went for the Spaniards and Portuguese who fled from fascist dictatorships. The German and Austrian Jews were a case unto themselves – they would have to wait until 1938 and 1939 respectively to be recognized by the Western countries as refugees.

Only after the Second World War, on 28 July 1951, did the Geneva Convention define the refugee, putting the emphasis on 'persecution'. It thus responded to the right to asylum that had been proclaimed in clear terms by the Universal Declaration on Human Rights a few years earlier, in 1948 (Article 14.1): 'Everyone has the right to seek and to enjoy in other countries asylum from persecution.' The Geneva Convention broke from earlier schemas that applied to groups, and provided the refugee an individual definition. A refugee was

> A person who, owing to a well-founded fear of being persecuted for reasons of race, religion, nationality, membership of a particular social group or political opinion, is outside the country of his nationality and is unable or, owing to such fear, is unwilling to avail himself of the protection of that country; or who, not having a nationality and being outside the country of his former habitual residence as a result of such events, is unable or, owing to such fear, is unwilling to return to it.

This definition is more ambiguous than it first appears. What does 'persecuted' mean? The motives that can drive an individual to leave their homeland are many, and extremely diverse; it is hardly set in stone that all of them have to correspond to the – generic, more than general – concept of 'persecution', as if this ought to constitute the decisive criterion. But, most importantly, the break with past schemas takes place internally to a substantial continuity. The refugee has the trace of the Soviet dissident. In the Cold War, it was the Western bloc that won and the socialist one that was defeated. The defence of civil rights thus prevailed over protection against economic forms of violence. This definition does, indeed, consider individual rights. The prototype refugee is the one fleeing from East to West. No space is granted to the victim of hunger or poverty, which remain losing causes. Thus, today's undesirable migrant does not find citizenship. Her exclusion is decreed by history.

The changing fortunes of the 'refugee' highlight the anachronism of a figure defined with ideological criteria and inserted in a bipolar universe where, rather than offer asylum, the Western countries wanted to be free to take in refugees from beyond the Iron Curtain. A subsequent protocol signed in 1967 extended this welcome to the persecuted the world over. For years and decades, the refugee had the traits of the exile who, in her opposition to dictatorship, could display the proof of her persecution. But the archives attest to a very generous praxis and a wide interpretation that bestowed refugee status on the basis of belonging, without dwelling too much on checks: it was sufficient to be Russian, Polish, Hungarian, and then Vietnamese, Lao or Cambodian. The need for a workforce further eased these measures.

It is worth underlining that the 'political' refugee arouses sympathy and sparks solidarity. Not only has she suffered an injustice as an individual, but added to that she is the exponent of an oppressed people, or some part of it, with which it is difficult not to identify: from the Spanish Republicans, expatriated with the *retirada* of 1939, to the Czechoslovak exiles who fled the Soviet tanks; from the Greeks who escaped the colonels' regime to the Chileans, Argentinians and other South Americans who reached the cities of Europe during the 1970s. Their political struggle was clear and engaging: it thus received support and agreement. But this did not stop asylum remaining an international affair regulated by diplomatic offices.

The situation changed when the borders started to close after the oil crisis of 1973, at the same time as the refugee's own profile seemed different. Less white, less educated, less wealthy, cast onto the tracks of emigration by factors that were both more complex and more trivial, she was accused of being a 'fake refugee', both because she did not correspond to the exile, to the dissident, to the 'real refugee', and because she wanted to pass off vulgar economic causes as noble political reasons. Together with the logic of selection, there was now introduced the administrative-bureaucratic procedure of the request for 'proof', undermined by the looming spectre of the lie. Those who aspired to be recognized as refugees, were, then, to be taken as always-already liars; they would always, it was to be supposed, resort to subterfuge and trickery in order to insinuate themselves under cover, in order to definitively move in. From this emerged the image of the 'clandestine'. The state flushed her out and and rejected her, thus restoring the truth.

In the final decade of the twentieth century, as the fall of the Berlin Wall failed to prompt the much-predicted invasion from the East, the number of those who fled not only the multiple international conflicts and incessant civil wars, but also from famine, drought, and violence of all kinds, grew beyond measure. The mobility corresponding to globalization favoured the circulation of migrants, and the migrant became a peculiar figure of hyper-modernity. The diasporization of the world, characterized both by the interdependence of crises and by the unprecedented participation in shared challenges, blew up both geopolitical and conceptual borders. The explosion of asylum claims would also wipe away the already fluid limit between the old categories of refugee and migrant.[18]

But, in the new millennium, the borders closed for those foreigners who are even more foreign than the rest: the poor. Separated from the migrant by an ever more insuperable barrier, the refugee remains, in her now-obsolete form, a necessary bulwark that administrative governance takes measures to strengthen by way of a new dividing line, which marks a further shift: the 'asylum seeker'. The 'seeking' becomes an indefinite condition to which the migrant is consigned, an unspecified wait, which can occupy her entire existence.[19] This is all the more absurd given that asylum itself – an ambiguous and antiquated institution – is systematically withheld, up to the ultimate violation officially sanctioned by the 18 March 2016 accord between the European Union and Turkey. According to this agreement, whoever reached Greek territory – even Syrians, legitimate asylum-seekers – would be pushed back behind the Turkish border. This treaty prevented potential refugees from even making an application, and thus obtaining asylum. The discredit cast on the migrant ended up applying to the refugee as well.

The term 'migrant' simply indicates those who migrate, without this having a positive or negative connotation; it does not correspond, like 'refugee', to any juridical category. For some time, however, 'migrant' has no longer been neutral and descriptive, but has instead assumed troubling and pejorative contours. A figure in transit, whose presence in the world is fluid and unstable, in her movement the migrant – destined to non-places, consecrated to the frontier – seems uncontrollable, invisible, elusive, evasive and invasive. Precisely the impossibility of defining her, if not by the fact of her blameworthy movement, exposes her to suspicion and reduces her to the wait that hangs over whoever is 'applying'. Yet, conversely, she can herself appear as the persecutor. For she has the sinister trappings of the adversary, the rival, the underhand and hidden enemy. She is the 'clandestine migrant', condemned to an everlasting exile, an interminable migration, a definitive invisibility.

Nor is the migrant – yet – the immigrant, the *sans-papier*, the seasonal worker, the commuter migrant, the foreigner and so on. The proliferation of labels is without doubt linked to the diversified profile of the new migrants. It suffices to think of unaccompanied minors or so-called 'climate migrants'. The landscape of migration has transformed. But all the labels remain within the semantic sphere of the 'migrant' and preserve the stigma attached to her.

And yet this new figure, who has been stripped even of the ancient dignity of the poor, could invoke a thousand reasons, a thousand often overlapping motivations, that pushed – or, rather, forced – her to get moving. The UNCHR has for some time now spoken of 'mixed flows' in order to indicate the arrival of migrants who are fleeing from war, violence and hunger. But this formula already admits the impossibility of applying old and rigid categories to untangling the unprecedented knot and selecting the good migrant from the bad. In the countless new political, ethnic and religious conflicts, persecution can have many different faces. It can have the face of drought. Or that of the semi-terrorist sectarian group that drives the peasants out of a village; if these latter leave their land, they may, wrongly, be considered economic migrants. Just as a Syrian, bizarrely defined a 'war refugee', may also be driven by some economic project, one who comes from Chad may have suffered political abuses her whole life. The criterion of national belonging has never been sufficient; now it seems entirely unreliable.

The distinction between the politically persecuted and economic migrants does not stand up. This is like arguing that the impoverishment of entire continents does not have political causes. The global civil war is not waged only with bombs. Exploitation, financial crises, capital flight, corruption, environmental disasters and fundamentalism are motives no less important than personal endangerment, torture and arrest. This ahistorical criterion is held up only by the logic of selection and the politics of rejection.

7 The metamorphoses of the exile

In a talk given in Vienna in December 1987, shortly before he was awarded the Nobel Prize for Literature, the Russian writer Joseph Brodsky, a Soviet exile in the West, asked what linked the fate of the exiled intellectual and that of the migrants, from the Italian and Turkish *Gastarbeiter* in Germany to the boat people of Vietnam, the Mexicans seeking entry into California, the Pakistanis who disembark in Kuwait or Saudi Arabia to get some job too lowly for the oil barons, and the Ethiopians fleeing famine:

Whatever the proper name for these people, whatever their motives, origins, and destinations, whatever their impact on the societies which they abandon and to which they come may amount to – one thing is absolutely clear: they make it very difficult to talk about the plight of the writer in exile with a straight face. Yet talk we must; and not only because literature, like poverty, is known for taking care of its own kind, but more because of the ancient and perhaps as yet unfounded belief that should the masters of this world be better read, the mismanagement and grief that make millions take to the road could be somewhat reduced.

What does the migrant have in common with the writer fleeing dictatorship? The answer is exile. This condition is the red thread that links the one to the other. As for the rest, there are very profound differences. And, as Brodsky himself emphasizes, 'the old gray mare of exile ain't what it used to be'.[20] Exile is no longer the exile of Ovid from Rome, of Dante from Florence. History is full of renowned exiles. Indeed, there are memorable pages which owe to many of these experiences.

Exile and literature constitute an established pairing. The exile condition, embraced with conscious pride or sometimes even actively sought out – think of James Joyce, who chose to live far from Dublin – is an inexhaustible source of literature. But the crudest and most merciless portrayals are instead entrusted to grand narrative. Perhaps the apogee of this came in *Amy Foster*, a story in which Joseph Conrad – himself a Polish exile – recounts the shipwreck and then the life – or, better, the survival – of Yanko Gooral, an Eastern European peasant who the sea had cast onto the coasts of Britain. Wholly alien in an indecipherable world, he was worn down in an agony that no word assuaged and no gaze followed.[21] Over the last two centuries, the literature on exile has become a real genre unto itself, almost as if in the attempt to follow the peripeties of that modernity unmasked by Nietzsche, ever more nomadic, estranged, divided, distant from the self.

Originating in the ancient practice of banishment, exile was first of all a radical form of dissidence. It was exclusive to a few – intellectuals, writers, political activists – and they were often able to turn this detachment into a position of privilege, and this loss into a possibility of redemption. The image of the exile changes over time. The epic of the noble and tenacious outsider, unmoving in her struggle against power, would peter out as it was submerged by the repeated waves of large-scale emigration. At the dawn of the twentieth century, the exile changed profile and was no longer even called an exile. This phenomenon, in all its complexity, ought not to pass unremarked: while emigration increased exponentially, the image of the exile broke apart and decomposed, instead giving rise to an ever greater diversity of figures, captured only in part by the various labels. Exiles, the stateless, the proscribed, fugitives, refugees, displaced persons, asylum-seekers, emigrants, nomads, 'illegals' – the list of more or less discriminatory terms varies across different languages and widens every time that new elements emerge in the multifaceted world of migration.

Though tied together by the fact of being exiled, only a distant family resemblance seems to connect the exile and the migrant.[22] Even to the point that it seems legitimate to ask – as the Palestinian-American intellectual Edward Said did – whether it is possible to hypothesize that they are one and the same phenomenon.[23] Yet, even without overlooking the real differences that do exist, it is preferable to opt for a continuity between them – which also allows, among other things, for present-day migration to be read in a historical key. This choice first of all finds confirmation in a few cases of slippage. Already, during the emigration of intellectuals from Germany to the United States between 1933 and 1945, the terms began to fluctuate, and exiles often defined themselves as *Emigranten*.[24] Adorno himself, in the section of his work *Minima moralia* entitled 'Refuge for the Homeless', a sort of autobiography written in exile, examined 'the needs imposed by emigration'.[25] The philosopher, who was fleeing Nazism, cannot be called a heroic oppositionist; he felt closer to an émigré, and admitted that he must reflect *aus dem beschädigten Leben*, starting out from life – even his own, mutilated and damaged one. One can identify in this terminological fluctuation not only the artificial character of labels, but also the problematic interweaving of different figures that do not come separately, one after the other, but rather intersect and overlap with one another.

8 Asylum: from ambiguous right to a *dispositif* of power

It is in this context, where definitions seem controversial and labels look like excuses, that the question of the right to asylum must be posed. This is an oft-hailed and declared right, invoked whenever there is talk – also in public discourse – of migrant reception. 'Sacred and inviolable' asylum is offered to the refugees who deserve it, and denied to the migrants who cannot lay claim to this right. The only protection set out for foreigners is revealed to be a prerogative of the state, which wields this prerogative in sovereign fashion. What kind of right is asylum, then? The right of the individual who asks for it, or of the state who grants it? In this question, there again emerges the tension between human rights and the immigration policy followed by states. But both the institution of asylum and its history conceal a further ambiguity.

The term comes from the Greek *ásulon*, made up of the privative alpha and the verb *suláo*, which means 'I depredate', 'I strip', 'I take by force'. Asylum is the space where 'capture', *sulé*, is not legitimate. The Greeks, the true founders of this institution, which then spread also elsewhere, called *ásula* all those places – from sacred forests to the mountains dedicated to the gods, from altars to the tombs of heroes – that ought to be considered inviolable. The fugitive slave and the prisoner of war sought shelter there, but so, too, whoever was stained by some crime, after having committed robbery or even murder. Once the fugitive had got to the altar, entered within the walls of the temple or reached the sacred forest, he absolutely must not be touched, violated or wounded. For he was protected by an immunity that radiated, almost as if by contact, out from the sacred site of which he had now become part. This principle of irradiation also applied to animals and plants. *Asilía* was the name for the right to inviolability, given by that place itself. The sacred character of the Greek 'asylums' is usually emphasized a great deal, though they also had a civic value, gradually also becoming the subject of treaties between cities. For the person who sought refuge could sometimes be a foreigner. These were, however, isolated cases. What often goes unmentioned, however, is that the fugitive could be either innocent or guilty, either executioner or victim. In its constitutive ambiguity, *asilía* did not distinguish; the right was thus bestowed on the basis of the criterion of place – within the bounds of the holy site.

It would be impossible, then, to speak of justice. On the one hand, the scope of *asilía* was, indeed, to offer protection to those who were fleeing violence; but it was also to grant shelter to those who who had committed violence. It was thus intended to break the infinite chain of blood. This is also apparent in the corresponding Jewish institution, the 'refuge-cities' where a person who had committed a crime non-deliberately and was being pursued by the victim's relatives could find salvation. It was thus also a way to stop the *goèl ha-dàm*, the 'avenger of the blood'.[26]

Opposed by the Romans, who saw it as an abuse, given that all sorts of rabble found refuge in the temples, the right to asylum was, however, very widespread in the lands of the East. It continued across the centuries, also thanks to ecclesiastical law, but then ended in the modern era.

It nonetheless reappeared, in another form, during the French Revolution; if it was not one of the rights proclaimed 'sacred and inviolable' by the 1789 Declaration, the Constitution of 1793 (Article 120) did, however, define it, stating that the French Republic 'serves as a place of refuge for all who, on account of liberty, are banished from their native country'. When it crossed into the sphere of international relations, becoming the right that was supposed to protect the foreigner, it maintained all the ambiguities of the past. Hence, great revolutionaries such as Giuseppe Garibaldi, Louis Blanc, Mikhail Bakunin, Giuseppe Mazzini, found asylum, as did many other political exiles. But asylum was also granted to Pol Pot in China, to Marcos in Hawaii, and to Stroessner in Brazil – not to mention the countless Nazis who managed to find refuge in Latin America.

Even as the figure of the exile has disappeared over time, there has flourished the whole constitutive ambiguity of asylum, its ethical ambivalemce, and the impossibility of distinguishing between innocent and guilty, between who deserves asylum and who does not – as shown by embassies, considered places of refuge. This invalidates the widespread idea that there is a right to asylum which ought to be accorded to refugees and not to migrants, once a careful distinction has been made. Nor is it clear why one should invoke this institution in order to speak of *Asylante*, or so-called 'asylum-seekers'. Indeed, it is hard to understand what a Syrian refugee can have in common with a deposed dictator or with a non-extradited criminal who has been offered immunity.

If asylum appeared as an ambiguous institution, at the limit of law, already before the great emigration, subsequently it ought to have wholly separated from questions of migration. And yet the opposite happened: asylum was broadened out, and repeatedly redefined. This caused a lot of confusion. The idea that those who receive asylum, or even those who seek it, are stained by some crime or have some connection with criminality has been inherited from the past.

Not even the explosion in asylum applications has changed this picture. Looking at recent developments, it is striking to see the vagueness of the concepts used to understand, for instance, persecution, a term which now has a very wide embrace, extending to include questions of human rights. But asylum policy has also been struck by two main shifts. On the one hand, the juridical and police barriers have multiplied (the crime of illegal immigration, penalties for those who aid migrants, administrative detention, expulsion), as have bureaucratic and procedural restrictions (for instance, the Dublin Treaty, which makes it compulsory for the application to be made from within the arrival country), with the none-too hidden goal of brushing off the application; the long waiting times, the uncertainty of the outcome, the fashioning of 'neither–nors' and all the difficulties in distinguishing between refugees and migrants ought to be read in the same light. On the other hand, asylum is 'outsourced' with apparently humanitarian objectives, creating refugee camps where applications are examined, offering temporary protection in some place close to the areas of conflict, and expanding the temporary forms of asylum. But this outsourcing is itself nothing but a way of keeping the migrants at bay.

This dual drift shows how asylum, at first a tool for regulating inter-state relations, has become a *dispositif* which states use to exercise – even in concert with one another – their power over migrants. If this may be ambiguous and arbitrary, this helps rather than harms the sovereign defence-at-all-costs of what is called, in a bizarre euphemism, 'asylum policy'.

9 'You're not from here': an existential negation

'Where are you from?' Even before whoever is questioned can reply, the recognition is there already: 'you're not from here!' These apparently banal words conceal a condemnation which nails the foreigner to an irredeemable negativity. Indeed, 'you're not from here' ought to mean 'you're from somewhere else' – you come from another country. Even if the genitive surreptitiously indicates a belonging to the place, rather than signalling a simple place of origin, the phrase does not seem to entail anything alarming.

In the present context, however, this formulation has taken on a specific valence and 'you're not from here' has come to be understood in the sense of the most absolute negativity: 'you do not exist'. Things are turned on their head, and essence precedes existence. Precisely because you are not from here, you do not exist. The migrant is condemned to non-existence by the autochthonous, who proudly insists on his own belonging, to this place, but also to his essence, to his existence. According to this view, then, one can only exist as the autochthonous, in the presumed naturalness of those born to the land in which they live. 'I exist' in that 'I am from here.' Whoever cannot lay claim to such an existence is condemned to an eclipse from which there is no escape: 'Get lost, you aren't from here!'

This is a political–existential reversal. The existence of the autochthonous is conjugated in multiple ways: since 'I'm from here', 'I have a right' to a house, to work, to healthcare, to social protection. And, on the other hand, since 'you're not from here', since 'you don't exist', 'you have no right to anything'. The 'you're not from here' negatively stigmatizes the foreigner, subjecting her to political non-existence.

Modernity has stripped away the foreigner's aura; she is no longer the one who comes from elsewhere. Things are rather more banal: she is the migrant who finds herself here even though she is not from here. The ultimate version of the contemporary misery, which surpasses even economic humiliation, the migrant projects no persuasive enchantment, no exotic fascination. In her dark and illegitimate nudity, she is the spectre of the guest who, denied in her very essence, no hospitality could make fully exist. The migrant is the foreigner stripped of her sacredness, of her epic elsewhere. The sun having set on the glory of her passage – still recognized in the twentieth-century landscape – the foreigner gives up her place to the new figures of that spatial-temporal disorder to which migration is reduced. She gives up her place – so to speak. The foreigner used to be able to lay claim to her place and hold on to it, because she came from another world, which secured her transit between the elsewhere and the here. She still enjoyed a power, by way of that mysterious halo that surrounded her world, of which she could become the bearer. The foreigner stripped naked, the migrant, has lost the reference to the elsewhere, and for that very reason no longer has access to the here. She is without-a-place in the unprecedented global struggle for a place. Here, simple presence does not justify her existence.

One analogous precedent is that of the mad person, an object of Michel Foucault's reflection. At first sacred, because it made up part of those dark powers of misery that gave her the right to hospitality, the mad person, that pilgrim of the senseless, arrives in modernity after being struck by a desacralization that already first struck against poverty, branded a moral failing. Thus, she can be hosted only alongside beggars, the destitute, *les misérables*, those interned within the walls of the hospital.

A familiar figure on the human landscape of the medieval world, the madman had come from another world. Now he stood out on the background, a problem of 'police', a matter of social order for individuals of the polity. Once, he was welcomed because he came from without; now he was excluded because he came from within, and the mad were forced to take their place alongside paupers, beggars and vagabonds. An ambiguous welcome awaited them, in the form of this public health measure that put them out of circulation: the mad still wandered, but no longer on the road of a strange pilgrimage – they just troubled the order of the social space.[27]

The ambiguity of hospitality – become internment, a police matter – not by chance also regards the migrant, the body, the remains left over after the desacralization of the foreigner.

And if the mad person and the foreigner were once the overlapping protagonists of a troubling and suspect errance, they later became out-of-place figures, who, in their superfluity, threatened the immanent dialectic of states. For this reason, it seems, they should be entrusted to an efficient exclusion policy, able to make the counter-empire of vagabonds disappear.

10 The migrant's original sin

It isn't just the recognition 'you're not from here'. The migrant also has to face the demand 'why are you here?' This question summarizes an incessant and reiterated process. Consubstantial with the act of migrating is, in fact, an original sin that the migrant will never stop having to answer for. The guilt will dog her forever. Against her own intentions, she will be caught between accusation and counter-accusation, blame-laying and self-blame. Whoever emigrates remains on trial for her whole life. However things happened, whatever its vicissitudes, whatever the story of her family or the condition of her country, and whether she has been pushed or even forced or instead acted with greater liberty – in any case, she is summoned to respond for her individual choice, for that decisive break. This, then, is the initial fault, the original sin that is migration itself, the political–existential act of making an irreparable break. And, just like the act itself, its effects are also political and existential.

Whatever attempt is made to make it look innocent, migration is suspect. Even just because it breaks the immediacy, the purported naturalness of nations, through which each person is due the place in which she is born. In this light, migration appears as an open wound in the integrity of the political order, a creeping and frightful subversion. Geographical atopia, political anomaly, an anomie that almost breaks out into anarchy, migration – movement through space – is also a moral deviation. It is thus an *original* sin in the ontological sense, even more than the chronological sense. All the other sins that follow – as they inevitably will – are contained in that first one, which no court sentence and no punishment can wash clean. The sin remains indelible, the stain impossible to remove, the stigma permanent.

Migration is illegitimate – in its two phases, both as emigration and as immigration. Even given the best of intentions, no discourse that remains within the outlook of state-centric thought can endorse migration. Nor can that frequent accounting exercise that measures its costs and calculates its benefits – thus reducing a complex historical phenomenon to numbers and statistics – succeed in so doing, as it tries to rationalize an arbitrary choice by vaunting the profits that immigrants offer to bring. Thus, the balance-sheets risk becoming endless points of dispute. The economy of the tax revenues that come in does not succeed in justifying any single individual's entry onto the national territory.

This illegitimacy reflects on the migrant herself, who, as such, is never a neutral figure. Indeed, she is accused of being where she ought not to be, of occupying someone else's place, which is not rightfully hers. Her presence is excessive – unforeseen, unwanted, unwelcome, abusive. 'This isn't your home – and don't forget it!' 'Go back where you came from!' The immigrant is a foreign body that disturbs the public order, a body out of place that does not allow itself to be swallowed up. It is obviously superfluous, but how it can be cast off is unclear. It has no right to be where it is. It is continually reduced to its in-existence as decreed by the others, the autochthonous, those who discriminate against it, who constantly rebuild the border around it.

This is even taken to the point that the immigrant herself perceives the in-existence to which she is subject, in all its tragic dimensions, and recognizes it and takes it upon herself. This is her limit-situation, from which she can find no exit route. She no longer feels either here or there. Since she emigrated, went away, it is as if through this rupture all ties had been broken. This is even a double inexistence: she exists neither in the place of arrival, where she is refused, nor the place where she started out, from which – despite every effort – she is absent. Rather, this absence – from which there is nowhere any shelter – is imputed to her, as her fault. Even if she will always still be there, in the country she left, her life proceeds elsewhere, lacerated, split, broken. Any attempt to desperately retie the threads after that break is bound to be futile. Often the migrant's life is exhausted in that effort, without still being lived, closed as it is in the trap of a cruel and asphyxiating coming-and-going. Abdelmalek Sayad has spoken of the 'double absence', by this indicating the paradoxical condition of the emigrant-immigrant who continues to be present where she is absent and, conversely, to be absent precisely where she is present.[28] The spatial split also has temporal side-effects: life is deferred in what becomes an enduring temporariness. Waiting to live, almost as if in transit, the emigrant-immigrant is herself host to the contradiction between the two irreconcilable times of the two communities – the one from which she departed and the one in which she has arrived – neither of which she fully belongs to. The temporal contradiction imprints the stamp of temporariness on her life, while the spatial split becomes more acute, to the point of becoming an uncrossable barrier. Even when she does make a return to her country, the emigrant that she has now become is a foreigner to those who stayed. Foreignness follows her around and dogs her. No longer is there a place where she is at home. Caught between two worlds that slip past one another, idealizing each in turn – in vain – she will not again recover the link that has been cut, and will instead be consigned to the in-between condition of a dual exclusion: the split with the community she started out from, and the rejection from the one in which she arrived. Like the absence itself, the guilt also doubles up. The emigrant-immigrant is everywhere forced to justify her existence. She accepts the process almost supinely, convinced that she has to constantly legitimize, in her eyes as in others', the original and unpardonable sin of immigration, as some accuse her of betrayal, abandon and perdition, and others of disturbance, intrusion, sedition. She will never free herself of this blame.

11 'Illegals': being condemned to invisibility

Precisely because immigration represents a latent crime, everything that the immigrant does will be judged on the basis of that previous aggravating factor. In this perspective, immigration is both a crime unto itself and a source of criminality. The guilt and the punishment double up.

The immigrant thus becomes the potential criminal, the underhand fraudster, the implicit terrorist, the hidden enemy. She is the spectre-like guest that no law of hospitality can make into a relative, a peer, a neighbour. There is no place in the nation for this sinister phantasm, who is always-already subject to prejudice (also in the sense of already having been judged), destined to inexistence, awaiting an even minimal recognition, a label, a stamp, a designation. The immigrant is a mirror-image of Ulysses, who, in Cyclops' cave, overwhelmed by terror, said that he was called 'no one' in order to be able to re-emerge a free man and make his return to his native Ithaca; but she, conversely, is called 'no one' by her terrorized hosts, who consign her to an indefinite suspension in a sort of spatial-temporal no man's land.

Language attests and sanctions the clandestinization of the immigrant. This alien, this *extracomunitario*, is designated with the simple stigma *clandestino*. If previously this term indicated the passenger who illegally boarded a ship, more recently it has been used for those who enter some territory without papers or who live there without official leave to remain. There is but a blurry boundary distinguishing the irregular migrant, the illegitimate guest, the underhand enemy from the regular, or regularized, migrant, whose documents may not be renewed at any moment; without leave to remain, she, too, would slip into illegality. While the actual number of 'illegals' is finite, the term 'clandestine' ends up being extended to all those immigrants whom the collective imaginary surreptitiously turns into *clandestine*. It is, sometimes, possible to redeem oneself from this clandestine condition, and to re-emerge by way of a temporary regularization. But the stigma remains: a bureaucratic contingency thus rises to the level of a constitutive property of a human being and her existence – or, rather, of her in-existence.

A closer look at the etymology can aid a better understanding of this illegitimate passage, which defies any logic. The term 'clandestine' comes from Latin *clam*, secretly, and *dies*, day: 'secretly by day'. The clandestine are those who conceal themselves, hiding from the light of day – those who dissemble, passing themselves off as something they are not, smuggling in their identity and insinuating themselves into the body of the nation, at the risk of undermining it.[29]

The immigrant is the clandestine person who, having entered furtively precisely because she has secretly mixed in, in turn deserves to be banished from view. She is condemned to invisibility. This is a way of decreeing her in-existence. Forced disappearances can take place by way of different forms and modalities. Clandestinization is one of them – and perhaps now one of the most recurrent. The borders are not only the borders of brick walls and barbed wire. It is easily possible to discriminate and exclude beneath the cloak of invisibility. The 'clandestine' person is allowed to dissipate and disappear in the dark limbo to which her very clandestinity has relegated her. In his novel *Invisible Man*, Ralph Waldo Ellison described this subtle condemnation, as lived by an anonymous African American in 1940s New York:

> I am an invisible man. No, I am not a spook like those who haunted Edgar Allan Poe; nor am I one of your Hollywood-movie ectoplasms. I am a man of substance, of flesh and bone, fiber and liquids – and I might even be said to possess a mind. I am invisible, understand, simply because people refuse to see me. Like the bodiless heads you see sometimes in circus sideshows, it is as though I have been surrounded

by mirrors of hard, distorting glass. When they approach me they see only my surroundings, themselves, or figments of their imagination – indeed, everything and anything except me.[30]

No recognition, therefore – not even the fleeting recognition of the gaze. The foreigners who inhabit the cities can be reduced to ghosts even without necessarily putting up walls, albeit with the same racist impulse. 'No, I am not a ghost', Ellison forcefully insists. For to be a ghost to other people means no longer really to exist. The ring of Gyges, which – as in the myth adopted by Plato – allowed one to commit the most barbarous acts unseen, has had its day.[31] Of course, it remains a hidden tool, but only for the sake of consolidating an already-established power. In the age of visibility, dominated by the motto 'I appear, therefore I am', invisibility necessarily reduces one to the impotence of the pariah.

The migrant's existence is a liminal one, which floats between the possibility of emerging into being and the possibility of disappearing forever. With the stigma of the term 'clandestine' – printed upon her even before she has made any landing – the politics of the performative simultaneously both accuses her of having something to hide, an inner vice that cannot surface, and condemns her to the absence of the qualities and of the prerogatives that cannot be attributed to her, to the point that she remains a ghostly 'other'. Relegated to the margins, she is never really assured of any berth. If the emigrant and the immigrant are, indeed, two conditions that exceed the bounds of invisibility, and which in part challenge it, it is, instead, the migrant who – being neither within nor outside, remaining between two shores, between one point on the grid and another – can succumb, trapped and immobilized in the apparent transit of a juridical enclave, and of a fatal political circuit. In order to avoid being caught, she must not be seen; and, on the other hand, in accepting that she will be invisible, she consigns herself to that tolerated clandestinity, that faceless existence, which authorizes not only indifference towards her, but even her total erasure. The life of the migrant in the transit zone is not so much subaltern, like that of the worker – which, despite everything, does allow a whole resistance and struggle – as it is a life in the shadows, in that underground invisibility in which one may only hide away and dissemble oneself, where one can make disappear something which is nothing but an absence. It would seem, then, that, in the life of the 'clandestine migrant', disappearance is the only, tragic exit route. The great political question posed by the *sans-papiers* is how to make this invisibility visible.[32]

12 The terms of domination: 'integration' and 'naturalization'

The first hostile condition of hospitality is that the foreigner should cease to be such, should make herself like the indigenous population, and should show her intention to try to assimilate and integrate into the identical Self of the nation. No matter, then, that no one is clear about what this identity actually is. So long as her arrival is taken for an intrusion – if not an outright invasion – it will at least be necessary for the foreigner to abandon her foreignness, or rather that the migrant declares herself ready to gradually reduce her troubling otherness. Perhaps one day she may even be naturalized, becoming 'natural', like the indigenous population. The minimal condition required by an open liberal society, able to integrate people, is that the other should become a little less 'other' as soon as possible, and provide tangible proof of this, with the effect that her presence on the national territory is not wholly illegitimate.

Her rights are suspended, in the wait for such proofs. In the meantime, the immigrant is directed to attend to her duties. The reversal is worth needs noting: rather than the guest's own rights being acknowledged and affirmed, she is instead reminded – indeed, as a potential enemy – of her obligations. It is up to her to take care of carrying out these obligations, as acts of generosity, unilateral and far from self-evident concessions she has to make. Hospitality is thought within the hostile perspective of a possible threat to the nation's purported integrity.

This, again, is a scenario in which the state-centric and ethnocentric imposes itself, reducing the *emigrant* to an *immigrant* who has to display her gratitude towards the benevolent community that has taken her in, overcoming the shortcomings that are tacitly ascribed to her. And, once again, since the immigrant is a non-national and thus apolitical, the attempt is made to depoliticize immigration by casting reception as a purely technical–moral question.

The vocabulary of domination is highly varied: it itself expresses the history of the consequences that explain why some terms, whose semantic history is already compromised, are scrupulously avoided. It is worth mentioning some of the most telling of these, from adaptation to inclusion, insertion and assimilation. In their different ways, all of these terms suggest a passage from otherness to identity. This apparently spontaneous process is in fact directed, oriented, piloted; the coercion is subtle and yet persistent. The official, usually irenic, version overlooks tensions and passes over the conflicts in silence, instead promoting the idea of a consensual and harmonious journey towards the identity of the self-same. It does all this, only for it suddenly to discover – as has happened even in the most recent past – that both consensus and harmony are lacking, and that, for this reason, what has taken place is exactly the opposite of the hoped-for result.

It is almost superfluous to emphasize that this vocabulary of domination reasserts the boundary between 'us' and the 'others' – indeed, setting out from this boundary in order to mobilize the whole performative charge contained within the magic word 'identity'. Between myth and bureaucracy, the standard of national identity is raised in order to block this – more or less tacitly imposed – journey, scattering it with impediments and barriers. It remains to be seen when and how the undesired foreigner does manage to become identical to 'us'. The test may never be over. Precisely when the success is confirmed, validated and corroborated by documents – indeed, 'identity papers' – issued for this purpose, it is impossible to rule out the possibility of failure. Just like how, in mathematics, the integral is the asyntotic curve that can be drawn out infinitely without ever touching the axis, integration never hits the target of identity. The imperative of integration, in which there resonates the echo of the absence, the lacuna that remains to be filled in – thus remains the sword of Damocles that hangs over the foreigner's head.

Each era has chosen different names for the passage towards identity, and through this name oriented its interpretation. This explains why some terms are so pronounced or sound anachronistic. Such is the case of 'adaptation', which designated the need for the worker to conform to the production line, to the rhythm and cadence of industrial production, and therefore the urbanization of the peasant-immigrants in the city, who otherwise risked becoming 'ill-adapted' misfits. More neutral, because it does not aim at any particular target, is the term 'insertion', which refers to the technical, almost ascetic, operation of grafting a foreign body into the great mechanism of progress.

For its part, the word 'assimilation' instead boasts a much longer and far more tragic history. Since at least the European Enlightenment, this term has indicated the change required of foreigners, or those perceived as foreigners, within the nation. If the nation assimilates, it is still up to these latter to become assimilated, to make themselves similar by abandoning their own peculiarities. This passage has, most of the time, been peddled as a way of overcoming particularism. Thus, assimilation has often ended up perilously slipping into becoming a synonym for emancipation. If this is no longer the case – at least, this association cannot be made with the same flippancy as in times past – that is because the devastating effects produced by totalizing universalism are now plain for all to see. One need only recall the history of the European Jews, their desire to be equal, their oft-unconditional allegiance, their aspiration to be recognized as citizens with the same rights – a history that ended, after their de-naturalization, in the concentration camps. Many philosophers have written on this already. And the colonial use of this term delegitimized it still further, leaving the mark of ethnocentrism branded upon its semantics and bringing out the digestive metaphor of anthropophagy – namely, the capacity to swallow and consume everything in the name of universal rights. Generation after generation, European society has assimilated immigrants, the ex-colonized, on whom the blame for any partial or total lack of success always falls.[33]

This is why, within the national-identitarian vocabulary of domination, the term 'integration' has ultimately prevailed. The word has itself had a winding path – at first used to designate the development that ought to have led to a cohesive, well-integrated society, and later rather more inflected to designate the inclusion of separate parts within the whole. Perhaps because it seems to hint, albeit very remotely, at the integrity of the individual, nurtured and not dissolved in the community, it is preferred to other terms with a more manifestly assimilationist content. Yet 'integration' – indeed, no less than 'inclusion', with which it contends for its place in public discourse – remains a term of obligation, of command, which directs the immigrant to attend to her duties, requires that she mould her own existence, daily altering it to suit pre-fixed models that ought to be spontaneously embraced. An infinite test, a repeated exam, without any advance to the next grade ever coming.

The immigrant, part of the underclass of identity, remains under observation even after years and decades. Even when she is already naturalized. The notion of 'naturalization', from the French *naturaliser*, is not as self-evident as some would have us believe. It is simple enough to break it down: it means becoming 'natural', like the indigenous children of the soil. The expression 'naturalized foreigner' refers to the immigrant who has applied for citizenship, at one time called 'naturalness'. This is a paradigm taken from biology, in which animal or plant species that spontaneously reproduce after being transplanted away from their own places of origin are defined as having been 'naturalized'. Juridical–political language retraces its empirical–scientific counterpart, as it uses this term to indicate the administrative process (different, in this sense, from the broader notion of integration) through which the immigrant must accede to national belonging. In the nation, which defines belonging by birth, there exists on the one hand a natural life, also precisely in the biological sense – namely the life of citizens, of co-nationals – and, on the other hand, a life that has been transplanted and has to be naturalized before its roots may sink into the new terrain. There is something artificial about this latter life, which makes it illegitimate, and demands an intense labour of cultivation even without there being any certainty as to the result.

Within the national order, then, immigration must necessarily repudiate itself in the naturalization into which it miraculously dissolves. This passage is a delicate transplant from one terrain to another, but it is also a blood transfusion, an outright transubstantiation. To enter into the nation is to melt into it, in order to avoid undermining its natural, political, moral and cultural order. But it needs to be underlined that naturalization is imposed by the nation's political orthodoxy. The economy, and especially the global economy, does not require this: it is not necessary for an immigrant worker to become a citizen. What pushes for homogeneity is, instead, the nation: the immigrant must be prepared to convert into a good national citizen, must accept this profound and complete annexation, which is in general passed off as an inestimable honour, a privilege granted with pomp and ceremony. In reality, thanks to an asymmetrical power relation, a citizen from another nation is simply annexed, often even including the replacement of their nationality. The civic oath with which one must renege on what one is and has been, in order to change 'identity' and become naturalized, is a form of institutionalized violence. For immigrants, this is no simple administrative procedure, but rather an often-painful antithesis in which they are caught, with no exit route: on the one hand, the betrayal of their country of origin, and on the other, the officially professed loyalty to the country of arrival. It is a reiteration of that first moment of rupture they made upon their departure, with which their emigration began; a betrayal that is duplicated, for they are deserting not only their former nation but also the group of non-nationals, which is to say the very condition of the immigrant.

13 When the immigrant remains an émigré

From the nation's point of view, the annexation of the immigrant is indeed the end point of migrating. Yet the reduction of the migrant to the immigrant is never entirely completed. What, in fact, does it mean to become an immigrant? Can one entirely become one? When she makes her home in a foreign country – whether or not in a lasting or definitive way – the immigrant acquires a certain status. This offers her certain guarantees and rights, depending on the particular situation. This status, which is based on the ideal of a well-inserted immigrant, is nothing but a hypothesis on paper, because it assumes the continued existence of something which is, instead, missing. The immigrant understood as a 'subject who can be integrated' is a bureaucratic construct that abstracts from her constitutive precarity, her indelible temporariness.

This is why the immigrant, who never ceases migrating, does not ever transcend or banish her condition as an emigrant, which remains inscribed in her status.[34] No bureaucracy can erase it. Despite every constriction complied with, every obligation answered, the logic of immigration does not decree the end of the emigrant. It does not overcome what remains a ghostly existence, a mere possibility, which continues to trouble also the immigrant herself. Rather, it particularly troubles the immigrant, who always continues to see herself as an *emigrant*. This word is based on the prefix *ĕx-* which refers to the 'out of' that has allowed for her not being at home, in her own place, and which denotes a point of no return. Ever since then, she has never reached another stable home of her own that could compensate for the one she has lost.

It may be more or less deep and more or less manifest. But the rupture of emigration cannot be healed and repaired. The emigrant bears its mark, branded on herself, to the point that, once she has become an immigrant, she is unable to remove it. Thus, the emigrant's existence not only precedes but also exceeds that of the immigrant, despite all the efforts the nation makes to neutralize and domesticate her. Rather than represent a lacking and unadapted figure like that of the immigrant, who lacks a home of her own, the emigrant is she whose broken existence subtly challenges the indigenous population's way of being from within, creating fault-lines and opening up cracks in the national soil. This itself reveals why she is so feared.

The emigrant interrupts the construction and the legitimation of the nation, opening up the breach to display the artifices on which it is based. The discredit that surrounds her owes to this disturbing action that she performs, even before she mounts any articulated political opposition; she challenges the hegemonic form of the nation from deep within, shaking its very foundations. An exponent of a pre-existing discord, the emigrant-immigrant de-naturalizes the nation itself – the one she has come from no less than the one in which she arrives. She introduces another external, extraneous, excess point of view that brings the artificial construct into view. Hence the accusation of deviancy, of pathology, directed against migration. The critical potential of this challenge is no less even where the 'good foreigner' is integrated according to the nation's own desires and requirements. So-called 'immigration policy' does not only resolve to 'govern migration flows' but also aspires to contain and neutralize this destabilizing action. And it does so in vain. For the immigrant, with her fluctuating, manifestly decentred self, to which the emigrant within her continually refers, is the figure of the temporary resident in which the other residents cannot but recognize themselves, detecting in her exile also their own.

14 The foreigner who lives outside, the foreigner who lives within

Omission, amnesia and caution have wrapped the foreigner in a veil of silence, and for centuries have left her in a clandestine condition. The foreigner has not obtained citizenship within traditional philosophy. Every now and then, one comes across some extravagance that would even make one pine for the old aristocratic tact that was at least capable of granting the foreigner the aura of mystery. Philosophical dictionaries and encyclopedias attest to this singular aphasia.[35] Only recently does the 'foreigner' seem to have obtained political asylum, but under strict surveillance, and under the looming threat of the first expulsion order.

In classical philosophy, the foreigner is kept at the margins. The more the difference between Greeks and barbarians took shape, the more there prevailed the need for a *logos* which, in its vertical rise, defined the ambit of the proper, thus restoring the order of the world – the *kósmos* which 'nothing is outside', as Aristotle put it in his *Physics*.[36] This order without an outside, the closed and all-inclusive Greek cosmos, is articulated only by its internal limits. Beyond it lies open the abyss of the *ápeiron*, the unlimited. Whoever goes beyond the limits, like Icarus in his ambitious attempt to conquer the sky, exposes herself to the risk of an ineluctable, deadly fall.

And yet in Greek thought there were also figures who did exceed the limits, or rather strained them. First among them was Socrates, who, with his *atopía*, his extravagance, his being out-of-place, set out from the edge to cross the *pólis*, almost as an expatriate in his own homeland, as he spread disarray and provoked disconcertment among his surprised and irritated fellow citizens. The philosopher, who could nonetheless boast of an extraordinary genius, was extraneous, already thanks to his unusual and strange questions, and his digressions which were just so many transgressions. Put on trial, Socrates proudly asserted: 'I am an extraordinary speaker.'[37]

But, elsewhere, Plato also opened the doors to the *xénos*, to the foreigner who, as he enters the scene, articulates decisive moments in thought and opens up new perspectives. How could anyone forget

Diotima of Mantinea, a prominent figure in the *Symposium*? But without doubt the most subversive character is the Foreigner from Elea, who pulls apart the fathers' doctrine, pushing Parmenides into a corner and inflicting the final blow upon him. Being is (*ésti*); it cannot not be. The identity of being is the inescapable foundation of philosophy. As becomes clear in *The Sophist*, however, there is the danger of exhausting oneself in the tautological repetition of this identity. The Foreigner intervenes in order to interrupt this exhausted repetition, and in order to save philosophy itself. And this is his impetuous, mad, visionary, *manikós* ('manic') provocation, for he pushes *not being* in a certain sense *into being*, showing that *not being* can mean not only 'not existing' but also 'being something else'.[38] With his question on the possibility of being something else, the Foreigner from Elea expropriates being of its presumed identity and subverts philosophy. The provocation is not, however, properly grasped: its consequences are taken no further than ontology. This is as far as the 'Platonic philosophy of the foreigner' goes: the *Xénos* introduces the *héteron*, the Foreigner introduces the other, elevating it to a philosophical category. But this other is not conjugated with Others. As Henri Joly has written, 'it remains a *category of the thing*, it is not yet *a category of the person*'.[39]

The foreigner remains rigorously outside of the Greek cosmic order, outside the borders of both *pólis* and *logos*. The exceptions prove the rule and take on a tragically exemplary character. Oedipus is the most perturbing example of this. A foreigner at birth, adopted by the king, Polybus, and alien to both Corinth and Thebes, after being consigned to exile once, the truth came out as to his incestuous marriage with his mother; destined to being outcast and *ápolis*, deprived of a city, finally able to see only thanks to his sudden blindness, he is a foreigner even in death and in his secret burial at Colonus.[40] No place is ever granted him, even for mourning.

Unthought over the centuries, the foreigner made her appearance in the most unknown and unforeseen trappings in that horizon of modernity which would be perilously restricted with the discovery of a spherical Earth. But the 'savage', who was now subjected to colonial conquest and entrusted to an evangelical assimilation, raised rather more of an anthropological question. Philosophy remained trapped in its ignorance, until the effects of the global order's loss of its centre rebounded in the decentring of the subject and in a new and plural articulation of reason. Not only did reason prove to be historical, but it also now appeared to be conjugated in different languages. And it was thus that the unfamiliar, emerging within the core of the proper, initiated modernity's adventures. But it would again take a lot more time before the unfamiliar was offered some space and the foreigner accorded a voice. Of course, philosophy did discuss estrangement – or, better, alienation. Hegel and Marx famously did so, in order to indicate that even self-awareness and even the fruit of one's labour – what most ought to be one's own – are instead exposed to a radical expropriation. Yet here the alien remains a difference to be removed, to be overcome, in the perspective of a victorious dialectical process.

Only in twentieth-century thought did the other, in her deep and inescapable otherness, open herself a path through the multiple currents of philosophy, from phenomenology to hermeneutics and deconstruction. If philosophy got back to understanding, this was because all that had previously been familiar suddenly revealed itself to be worryingly unfamiliar. It was impossible to still feel at home in the world, even as the subject lost her ancient mastery over her own self. The starting point could no longer be the *cogito* of the ego, when it was also necessary to take into account that elsewhere from which the ego always comes and which makes this latter – more than an *alter ego* – an *alter tu*. Otherness does not, therefore, spare the id that discovers itself to be another, an alien. And this is a discovery both thick with fears and laden with promises.

The stranger engraves her particularity in her most private and familiar recesses, in the properties of hers that can most be taken for granted. This does not mean, however, that the challenge from the unfamiliar is welcome. If it does not end up being overlooked entirely, it often remains the ambiguous privilege of the margin, which offers introspection into the estranged self. But the decisive step from the margin to marginalization is not made. The stranger's prodding can even give rise to an almost complacent basking in altruistic reflections on otherness – one's own, and others' – without this meaning that space is given to the foreigner, or, therefore, that the political question is unpacked.

Who is the foreigner? How is one to define her, if she seems to evade any definition? If it only seems possible to characterize her in negative terms? How to talk about her without drowning out her voice with one's own, without supplanting her, even before having granted her hospitality? These are the questions raised by Bernhard Waldenfels. Repeatedly, indeed in various works, he has outlined a phenomenology of the stranger which is at the same time a topography of the foreigner. And topography should here be understood in the literal sense: writing on a place, or places.

This, at least, is beyond doubt: that the foreigner as such does not exist, and nor does the foreigner exist in the absolute. More than a concept, the foreigner indicates a *tópos*, a place – or better, is herself indicated by some place. The etymology of the Italian word for foreign, *straniero*, itself shows this, much like the English word 'strange': they come from the Latin *extranĕu(m)*, and thus always refer to the 'extra', which is to say 'outside', dimension. And, moreover, this is always an outside seen from within, a there which is not here, in a spatial relationality that should not escape us, because it is within this relationality that a Left and a Right, an above and a below, are also situated. The unfamiliar and the proper are thus always correlated. For the foreigner is always determinate and contextual. We could even say that 'foreign' means nothing other than a relationship.

Simmel was well aware of this. In his famous *Exkurs über den Fremden* – a few significant pages written in 1908 – he identified spatiality as the ambit in which the foreigner is situated; the foreigner *per se* does not belong to the internal, but rather comes from the external. In this reciprocity of distance and closeness, which articulates human relations, 'distance means that he, who is close by, is far, and strangeness means that he, who also is far, is actually near'.[41] This already suggests that the condition of the foreigner, expected to make an impossible synthesis between close and distant, is less a condition than a mobility. The foreigner is the person who moves *par excellence*. Indeed, this is true also because she is deprived of property, a base, a terrain. The European Jew would provide the highest example of this figure. Simmel did not stop at the interplay between *Fern* and *Nah*, distant and close. Rather, he was the first to pose the question of the foreigner determined upon staying, of the migrant who becomes an immigrant.

> The stranger is thus being discussed here, not in the sense often touched upon in the past, as the wanderer who comes today and goes tomorrow, but rather as the person who comes today and stays tomorrow. He is, so to speak, the potential wanderer: although he has not moved on, he has not quite overcome the freedom of coming and going.[42]

The question would be picked up anew years later, with much more dramatic accents and a certain autobiographical touch, in Alfred Schütz's short 1942 article entitled 'The Stranger'.[43] Compelled to leave Austria in 1938 to reach first Paris and then New York, Schütz was influenced by Husserl. The ambiguity that phenomenology had shown in dealing with unfamiliarity, which constituted itself 'within and by way of' the familiar, which is thus always originary, again emerge in Schütz's text.[44] But his merit lay in the fact that he introduced the figure of the immigrant, which he talked about in the first person, specifying that 'the term "stranger" shall mean an adult individual of our times and civilization who tries to be permanently accepted or at least tolerated by the group which he approaches'.[45] Unfortunately, Schütz did not outline a phenomenology of the immigrant. Here and there, there does emerge the negative experience, the bitterness of those who feel out of place, the disorientation, the blow inflicted on one's confidence in the habitual way of thinking and of living. There is more than one insight: Schütz detects the novelty of the 'crisis', grasps the difference between the tourist (a detached spectator) and the foreigner who needs to make her home, and sees the need for the translation from one cultural model to another – a far from self-evident path, given that the new country is not just a refuge for the immigrant but a field of adventures. But missing are the wider political coordinates that appear – for example, in Arendt's reflection – dating to this same era. Schütz saw the immigrant as an 'aspirant', the future husband, the recruit enrolling for service, the farmer's son who goes to university, the new member of an exclusive club – images destined to reappear in the English-speaking debate. But these images wipe away the relationality of the foreigner, her being out of place, which cannot but also have repercussions within the community.

Hence the importance of a phenomenology which – without giving in to the will to capture, dominate and domesticate the foreigner, neutralizing her explosive charge – instead limits itself to indicating her place within a topography that ends up also proving to be a typology. Only thus is it possible to safeguard what Waldenfels calls the 'radicality of the alien', a not entirely convincing formula but one that seeks to underline the impossibility of deriving the unfamiliar from the proper or of transcending it in the universal. A recap of the many ways in which the unfamiliar has been and is spoken about in both classical and modern languages brings out at least four semantic tonalities which allow us to distinguish between a similar number of facets.[46] And place seems the most relevant aspect, in this regard:

- The foreigner is the *xénos, externus, peregrinus, straniero, extranjero, étranger, Fremd*. She is external, outside of some within, in an attribution of places that determines limits, marks out thresholds, and opens or closes passages. The territory has already been occupied and the borders traced. So long as the foreigner exists, the border is necessary. The foreigner comes from elsewhere and lives beyond the borders. This line of discrimination makes it possible to distinguish the external from the internal, to exclude and to include, according to schemas which, while being conventional, should also be flexible. The territorial determination in general follows a concentric order, centring things around an axis. The internal is a centre surrounded by an external periphery. The foreigner is, therefore, by definition peripheral, relegated to the provinces, which is to say, not urbanized.

- The alien is the *estraneo, allótrion, alienum*, in opposition to the proper and property. This is a determination based on ownership and belonging – according to Hegel's triad, another family, another civil society and another state. The foreigner is alien because she presents documents that attest to another identity, she speaks another language and she has another passport.
- The foreigner is the extravagant, strange, *insolitum, extraño, sonderbar* – she who is heterogeneous with respect to what ought to be familiar. She appears as such in her manners, her style, her appearance, her clothes. She deviates from the norm, she appears bizarre, she strikes a jarring note in the presumed collective harmony. This is the strangeness of what on the one hand precedes in time, according to a phylogenetic or ontogenetic sequence, and on the other hand runs parallel as it falls into the pathological vertigo. There thus alternate the figures which traditionally delimit reason – the child, the savage, the mad person, the fool – to which one could also add the animal and the machine.
- Finally, the foreigner is the extraordinary, the *deinós, insolitum, außerordentlich*, which goes beyond the borders, exceeds the limits of order, and is extra-ordinary. She exhibits singularities, exceptionality, perhaps even friendliness. When she passes through, the order is no longer the same. She is a subversive, a founder, a poet, a revolutionary, or even a terrorist.

Even if these different facets bring the figure of the foreigner into focus as in a kaleidoscope, she eludes being pinned down or defined – and she thus continues to be defined in negative terms. It is impossible to grasp the foreigner as such. Hence the appealing and troubling ambivalence of her polyhedric and iridescent figure, the promise of new ties and the threat of division and explosion. The foreigner oscillates just like the limit between within and outside. The criteria for distinguishing her continually capsize and turn into their opposite. But what, then, of the identity of her opposite, of the non-foreigner? This question is more than legitimate, considering that the foreigner often provides a more or less tacit criterion for defining the identity of others. In the attempt to counterpose her to the *xénos* who came and went, the Greeks called the owner of a piece of land the *idiótes*, from *ídios*, 'own'. The identity identical to the self, property stripped of direction, is the obvious, taken-for-granted idiocy of normality. Only the foreigner can salvage it with her incursions.

But does the self-identical truly exist? Is this not, perhaps, a powerful fiction? Strangeness is not an absolute outside. One then ought to believe that the foreigner is not only she who does not live with me, but so, too, she who lives within me. Freud suggested this already with his *Unheimlich*, the uncanny which deeply perturbs the ego. Extraneousness, unfamiliarity, is an outside that can come from within, which can chip away at ipseity. The id is another – a stranger, a foreigner to itself, even at the strongest sites of its identity. Starting with birth and death – confines that the id does not master, emblems of unfamiliarity within the heart of one's own.[47] Existence is a temporary hostel to which one will never have the keys.

Julia Kristeva entitled her successful book *Étrangers à nous-mêmes*, 'Foreigners to ourselves'.[48] This is what is discovered during the foreigner's journey in extraneousness. The discovery is not circumscribed to the unconscious, to the spur-of-the-moment idea, to obsessions and dreams. Experiences multiply and affect even the realm of the body. And this means that extraneousness shows up in flesh and blood. It is the body that perceives itself, the gaze that looks at itself in the mirror, the name that hears itself said. Not even language is a sure anchoring of identity, given that language is always-already the other's, and speaking is but a continual estrangement from the self.

The foreigner poses a challenge to whoever imagines themselves sure that they are identical to their own property. If they acknowledge this challenge, at least in part, it reveals a world in which no one can feel at home any longer. Yet the conclusions to draw from this are not only existential, but also political.[49]

15 Clandestine passages, heterotopias, anarchic routes

The sea is not at the beginning. It is a passage that opens up in the wake of other passages and crossings – of deserts, of uplands, of mountains and plains. The expanse of water merges into the horizon as it turns into sky. And it blends into this indistinctness. Favourable, auspicious waves will map out the route and assist the voyage. But the liquid bridge can suddenly erect itself as a wall that is impossible to surmount. Hence the ambivalence of an in-between that opens and closes, links and separates.

The sea is an anarchic passage; it evades any borders, it cancels out any trace of appropriation, it contests the *arché* of order and subverts the *nómos* on land. For this reason, the sea also preserves the memory of another clandestinity, that of oppositions, resistances, struggles. Not the clandestinity of a stigma, but rather that of a decision.

The anarchy of an extra-ordinary passage, a transgression that navigates out of place and against the times. What Foucault would call heterotopia. Understood as a 'challenging of all other spaces'. And in the ucronic counter-spaces of the sea, 'the ship and the heterotopia *par excellence*'.[50]

In his *History of Madness*, Foucault reconstructs the mysterious, disturbing case of the *Narrenschiff*, the *stultifera navis*, the ship of fools. Attested in literature as in the visual arts, from Sebastian Brant's satirical poem to the Hieronymus Bosch painting, this ship was not just an artistic creation. Rudderless vessels tossed about on the water; they drifted along the rivers towards the estuaries, and then out into the open sea, never to return. They carried with them a cargo of mad people whom the cities did not know how to get rid of. At the dawn of modernity, the *stultifera navis* gave rise to the madhouse. In the medieval landscape, the mad, most of them vagabonds, were expected and tolerated. But for the most part they were abandoned to themselves – indeed, outside of the cities. Not that there were no hospitals, dormitories, special houses and outright sites of detention. But a space of hospitality was still reserved for fellow citizens only. It seems, conversely, that the custom first of all struck against foreign fools, mad foreigners, who ended up crowding into the sites of pilgrimage. Foucault advances the hypothesis that, at first, the ships were simply meant to take the mad on a symbolic voyage in search of their lost reason. Subsequently, the concern to exclude prevailed over the concern to cure. The mad thus gathered in the main centres of transit and of market exchange; there, they were entrusted to sailors, so that they would take these fools away with them and thus free the city of their presence. Consigned to the tacit folly of the sailor who risked the open sea, the insane now had to confront this immense, agitated expanse, having lost any links or ties to their homeland – indeed, at the risk of losing not only their reason but also their faith. The heterotopia of the sea, and of madness. These were the years of great discoveries and large-scale expulsions. The departure of the mad was, however, less part of the fleet of dreams than it was inscribed in the legacy of ritual exiles. It is impossible to find a precise reason for this vessel crammed with the mad, the alienated, vagabonds and foreigners, which set sail without even a helmsman. But it is not difficult to imagine that this was a purifying ritual. The ships departed from the Rhenish cities, but also from Belgian ones. Even from Venice. It happened at the end of the Carnival, in preparation for Lent.

The highly symbolic value of this troubling ritual, which still retains a deeply present-day relevance, ought not to go unnoticed. Of course, the recourse to the *stultifera navis* sought to evict a troubling presence from the city. But the dark mass of water not only took this presence away but was also meant to purify. The mad person departed for the other world, as indeed did the sailor, who did not know whether he would ever return. Every departure was – and is – potentially the last. And yet the mad person's voyage was a definitive separation, an absolute passage.

A prisoner of the sea from which she could never escape, the mad person was handed over to the thousand-fathom river, the thousand-route sea, to this great uncertainty outside of everything. She is a prisoner amidst the freest and most open of routes: tightly chained to the infinite crossroads. She is the Passenger *par excellence*, which is to say a prisoner to the Passage. And the country which she would reach remained unknown, just as, when she did set foot on dry land, it would be impossible to tell what country she had come from. She had neither truth nor a homeland, if not in this infertile expanse between two lands that could not be hers.[51]

The heterotopia of the mad, the marginalised, pushed out of the gates of the city, could prove to be a privilege. One can see the subversive potential concealed within the liminal situation. Then she was no longer even granted the limit itself. She had to be dealt with in the site of passage itself, relegated to the outside of a within – the city – and confined within an outside – the sea.

This, precisely in order to take away her extra-ordinariness. In the hetero-topography traced out above, this is part of the fourth facet mentioned: the stranger who no longer has anything extra-ordinary about her, who no longer transgresses the limits, who does not exceed the given order, because she is blocked along the way. No longer would any anarchic route open up.

The migrant boats are the recent version of the ship of fools. The migrants are like the mad, for they recklessly risk their fate, earning them the senseless end determined by the waves. And there is no contrition for these extra-terrestrial prisoners of the sea. 'Let them drown!' The historical imaginary of Europe's geography is the horizon looming over them.

But to take away the stranger's *atopía* – the fact that she is out of place and against the times, her heterotopia – means closing the space beyond the borders in which the future place of utopia can alone be anticipated. All that would remain would be order – an order reasserted by police methods, under the banner of normalization and straightening things out. This would doubtless also come at the expense of the stranger found within. Accepting, that is, that the idiocy of property can long preserve itself without the stranger.

The anarchic sea route instead indicates the challenge of the elsewhere, the reversal of order, a fundamental upheaval. An upheaval that ensures that the 'poetics of space' does not lack any *ex-*, any outside, any outsider.[52] And yet it is not enough to start out from the stranger within, and still less is it enough to eulogize the otherness of the other, in a xenophilia – opposite to xenophobia – which has often risked being mistaken or reduced, or indeed has risked limiting itself, to an ethics without politics. What is instead needed is a politics that takes its cues from the foreigner understood as a foundation and criterion of community. She is a dative, who ought to be allowed passage.

3

RESIDENT FOREIGNERS

For the first time Jewish history is not separate but tied up
with that of all other nations.

Hannah Arendt, *We Refugees*

The land must not be sold permanently, because the land is
mine and you reside in my land as foreigners and strangers.

Vayikra/Leviticus 25, 23 [New International Version]

1 On exile

The new millennium is the age of the diasporization of the world.
For centuries, modernity has denied exile and everywhere wiped
out extraneousness. This has been a powerful but ineffective way
of combating the two great waves of migration. The political result
of this removal has been to imprison peoples within nation-states,
a form of habitation in which the self and the place converge. Yet
this convergence has buckled under the pressure of communities
which in fact extend beyond the state, and the relationship between
self and place has almost dissolved. There has thus emerged the
phenomenon of a self which, being able to live in different places,
no longer feels at home in any part of the world. In history, there
has been just one precedent for this: the Jewish exile, an apparent
paradox and an outright scandal for the other peoples. But after the
sedentary era, the norm that a self should identify with a place is in
fact no longer a norm. If a deterritorialized self can exist, then land

should not be considered the *a priori* of existence. Diasporization makes it possible to glimpse the possibility of a new form of habitation that makes what had previously been the exception – the condition of the exile – into a norm.

Whether or not they are themselves tested on the paths of immigration, everyone is an exile, unaware that this is what they are. In her exposed nakedness, the foreigner – lacking either roots, a homeland or a refuge – brings out into the open the exile that deeply troubles each person's existence. Hence the horror which she provokes. In each particular case, her historical and biographical circumstances unveil the intimate connection that binds exile and existence. Even if the etymological comparison is uncertain and remains a matter of controversy, 'exile' and 'existence' do each share the prefix *ex-*, which indicates an emergence from, a step outside, a way out. Exile pushes existence to recover this same value, tearing it from its inertia and its carefree obviousness. Before exile, it does not know how to exist, if to exist means to extend beyond, outside one's own self.

Exile suddenly comes down with the violence of a storm. Nothing is like before. A definitive rupture, an irreparable split, exile breaks the identity between self and place and interrupts the immediate relation between the individual and her world, expropriating her of any firm possession. Existence can no longer imagine that it is still at one with the Earth, that it is a natural secretion, the product of the soil. A traumatic event and one that is passively suffered, exile is an irreparable rupture that even a whole life is not enough to heal.

It is the actual moment of departure that marks this interruption. But in that moment, stunned in the bitter spasm of taking one's distance, this moment evaporates. Only in the memory will it continue to appear more clearly. Privation, disappearance, ruin: everything seems lost forever. The baggage of the exile are the scraps of past happiness, as she now floats almost weightless. A long chain of generations, thousands of lives, press to demand their own survival, as the peril of drowning looms over them. Centuries are recapitulated in this moment in which each of those who depart takes a last look at the tombs that she is leaving behind. From the shore, she promises a future memory.

As familiar images and fragments of familiar voices disappear into the distance, the sounds, colours and perfumes of the native landscape dissipate. Plains, hills, water courses, woods, beaches: these places were the intimate recess of her sensibility. The world will always have these contours and these lights. Yet only from a distance does she begin to see them clearly. Never will she be able to rediscover this immediate intimacy. Exile has torn her from her land, in which every fibre of her being was immersed and enveloped. She feels like an uprooted tree. This is the dramatic experience of being uprooted. Her roots are laid bare, left exposed. They will not again be able to sink into some other land; the only space she can still stretch out into is the sky.

This uprooting is the definitive separation from the land, which now appears as a distinct entity, and an irreparably lost one. And yet exile has a surprise in store: for in a certain sense the land becomes more present as the exile runs over it again in her memory. She then discovers that it is land that inhabits her. Liberation from one's natural assignation to a given place is the beginning of an unprecedented freedom: space becomes temporal. The land itself acquires a new presence. It is not the muck of the past, but the promise of the future.

Turning around, the exile looks at the life she shared, at the way of being to which she had unwittingly conformed, and which suddenly now appears to her as just one among many habits; it is just that she called this inhabitation her homeland.

Shipwrecked, having survived the storm, she is abandoned on the shore, reduced to herself, while the sea retreats. And so, she feels that she no longer has a place in the world – or, rather, that she no longer has a world, for this has drifted away, along with the sea. No longer is there anything to support her. But in this abyss, where she can count only on herself, she understands that it is not the world that carries her, but rather she who is carrying the world.

Perhaps this is the brief moment of her absolute identity? Unbound from any ties, what else ought to be left to her? Even as she looks to survive beyond interruption, almost akin to a death, it is as if the eyes of some other were scrutinizing her from deep within. She feels invaded by an intimate unfamiliarity. This is a troubling duplication. She cannot escape the gaze of these eyes, which contemplate her in the nudity of her uprootedness. And yet, precisely in this rift, she glimpses the cadaver of her first identity. There lies the rooted person – destroyed by her newfound uprootedness – who seeks another life in her own self. Two faces clash within her – and this is a chasm she could fall into. The unease overwhelms her. And yet the destruction of the old abode brings to the surface a new possibility. If she is reduced to herself, this is not as herself, but rather as her potential-to-be. In losing all her supports, she awakens to herself, is born to herself. For this reason, to be in exile means to escape from the firmament of birth, from the identity which descended on the self in such an untimely way – the identity with which, in her inertia, she thus had believed herself identical.[1] But unfamiliarity, which is now at home, pushes her to shake off her self, to be born again.

This is, then, a providential encounter with the stranger who crops up from among the miserable baggage that had accompanied her on her impetuous flight. Or, rather, it is precisely this stranger that directs the exile in her migration, which in turn finally takes on some sense. 'Head towards yourself!' Thus resounds the appeal, as ancient as the imperative injunction to Abraham: 'Go from your country, your people and your father's household to the land I will show you.'[2] The exile leaves the ruin behind her and projects herself beyond, into the immensity of exile, where the void opens up to her a sky of light and reprieve.

2 Neither rootlessness nor roaming without direction

After taking her leave, the exile can sink further into rootlessness or consign herself to directionless wandering. If it is nostalgia for lost roots that prevails, then regret becomes the cipher of existence. The uprooted person lives with their eyes on the past, in continual disillusionment, in a tragic wait. Nothing can console her. The happiness of rootedness has dissolved forever. But was this blessing truly happiness? Already for some time, the rooted person was pervaded by a distressing uncertainty. Her uprooting is but the definitive proof that she no longer inhabits the garden of Eden. The rooted person is, in fact, an uprooted one who is unaware of what she is, who imagines herself a tree planted in the ground.

Just as exile cannot be reduced to rootlessness, nor is it mere directionless wandering. The abode has crumbled because it was only ever a chimera. It would thus be impossible to inhabit it. Thus, the uprooted person is bound for a nihilistic desperation, and gets dragged along the routes of errancy. Hers, too, is a gloomy mourning for her lost roots. Except here what dominates is the disenchantment of a present lived in an obsessive dizziness. The wandering person heads into the void without direction or purpose, dangerously wallowing in the desert, abandoning herself to chance and handing herself over to the senseless, even if she does ultimately hope to find some direction, some meaning. But she does not believe in the possibility of a return.

Even before delving deeper into the return, it is worth questioning further the meaning of 'inhabiting' and of 'migrating'. In order to understand what role residency can play in a politics of hospitality, it is worth making a journey back in time, although not according to a chronological order. The stages in this journey are Athens,

Rome and Jerusalem. These three historical models of cities and citizenship remain ideal types.[3] The open citizenship of Rome distinguished itself from the Athenian autochthony, which explains many of today's political myths. Conversely, in the Biblical City, extraneousness reigned sovereign; the hinge of the community was the *gher*, the resident foreigner.

3 Phenomenology of habitation

In the realm of philosophy, only very belatedly has the question of habitation come to light in all its complexity. It emerged when the organized ruin of the Earth began its fearsome work. This destruction process made the world less a snug and welcoming womb than a planet criss-crossed and explored even in its remotest corners, one that was dug and ploughed far and wide, squeezed and crowded by buildings and habitations, and, indeed, systematically domesticated. Paradoxically, precisely as the Earth began to appear as a familiar abode, its inhabitants, who could finally feel at home everywhere, were no longer at home anywhere. As humans settled into the world, this irreparably turned into a sense of being unsettled. It is as if it were no longer possible to lay down roots in the technological–industrial domain that covers the Earth and uses it for its own cosmic calculations – as if the gradual elimination of unfamiliarity had undermined the very possibility of any relation.

Too intimate and close-at-hand a phenomenon to be considered from a proper distance, habitation became a philosophical question precisely when it stopped being self-evident. The reference to 'habitation', here, understands it not as something intended to be built – on which there is indeed a developed reflection in the architectural context – or in terms of the 'housing question', concerning the housing crisis and the shortage of accommodation, which Engels exposed already back in 1873.[4] Rather, the philosophical question regards the meaning of human habitation.

The Latin *habito* is a frequentative form of the verb *habeo*: it means 'to habitually have, to continue to have'.[5] Right from the outset, property and belonging insinuated themselves into this verb. Reiteration changed into habit, and in turn habit gave rise to domination and command. First of all, over place. To possess, to remain, to move in, to settle, to establish oneself, to make one's own, to identify, to bind to oneself, to become attached – habitation, understood as a re-elaboration of the surrounding world, is commonly held to correspond to all these things. The subject, the protagonist of habitation, digs into the ground and draws boundaries of appropriation around herself. The body moves into a space and immerses itself therein, almost to the point of merging into it, of becoming wholly at one with it. This space belongs to her out of the frequency, the habit, with which she inhabits it. It is her place of habitation; her physicality, incarnated there, has grown together with its organic matter and can no longer be separated from it. This could come only at the cost of an amputation, of the violent cutting of the living arms and legs solidly attached to this site, rooted in this terrain, enveloped in this soil. The amputation would also extend further and concern the 'things' that populate this space, which have become attached to a strong sense of belonging. Habitation would, then, be a possession which even becomes a convergence, a mutual belonging. The self identifies with the place that it inhabits and draws its identity from this place. This is why the expropriation of this place would bring an irrevocable loss of identity. The fact of the inhabitant becoming-at-one with the place inhabited – a fact perpetuated and renewed over time, leaving traces that supposedly provide her with proof of possession – gives rise to 'the home' and *feeling at home*. Only in this space chosen for inhabitation – even in the solitude and in the misery of an austere hovel or some bare refuge – can the flame of the hearth be lit, and only there can a being's singular experience unwind in a place of its own. The place is preserved by way of the self, and self is preserved by way of the place.

The semantics of habitation are based on a series of consecutive passages that range from 'stays there' to 'possesses'. As if 'staying there' represented the legitimate foundation of possession. There thus imposes itself the idea that staying – stopping, remaining, hanging around – provides exclusive access to a place, and affords the right to property over it. While this is particularly obvious in Latin and in the Romance languages, the closeness of 'habitation' and 'having', prescribed by the frequentative, is apparent also elsewhere. The German verb *Wohnen* which, as the Grimm etymological dictionary suggests, derives from the ancient *wunian*, initially meant 'to have the habit of', and then came to indicate 'to remain, to inhabit'. An analogous shift took place in Latin: 'I am in the habit of being here', thus 'I inhabit', 'I have this place.' The two meanings, which can combine with one another, survive in German still today.

One can thus get a sense of the difficulty of unbinding 'inhabiting' from 'having' and instead attaching it to being – that is, the difficulty of inscribing it in existence and making it something existential. This is what happens in the famous § 12 of *Being and Time*, which for this very reason marked a turning point in the reflection on habitation. Heidegger repeatedly returns to this theme, almost a red

thread that connects together his work. For habitation is a constitutive characteristic of human existence, which dwells in the world
in different forms, under the most varied historical constellations.

According to the criteria of traditional metaphysics, existence
ought never to be understood as what is real, as what is simply
present; rather, *ex-sistere* means 'to come out', 'to emerge from'.
Existence, in its dynamism, in its continual potential-to-be, is always
ecstatic and eccentric. How, then, should its being *in the* world be
understood? What is the meaning of this *in*, the preposition intended
to indicate the place that existence occupies within space? Heidegger
revolutionized not only the relationship between being and time,
but also the one between being and space. Being-there, *Dasein* – as
he preferred to call existence, to underline its 'already-being-in', the
finished condition to which it is consigned and from which it each
time emerges with some effort – is always a *being-in-the-world*. One
is usually led to believe that being-there exists autonomously and,
moreover, that it is to be found in the world – or, better, within the
world. In short, what is imagined is a spatial relation, through which
it stands within the world as if within a container. But, to deconstruct this belief, one need only look back to the etymology of *in*,
which derives from the ancient Gothic *innan* – or *wunian* – which
is to say *Wohnen*: in Latin, *habitare*. Heidegger specifies that here
an indicates being usual, habitual – that is, it corresponds to familiarity.[6] Being-in-the-world does not mean standing within the world,
occupying a place, but rather implies a relation that manifests itself
in staying in the world in a close bind of intimacy.

Unsurprisingly, Heidegger deduces the most radical consequences from this relation, even to the point of arguing that only
where *Dasein* exists does the world come into being. For it is this
being-there which, in making its stay within the world, on each
occasion brings the world to light. On the other hand, nor can
this being-there come about without the world. Being-in-the-world
indicates existing, in its deepest and broadest sense, in which
being-there emerges from its already-being-in to disclose the world
and, in turn, itself to become worldly. Inhabiting, therefore, is the
fundamental characteristic of existence.[7] Hence why it deserves
contemplation.

The phenomenology of habitation delineated by Heidegger – an
unprecedented philosophical novelty – revolves around the theme of
the sojourn, of the temporary abode, of a brief stop on this Earth.
This has nothing to do, therefore, with having, with the occupation
of a space, the possession of some lodging. That, rather, is the
reductive way in which habitation has always been conceived. But
the 'habitation crisis' does not consist of the lack of habitations;

rather, it lies in the need to rethink humanity's sojourn on this Earth. It is necessary, then, 'to learn to inhabit'.[8]

The obsessive quest to possess must cede its place to a reflection on the way of being in the world that distinguishes 'mortals', who take this name precisely because they are born and die. For theirs is not a permanent stay; they are but passing through. This transitoriness marks their stay here and delimits their 'sojourn' – a lapse of time and of space that lasts until the sun sets and the light disappears. It is the interval between arrival and departure. Whoever makes this stay cannot forget it. The risk would lie in overlooking the real measure of this sojourn, of mistaking it for a presence that will continue to endure. This passing-through is extended into an indefinite deferral, into the pretension of escaping the temporary, into the obstinacy of an existence that does not quieten into the steadfastness of letting things go. Rather, it takes a dogged stance that insists on remaining and, in becoming at one with its sojourn, becomes disrespectful and sets itself up against others.[9] If this persistence in a simple presence goes for the existent in general, it cannot however apply to 'mortals'. For them, existence is a temporary passage.

4 What does it mean to migrate?

To inhabit means, then, to make a stay, to hang around for a while, like on a journey, as much as is necessary to habituate, to familiarize oneself, but without ever really being able to establish ties or sink roots. For the journey always requires some detachment. To inhabit means to migrate.

The word which Heidegger draws on is *Wanderung*, 'migration'. Here, it is necessary to capture the echoes of a usage that has already been philosophically attested, in which the Latin *migrare* not only indicates physical movement or the crossing of some limit but also is the metaphor for the most extreme of passages. Thus, Cicero spoke of *migrare ex hac vita*, in the sense of leaving this life behind.[10] Nonetheless, for Heidegger, to migrate does not only designate the 'earthly' sojourn of mortals, in a Christian-metaphysical sense, and does not mean a beginning and end, but rather shapes existence, in the 'ec-static habitation', in the continual leaving of the self, the self-separation, that is a perennial migration.[11]

His break with the dictionary entries that have traditionally delimited the semantics of inhabitation – staying, possessing, appropriating, identifying – could not be any more drastic. In the landscape that Heidegger heads into, neither permanence nor rootedness seem to be present; nor, still less, the immobility of a perennial being-oneself. On the contrary, existence appears decentred, in a movement that is always also an engagement with the other.[12] Habitation is a migration that recalls the flowing of a river.

Water, then, and not earth. But this is not the vast expanse of the oceans; rather, it is the current that funnels through a riverbed, deepening and shaping yet also following it, even as it marks out patterns, opens paths, and discloses places in which the light shines on open spaces and the trees thin out, leaving clearings or even abodes in the woodland. 'Current', because inhabitation cannot be conceived as a being-here. It should instead be understood as a being-here-and-beyond, where the river is headed. Ec-static inhabitation finds its habitat precisely in this current, where, paradoxically, being-in-oneself is always-already being outside oneself, according to the eccentric dynamic of existence.

If the site of humanity's sojourn on this Earth is the current of a river, and this is its only domicile, then inhabitation cannot draw its legitimation from blood or soil. It cannot draw legitimation either from Nazi *Blut* or *Boden*, or even from the *ius sanguinis* or *ius solis* that continue to exist in various different forms. In vain would one search, in Heidegger, for an apologia for the sedentary, a cult of place, a eulogy to rootedness, an unconditional bond with the Earth. The current takes away with it any deeds of property, any pretension to inheritance. In its current, there remains only the promise of a temporary stay.

This elemental change – from earth to water – ought not to go unremarked, for it makes it possible to mark out a new phenomenology of inhabitation. Heidegger follows Hölderlin and his hymns, in which the song of the rivers merges with the song of poetry. But the rivers are not poetic, metaphorical images, just signs that point to something else; to interpret them like that would be a grave misunderstanding. The river is *Wanderung*, migration 'in a singular and consummate way'.[13] It is this going away and beyond, in which the transitory can only become a here, a locality. The current, Heidegger specifies, 'guards this locale in its essence, it is its locality'.[14] Thus comes to light the enigmatic movement of the river, which is at the same time the 'locality of erraticness' and the 'erraticness of the locality'. As they repeatedly dovetail, the two words *Ortschaft* and *Wanderschaft* mark out the course of the water and bring out into the open the secret law of the river. Even as it inhabits, the river allows for habitation; it offers an abode that is in no sense stable but rather grants the pause of a haven, the peace of a sanctuary, a passing refuge. Through its fluvial essence, place is always erratic. Humanity's historical habitation ought to be identified in this migration, in the incessant flowing and passing in which the locality of a possible sojourn emerges. The current is humanity's domicile.

To migrate means to go away. But go where? What is the end goal, the destination? Or is this simply a matter of errant wandering? Being erratic ought not to be confused with errancy. The path of the river, followed by Hölderlin and retraced by Heidegger, does not simply lead elsewhere or proceed from the own to the other, but rather returns from the other to the own. The destination is the *Heimat*; the way there is a 'making-one's-home' that discloses itself only after it has withstood the test of the most remote distance, after it has endured its engagement with what is most troubling about it, after it has crossed the path of the non-habitual and the uninhabitable, up to the extreme limit of unfamiliarity.

The route is disconcerting: it does not lead from the homeland to the elsewhere, but rather from the elsewhere to the homeland. It is a making-one's-home in being *not*-at-home, a *Heimischwerden* in an *Unheimischsein*, in which this being-disoriented always precedes familiarity. Already in *Being and Time*, Heidegger had noted that the 'not-at-home', the *Un-zuhause*, is always the phenomenon that comes first.[15] To inhabit means to return. And yet *to return* does not necessarily mean *a return*. One ought to be cautious and make sure not to take an arrival for a return.[16] The slow path which leads home is, if anything, an incessant getting-closer. The separation, which is always-already required upon departure, does not follow the reaching of the destination. In its secret, in its *Geheimnis*, the *Heimat*, the homeland-abode, remains beyond grasp; it is always beyond, in an immemorial elsewhere.

For this reason, to migrate is a continual pushing-beyond, which corresponds to the very heartbeat of existence, to its constitutive eccentricity. One could say that the movement unfolds in a spiral, spreading from the inside to the outside, if it were not for the fact that inside and outside are already terms of a metaphysical dichotomy. The movement is, rather, that of the surges of a river, in their whirling, sinking and re-emergence. Between the rivers that Hölderlin 'sets in poetry' – from the Main to the Neckar and the Rhine – it is the course of the Danube that sheds most light on this singular journey of return.

Heidegger elaborated on the theme of migration, in its profound philosophical relevance and powerful historical thrust, in two famous comments – one on the hymn 'Der Ister' in 1942, and the other on 'Andenken' in 1943.

What kind of river is the Danube (der Ister)? Hölderlin's elegy begins by evoking a light that appears in the night of time, the flame of the origin, the sun of civilization. 'Eager are we to see the day.'[17]

This yearned-for moment arrives only when this remote errancy seems to be held back at the riverbank. For it is rivers that fertilize the Earth. 'Here, however, we wish to build.'[18] But the river already has a name. 'This one, however, is named the Ister. Beautiful he dwells.'[19] Ístros is the name that the Romans, following the Greeks, gave to the lower Danube, whereas the upper one remained the *Danubius* – in German, *Donau*. Two names for a river whose identity appears suspended, almost split, between its source and its mouth.

On the one hand, the yellow shores and the black of the forest of firs, the *Schwarzwald*; on the other the fiery isthmus in search of shade, the delta of the waters that open out into the Black Sea, in ancient times also called the Pontos Euxeinos, the 'Hospitable Sea', a basin within the Mediterranean that both divides and connects Europe and Asia. But the Ister–Danube solidly connects Greece and Germany, in a capsizing of the spatial-temporal coordinates and a remixing of historical times. Its flow runs backwards, *rückwärts*:

He appears, however, almost
To go backwards and
I presume he must come
From the East.[20]

Its surges shift turbulently and, sometimes stagnating or hesitating between the rocks, they push back towards the source the water that comes from the place at which the river opens into the foreign sea.[21] Thus, between its swirls, its twists and its obstacles, the river brings that Greek dawn of civilization back to the nocturnal German source; it conjugates the beginning with the end and the end with the beginning, as it mixes the waters between the mouth and the source. Danube–Ister, Ister–Danube. After having immersed itself in the sea of unfamiliarity, that of a Greek Orient which is itself already distant, more Balkan than classical, the river – as if suspended in the *aporia* between these two directions – turns back home, loyal to the source towards which it never ceases to make its return.

Of course, only she who has departed, she who has made her way through the unfamiliar, following the course of the rivers, can indeed make a return. 'It is precisely that [belonging and going along with the rivers] which tears onwards more surely in the rivers' own path that tears human beings out of the habitual midst of their lives, so that they may be in a centre outside of themselves, that is, be excentric.'[22] She who presumes that she is at home cannot become-at-home. Nor can she feel nostalgia for the *Heimat*. Only she who is distant is consumed by her homeland and, in this troubling unfamiliarity, learns to make the return to her own, learns to inhabit. An exemplary figure, in this regard, is she who heads out so far that she ends up on the sea. Even in their fear, those who set sail separate themselves from the shadowy forests of their homeland and make their route out into the open, trepidly remaining on the alert even by night. Those who navigate are the poets who do not lose their route even on the high seas; they follow the way indicated by destiny, towards the homeland which awaits them and to which they aspire. They are no adventurers, and nor could they ever become that. For adventurers, the unfamiliar is but the exotic; it has the flavour of a drug, the appeal of the extraordinary. For this very reason, they do not even have a route – they lose themselves in an errancy without return.[23] Conversely, those who navigate maintain their focus on their route and, in passing through the unfamiliar, are right from the outset always-already making a return towards their own. And they do so without ever being able to appropriate anything for themselves.

5 The global uprooting

Heidegger pointed to the double trick that is concealed within habitation. First of all, the tricking of those who are convinced that they are already at home, solidly rooted in the native soil, in a sure belonging, an unshaken identity. Together with this – this naïve sense of stability – there takes form the alternative of an errancy that knows neither route nor destination nor return. It is the trick of uprootedness, of the mobility that is supported by technology. If habitation is a temporary stay, then it cannot be understood as stably making one's home on the land, or indeed taken for the complete renunciation of the land, through that *Bodenlosigkeit*, that lack of soil, that risks making modern man into a 'planetary adventurer'.[24]

In his *Letter on 'Humanism'*, Heidegger denounces the 'homelessness' – the *Heimatlosigkeit* – which, having become a 'world destiny', risks irredeemably damaging the 'human essence'. That is to say, the ec-static existence that must always take hold in order to emerge once more, leaving the traces which attest to itself and constitute its historical habitation. But what happens where – as Walter Benjamin already cautioned – the new architecture of glass and steel makes this impossible? The unprecedented experience of 'inhabiting without trace' risks being reduced to an empty habit which can be transported anywhere.[25]

Precisely in the planetary era, in which the mounting impossibility of inhabiting this Earth proceeds in tandem with a growing uprootedness, it is necessary to learn how it ought to be inhabited. That comes well before any discussion of building or continuing to build. For Heidegger, here the terms of the question are reversed: one does not build in order to inhabit. Only those who are able to inhabit know how to build. In its most eminent sense, to build means to cultivate, to curate, to take care; it again makes up part of inhabiting.[26] But learning how to inhabit also demands that one go back yet further – and this is itself a way of inhabiting – to the point where Hölderlin's verse: 'poetically Humans dwell upon this earth' emerges in its all its richness.[27] It is the poets who, in naming things, call them into being; who, in giving a measure of the world, articulate it. 'Poetry is the original admission of dwelling.'[28] Dealing with what would otherwise pass fleetingly with the current, the poets institute what remains; they are the architects of the world-as-abode.[29]

'Planetarism' is that era in which the dominion of industry and technology covers the entire planet. This latter is inserted into that calculation which is already preparing cosmic and interstellar space as a future habitat. Governed by the excess of calculation and troubled by the inability to measure, this is the impoetic time of a global disorientation. It becomes ever more difficult to keep open the space of a possible habitation. For what is lost is not only, and not so much, the home in which one can happily find some peace, the calm of the hearth, as the sanctuary of poetry, the respite from the other's speech, the only refuge that remains amidst the planetary exile. 'We today wander through the world-abode which lacks the "friend of the house".'[30]

6 'The earth-born': Athens and the myth of autochthony

Among most Indo-European languages, human beings are called 'terrestrials' because they inhabit the Earth and not other planets, because they have their abode on the Earth's surface and not in the depths of the water or in the rarefied heights of the skies. But they are also called this because it is as if they originated from the earth, as if they were created with this element – thus *homo* and *humanus* both come from the Latin *humus*, earth.[31]

In Greek culture, this link with the earth is a very robust one. In that culture, it assumed unprecedented forms and singular contours. Before they were called 'terrestrial', human beings were 'mortals' – *brótoi, thnétoi anthrópoi* – in the sense that what defines them is their extreme limit, death. They are born mortal, consigned to a brief sojourn, destined to a life over which death is always looming. And it is this that determines their irreparable distance from the gods, their baleful caesura from the immortals.

Because of this destiny which linked them back to the land – almost a prison from which they aspired to free themselves – mortals were also called *epichthónioi*, 'those who inhabit the Earth'.[32] This word is made up of *epì*, 'at'/'on', and *chtón*, the earthly soil, between the depths of Hades and the Olympian skies, on which humans found their cities and have their homes and their tombs. The soil, *chtón*, which remains connected to this habitation and to the *pólis*, continued to have a political meaning.

The primordial earth was instead called *gê*. In Greece, there was no account of the beginning like the Jewish Bereshit, a genesis that connected the human being back to some act of creation. Nonetheless, there was no lack of myths that dated back to the most remote eras, which narrated men's birth to Mother Earth. While these different versions were richly textured and varied greatly among themselves, there prevailed a shared agreement that humanity had come from the earth. In this, there were, however, two opposed models. In the one model, the earth was a malleable material, clay modelled by a demiurge, an artisan-god who fashioned the human creature just as a sculptor or a potter would. In the other, the earth was itself the mother from whose spontaneously fertile womb – or one fertilized by some fortuitous seed – men were born. They emerged from her womb just as plants spring up from the soil. Between the two models – that of the artifice and that of fertility, which sometimes overlapped, where the clump of soil became clay – the one that prevailed was the one in which the Earth, the solitary archetype of all the feminine roles, the power that produces life, took form as Mother.

Hence the eminently Greek myth of the Mother-Earth, of which humans are the offspring. Asserted in the Greeks' origin stories and attested in the cities' ancestral traditions, the myth found its most famous formulation in Plato's *Statesman*, in the discussion of that first race of beings that did not derive from mating but rather immediately sprang from the life of the Earth itself. They were thus called *ghegheneîs*, the 'earth-born'.[33]

Like any origin story, this one, too, posed question marks and raises difficulties. How could one explain the passage from the immediate birth of the 'first humans', to their progeny, who instead descended from the reproductive cycle? Hypotheses abounded and interpretations were thrown together. From the golden age to the silver age and the age of bronze, various disparate eras were interposed between that first, mythical beginning and the human epoch. In all this, woman herself represented an enigma: her presence appeared fundamentally awkward. For it was beyond doubt that human beings, *anthrópoi*, had emerged from the womb of the Earth, before woman could have any role and even before she had existed. And it did not matter that this propulsive power itself seemed like a precocious imitation of woman's own functions. What counted was that this divested woman of her role. Gea, Earth-made-goddess, was the great Mother. Woman was left in her shadow, like a stranger, and makes up part of the human *ghénos* – indeed, even subsequently maintaining an ambiguous place within humanity. Conversely, the *anthrópoi*, calling themselves as such in opposition to the gods, became *andrês*, 'men', as distinct from women. And this did not free them of trouble, because they would still have to pass via the *ghuné* – this other from the self, a surrogate for Mother Earth – in order to reproduce. But no matter how one works one's way through the dense web of myths on the 'earth-born', one will not find a single autochthonous daughter. And yet it is woman, already in the mythical-poetic figure of Pandora, who would have to assume the role played by the Earth.

Conversely, there could be no room for doubt on the role attributed to the *andrês* who constituted the body of the *pólis*. Each city celebrated the tradition of the founder of its bloodline, an 'earth-born'. This did not mean they had a problem with there being certain contaminations of this bloodline. But the founders were necessarily divine. Perhaps the most famous of these, Erichthonius of Athens, was at the same time both the 'son of the gods' and *autochthon* – a key term composed of *aúto* and *chthôn*, 'same' and 'soil' – born in the *soil itself*, not only from the earth but within the circumscribed territory of the city.

This was the foundational myth of autochthony. This Greek myth did not aspire to offer a vision of the dawn of time or seek to lay claim to the first-born forefather who had the honour of giving rise to humanity. In its multiple versions, suiting each of the different – often rival – cities, the myth served not so much to underline the nobility of a heroic and archaic genealogy, as to assert exclusive possession of the *chthôn*, the civic territory from which, in a collective attribution of autochthony, the citizens were born and to which they belonged.

No lack of cities or regions gloried in having been founded by some prestigious foreigner who had come from elsewhere. The Peloponnese owed its origin to Pelops, a Phrygian. But, in general, the Greeks preferred accounts that evoked some autochthonous hero, who had sprung from the civilizing earth. The celebration of this origin served to reaffirm the purity of the self-same, the *autós*, which had to prevail and did prevail even among the descendants, by way of the line of filiation. It was as if, even though the descendants had been born to women, they, too, had all emerged from this same land itself, like the first-born themselves. This, in turn, legitimized a property relation – their ownership over this land. In order to avoid this relation being dissolved, it was necessary to ostracize anything distant and make sure that the present remained linked to this original past. On the one hand, therefore, this was a matter of temporal proximity – the memory of the transmission of that soil. On the other, it was a matter of stability, their continued presence in this same place. Herodotus repeated this, as he credited with autochthony those peoples, such as the Arcadians, who remained temporally and spatially faithful to their origins.[34]

If Sparta was the Doric city of immigrants, Athens was the homeland of the self – the brilliant and unattainable example of pure autochthony. The two cities' atavistic rivalry was also due to these opposed forms of provenance. Nonetheless, Athens did not limit itself to celebrating its origins, but reiterated them. The mythical purity of the past, when the autochthonous people had acquired the soil which it inhabited in the very moment of its birth, without ever having had to reside on others' lands or hunt out previous occupiers, was indispensable for legitimizing the Athenians' right to possession in the present. In return, the present reinforced and validated the past. In remembering that beginning, the Athenians assured their own identity, as they remained solidly entrenched in the *chthôn*, the territory of Attica. After the Athenian mothers had been erased from the genesis of the *pólis*, the Earth's own maternity was itself ever more hidden. As Demosthenes proclaimed in the funeral oration given for the dead of the Battle of Chaeronea, Athenians were autochthonous sons of the originary homeland.[35]

The Attic soil was the *arché*, the absolute principle, the beginning of humanity and of the world, the absolute foundation of the City, the origin from which the patrilineal order unfolded – the order of the *patria*, of progeny. The *arché* is the principle of the homeland.

Sons of their own soil, from which they had never moved, the Athenians remained 'the same', tied to the identity of their origins, and guaranteed the purity of the *génos*, of birth and of the bloodline. In its peerless autochthony, Athens proclaimed itself the authentic Greece. Numerous accounts by historians, poets, tragedians and orators eulogized it in these same terms. But it was in Plato's *Menexenus* that the celebration of Athenian autochthony reached its apogee. Here, the myth seems to have found philosophical legitimation. But this should not be misunderstood; in fact, in parodying the patriotic prose of the funeral orations, Plato related an immemorial theme of the archaic Greek tradition, a rhetorical motif of whose powerful political purpose he was himself aware.

Autochthony was conjugated with *eugéneia*, literally meaning 'good birth', and both made the Athenian *génos* into a single bloodline, the ancestry of one same family. No adopted son, no bastard, no intruder, no immigrant. It was, indeed, movement that brought mixing – including the mixing of blood:

Now as regards nobility of birth, their first claim thereto is this – that the forefathers of these men were not of immigrant stock [*metoikoûntas*], nor were these their sons declared by their origin to be strangers in the land sprung from immigrants, but natives sprung from the soil living and dwelling [*oikoûntas*] in their own true fatherland; and nurtured also by no stepmother, like other folk, but by that mother-country wherein they dwelt [*oikoûn*], which bore them and reared them and now at their death receives them again to rest in their own abodes [*en oikeíos topois*].[36]

Not only birth, but also death, unfolded within the terrain of the authentic, the proper. The dead must lie in family plots, returned to the womb that had first given birth to them. The life cycle ended by returning to its own beginning, in confirmation of the nobility of the pure origin. Democratic Athens tacitly endorsed the values and advantages of aristocracy. But this question also has further implications – indeed, ones that are very much relevant today – insofar as it relied on a genetic unity, the homogeneity of the bloodline, in order to legitimize democracy. Paradoxically, autochthony and 'good birth' were taken to be the unavoidable preconditions for a valid and effective democracy. Plato immediately offered the reason for this: namely, that the equality among citizens is not *sought*, but rather *presupposed*, and is originary – or, rather, comes from the bloodline itself. A juridical and political equality can be established only on the basis of this genetic equality.

For whereas all other States are composed of a heterogeneous collection of all sorts of people, so that their polities also are heterogeneous, tyrannies as well as oligarchies, some of them regarding one another as slaves, others as masters; we and our people, on the contrary, being all born of one mother, claim to be neither the slaves of one another nor the masters; rather does our natural birth-equality [*isogonía*] drive us to seek lawfully legal equality [*isonomía*], and to yield to one another in no respect save in reputation for virtue and understanding.[37]

Hence the difference between autochthonous Athens, where all were 'brothers' born to one same mother, and the other cities that proved unable to maintain the purity of the Hellenic line, instead mixing among themselves or even with barbarians. Plato had no hesitation about bluntly speaking of 'metics', the term used to designate resident foreigners. If each autochthonous Greek was necessarily earth-born, not every earth-born was an autochthonous Greek.[38] Whoever had left the place in which he was born and moved elsewhere could not be autochthonous – rather, he was, at most, an adoptive son.

This definition advanced through division – or, rather, through exclusion. The discriminating criterion was that of the pure *génos*. On the one side, the Greeks; on the other, the barbarians.[39] This was the initial divide within humanity. Then came the divides within Greece: on the one hand, the Athenians – 'the only people', Herodotus emphasized, 'that never emigrated', and in whose autochthony he exalted the paradigmatic Greekness; and, on the other hand, the rest of the Greeks, relegated to the margins, pushed back to the boundaries with the barbarian world, and who were themselves, in turn, impure Greeks or semi-barbarians.[40] In *Menexenus*, the Athenian imperialism of the self triumphs in emphatic and extreme tones:

> So firmly rooted and so sound is the noble and liberal character of our city, and endowed also with such a hatred of the barbarian, because we are pure-blooded [*eilikrinôs*] Greeks, unadulterated by barbarian stock. For there cohabit [*sunoikoûsin*] with us none of the type of Pelops, or Cadmus, or Aegyptus or Danaus, and numerous others of the kind, who are naturally barbarians though nominally Greeks; but our people are pure Greeks and not a barbarian blend; whence it comes that our city is imbued with a whole-hearted hatred of alien races.[41]

Autochthonous Athens, authentic Greece, pure self, solid Centre of the world, the City *par excellence*. Here, where everything was set under the sign of the proper, of the *oikeîon*, of what was intimate and familiar, the Athenians steadfastly inhabited the ancestral soil on which they were themselves born; and they moreover inhabited it among others who were the same. Habitation, *oikeîn*, was itself integral, uncontaminated, without extraneous traces – it was neither a *sunoikeîn* (the co-habiting with which the foreign, barbarian bloodline tries to insinuate itself into the city), nor, still less, a *metoikeîn* (the residency conceded to the metics). Composed of *metà*, in the sense of 'change', and *oîkos*, 'house', the term 'metic' indicated those who have left their home in one city and moved into another –resident foreigners.[42] The separation between the territorial border and the barrier to citizenship clearly emerges within this figure: inhabiting the territory of the city is not the first step towards integration into the civic body. For the *pólis* is not only the name of the place inhabited by the city, but also the name of the community of citizens.

Here come to light the political consequences of autochthony. Imagined as a permanent presence, at the same time it is the response to an apprehension that slithered through the Greek cities of those years. There are echoes of this in Aristotle's *Politics*, which delves into the identity of a *pólis* that cannot remain the same if the population continues to vary and, picking up the theme already underlined by Plato, draws the attention to a question that no statesman could ignore: the political stability of a city where not only the *ghénos* but also the *éthnos* remained the same. Maintaining one same bloodline – one same 'race'? – was the guarantee of stable government. Even democracy would, then, be a question of family. For this very reason, 'citizenship is not constituted by domicile in a certain place'.[43] This argument was destined to great success even in the modern era. The Greek model of the *pólis* was based on a fine homogeneity that kept itself intact and was neither spoiled by foreigners, upset by new arrivals, disturbed by immigrants, nor troubled by slaves. Within this perspective, the perfection of the political regime should be deduced from the purity of the city's origins, and democracy from autochthony. The only city to have accomplished this, Athens was the City at peace with itself.

The further, decisive consequence of autochthony was thus citizenship. Only legitimate sons were *polîtai*, and only Athenians were citizens. All the 'others', those who arrived from elsewhere, the intruders, were not and could not be citizens. While in other cities founded by foreigners, such as Thebes and Sparta, various degrees of citizenship were stipulated, Athens once again distinguished itself in this particular regard. It set down a divide between citizens and resident foreigners. These latter inhabited the city, where they were also integrated, but they did not share the same civil rights. To be more precise, one would have to reach the additional conclusion that the Athenians were the only citizens in the world.

The other Greeks could also fashion themselves such a title – *polîtai*, 'citizens' – but this was, in Plato's argument, a matter of convention rather than of nature, given that in the cities in which they resided they were adoptive sons, the descendants of distant immigrants. To be precise, they were only residents, who remained foreign, even if they aspired to the right to citizenship. But, given that the *chthón*, the ancestral soil, and birth on the ancestral soil, decided citizenship, it should be added that only Athenians were citizens, while all the others were simply 'natives'. What distinguished their relationship with the city was residency, inhabitation, *oikéo*, which is never pure, if only because it is the point of arrival after some movement, a prior errancy. Before the inhabitant there was the wanderer, the *metanástes*, the migrant, the one who comes from outside, *állothen*, who is to be reproached for having moved, or for having been born to someone who had moved.

Movement is a wrong, a fault – it is the error of errancy. The autochthonous self is defined by negation, by the absence of movement, by immobility. More than inhabiting, it remains, *hístemi*, in a stability which supposedly exhibits a different dimension – not horizontality, but verticality, within the terms of a deep rootedness and the edifice built upon these roots. These are thus two opposed ways of residing. Except for the fact that *hístemi* is less stable than is presumed, and its meaning – besieged by the numerous prefixes that all introduce a sense of movement – is continually destabilized. Even to the point that one ought to ask whether there really does exist an immobile *hístemi*, or if this is, instead, a metaphysical fiction, like the whole *logos* of autochthony.

This is especially true given that not only *hístemi* but also *oikéo* seems rather unstable. It is impossible to see in what sense *oikéo*, this Athenian sense of habitation, is supposed to be any different from others' forms of habitation, if not through the reiterated assertion that 'it is us who inhabit Athens together with self-same Greeks'. This stipulation does nothing to make the verb *oikéo* any more pertinent or proper – indeed, with good reason it is assigned also to others, to foreigners, to metics, to the immigrants culpable for having come to occupy lands which belong to others, which they nonetheless inhabit. It is as if the self were defined always and only in opposition to the other, on which it thus depends; similarly, autochthonous inhabitation is a fictitious continuous presence which in its very claim to perfection risks turning into a tautology, into the immobile repetition of the self. When it situates itself on the terrain of others, it appears as a stability so precarious as to instantly give way to movement. Autochthonous identity here vanishes, just like its myth.

7 Rome: the city without origin and imperial citizenship

Athens was a city closed in on itself, jealous of its own identity, and in which citizenship was handed down from father to son. The need to protect the ethnic purity of the Athenian lineage was first decreed by Pericles (in 451–450 BC) and then imposed with the prohibition against mixed marriages (341–340 BC). The myth of autochthony shaped citizenship; the ideology of rootedness dug a political moat, an axiological gap between the citizen and the resident foreigner. There was no right to the city: the community of Athenians affirmed its own freedom, its own autonomy, its own autarchy, taking the sovereign decision to close the gates.

What about Rome, though? Did there exist a 'Roman path' to citizenship? From its origins a foreign city, Rome was an open city, an unfinished and incomplete one that was prepared to welcome those who came from outside into its already-immense population of free citizens.

The foreigner's place in the city provides the clue and the evidence thanks to which we can make out the two opposed models of community and belonging specific to Athens and Rome. Beyond the creations which they historically produced, these models were destined to represent two ideal paradigms. The mirror-image relationship between them was even expressed in the words used: for, if the Greek *pólis* defined the *polítes*, conversely the Roman *civitas* was defined by the *cives*.[44] In the Athenian model, it is the community that prevails over the individual, while in the Roman model it is the individual that determines the community. Hence also their diverse relationships with the foreigner, and their two different forms of citizenship: the Athenian form was exclusive and static, whereas the Roman one was inclusive and dynamic. The foreigner represented a threat to Athens, for he might change the finite and perfect community and alter its identity, even to the point of making it disappear. No such risk existed for Rome, whose unity, which widened and extended according to inclusive criteria, could not be undermined by the foreigner. It is hardly much of a leap to recognize in these two historical models of city and of citizenship two ideal-types that continue to operate at the borders. Often, as indeed always happens with ideals, this translates into mixed and hybrid forms. It nonetheless remains the paradigm of reference, in responding to the questions raised by the foreigner's entry into the city.

In contrasting these two models, it is also, however, necessary to note their almost incomparable proportions: Athens was a direct democracy constituted by an assembly of around 30,000 citizens, which all-in-all lasted no more than a century, whereas Rome could boast a continuity of over six centuries, in which it could accord citizenship rights to a multitude of peoples which, once defeated, were integrated into the Empire. One can, nonetheless, turn the argument on its head by arguing that, at the moment that the sun set on Athens, Rome, precisely because it followed a different policy, was able to become an imperial power off the back of its vast population of foreign-origin free citizens. This, moreover, was recognized by Dionysius of Halicarnassus, the Augustan-era Greek historian, who paid tribute to the wisdom and the openness of the Romans.[45]

Already from the first century BC, Rome conferred a collective citizenship on the free Italic peoples which, though defeated and constantly in revolt, were not subjected. Rather, they merged into the *populus romanus* while also conserving their own original belonging. As early as 90–89 BC, there were two laws which sanctioned this approach: the *lex Julia* and the *lex plautia papiria*.[46] This gradual extension of citizenship reached its apogee in Caracalla's famous edict in AD 212, which granted citizenship to all the freemen of the Empire. This was born not of generosity but of expansionism. This unstoppable cosmopolitan push led to a subdivision of the world between Romans and non-Romans, corresponding to the Empire's borders. The very concept of the foreigner declined; he now appeared as a non-Roman – or, better, as a not-yet-Roman. In fact, it was a division that only applied in law. Hence, therefore, the novelty: the Romans introduced juridical citizenship. To this end, they clearly uncoupled citizenship from the city, right from politics, individual from community. Citizenship became ever more transportable. This was a need which tallied with the transition from the Republic to the Empire, which itself also marked a morphological change in the much broader and more varied political landscape, in which the citizen appeared in the trappings of the *Homo legalis*. If citizenship was collectively bestowed on entire peoples, it was nonetheless the individual who became a Roman citizen, most importantly acquiring civil rights. As can easily be imagined, however individual and egalitarian it may have been, citizenship proved to be politically discriminatory.[47] Ultimately it was the master who decided whether he would free a slave – that is, whether he could allow him to be a *cives*.

Residency did not ensure citizenship. There thus remained the complicated figure of the resident foreigner – that is, he who inhabited a place within the Empire's borders but came from a colony or a municipality that had not yet received citizenship. However, Roman law continued to integrate the foreigner. It did so by uncoupling domicile from citizenship, which was instead connected to provenance: to *origo*. The peculiarity of Roman citizenship was condensed within this magic word.[48] But what does that mean? It was a legal fiction without any counterpart in Greek philosophy. Each citizen had some site of anchorage within the Empire, an *origo*, inherited from father to son, which linked him to some city, some colony or some municipality which had collectively received citizenship from Rome. This could be some remote village on the Eastern shores of the Mediterranean, a Spanish city or a municipality in Latium itself. Each Roman thus had a dual citizenship: that of the place from which his family came – even if he had not been born there and never lived there – and Roman citizenship. To note one illustrious example, Cicero proclaimed himself 'from Tusculum, by origin' and 'Roman, by right'.[49] Juridical citizenship was thus uncoupled both from birth and – most importantly – from domicile; the *origo* was enough to link the Roman citizen to some place in the Empire's territory. *Origo* designated a citizen's bond with some place, which still applied even when he was distant from it. One could be a Roman citizen precisely *as* a Greek, a Jew, a Dacian and so on. Thanks to this dual citizenship, of origin and in law, Rome could easily extend its dominion while safeguarding the otherness of the peoples included – starting with the Greeks.

Did Rome not itself hark back to a foreigner? Who does not know the story of Aeneas? Having escaped the destruction of Troy together with his father Anchises and his own son Ascanius, he found refuge on the shores of Latium, where he married the daughter of the king, Latinus, and founded Lavinium. Not far from there, after Aeneas' death, Ascanius himself founded the city of Alba. Many generations later, from Alba came the twin sons of Rhea Silvia – a queen dispossessed of her throne, and whom Mars had impregnated – namely Romulus and Remus. The twin brothers abandoned to the currents of the Tiber in a basket were saved by a wolf, which brought them to land and nurtured them. Together with the band of brigands, nomads and shepherds with whom they grew up, it was these twin brothers who founded Rome on the Palatine hill. After the death of Remus – who had committed sacrilege by crossing the perimeter where the walls of the city were meant to be built – Romulus was left to reign alone. Thanks to the establishment of the sanctuary on the Capitoline hill, where all the exiles from nearby cities could find refuge, Rome prospered to the point of becoming the capital of the Republic.

This legend, which exists in very many versions – some have listed twenty-five of them – is still the subject of a great deal of discussion.[50] Indeed, even for ancient historians, it appeared something of a head-scratcher. In this narrative labyrinth, fantastical themes mixed with mythological characters and pseudo-historical accounts. What was certain was that this one legend spoke of at least two foundations – of Lavinium, and of Rome – which were difficult to link together, and that there were two great protagonists, namely Aeneas and Romulus. As for the rest, this account, which is usually taken as a founding myth, a representation of the original identity, proves very difficult to disentangle. Ultimately, all that the different versions shared was the proper noun Rome, whose etymology is an enigma. The Greek calque of the Latin name leads us to *rhóme*, 'force' – in Latin, *valentia*. There was a Valentia before there was a Rome.[51]

But what was the significance of Aeneas and Romulus? And why this double foundation? Even though he was a Trojan – and ultimately the Trojans were not so distinct from Greeks – Aeneas represented a Greek provenance. And it is known that a city is either a *pólis* or it is not – there do not seem to have existed any alternative models. Rome recognized itself as a Greek city of a Trojan variant. Even the Greeks themselves considered the Italic peoples as being of Greek origin, wth some archaic traits. It was the ancient Pelasgians, or perhaps the primitive Arcadians, who mixed with the locals, the Aborigines, and introduced civilization to the peninsula. For some historians, however, even the Aborigines were Greeks. Nothing is ever truly certain in Italy, starting with its origins – though its peoples were not, in any case, autochthonous. This applies to all the Italic cities, and thus even more so to Rome.

When Republican Rome recounted its origins, it relied on Greek fables. Yet in such a privileged position as it enjoyed – open towards the Mediterranean, the crossroads of ceaseless migration from East to West, from North to South, and vice versa – Rome was not entirely Greek, and nor did it want to be. The rituals of public worship, strictly observed by the Roman people, reveal something further. In Lavinium, they offered sacrifices to the *Penates*, gods who protected the household, whom Aeneas had brought with him – or, rather, who had shown him the way. This was thus a worship that had come from afar to the place where Aeneas' errancy had reached its end, albeit without this itself giving rise to anything. Rather, between Aeneas and Romulus, there was a hiatus, represented by the distance between Lavinium and Rome.

If Athens was a *pólis* that identified with both the territory and the citizens – the Athenians, all of whom descended from Athenian mothers and fathers – the *Urbs* was very careful not to limit itself to the *populus romanus* circumscribed within a geneaological definition. Anchored in the soil and very much earthly, it did not, however, possess a unified territory. The *imperium romanum* did not coincide with Rome, but rather gradually extended as it added new municipalities and provinces. In this sense, the *Imperium* was like a constellation moving through space. The Romans never founded, and never made any pretence to have founded, a territorial state. The *Urbs* was the site of an open citizenship.

And what about the Roman citizens from Rome itself? Were they not, then, more citizens than others were? No: there was no difference. They had themselves come from elsewhere, from another city, from Lavinium. They were thus in debt to the 'father' Aeneas, not as the initiator of a geneaology, but rather as he who, through the worship of the *Penates*, had transmitted to the inhabitants of his 'home' his rootedness in the soil where he had stopped his journey, the *origo* which allowed them to be Roman citizens. This put them on an equal footing with the citizens of the other Italic cities. Strictly speaking, no one was a Roman citizen in the pure sense. All Roman citizens came from elsewhere and had some external *origo*.

Things would have gone very differently if Aeneas and his *Penates* had gone as far as Rome, rather than stopping short in Lavinium. Rome would then have become yet another finished, complete Greek city, limited to its lineage. What goes for Romans also goes for the *Urbs*: Lavinium was, so to speak, its external *origo* which opened up Rome to the world.

If a Roman, forgetting his provenance from Lavinium, wanted to boast of having been born within the perimeter of the *Urbs*, then he would have had to grapple with Romulus who, more than founding a city, welcomed into the sanctuary all those who could be called 'the earth's rejects' – bandits, brigands, outlaws and fugitive slaves – in order to make them into Romans, the *patres*, the forefathers of the future senators. In short, he would have had very little to boast about. If the Greek historian Dionysius of Halicarnassus, convinced that the Romans were no more or less than Greeks, cried outrage, denouncing what was only a lie, Livy openly laid claim to Rome's inglorious foundation, emphasizing that it was preferable for Romans to admit this truth – in any case a commonplace – rather than pass themselves off as 'autochthonous' and earth-born.[52]

On the contrary, the Romans knew that they had been foreigners before they became Roman citizens. For they symbolically came from Lavinium, a city in Latium. They owed this origin to Aeneas, a foreigner who was a little Trojan and a little Greek, and indeed so much a foreigner that he had not come so far as to be Rome's founder. It would take another three generations for Romulus to come along, and this period represented the Roman time of memory and oblivion. The Romans thus had an at least double extraneousness, and similarly two-sided was the separation which marked the act of the *Urbs*'s foundation. The reference to Aeneas and Romulus impeded any direct genealogy and forbade any mythical autochthony. As for the Aborigines – another way of referring to the Italic peoples, or Italians – their name, which betrayed their *origo*, meant those who had been there *ab origo*, from the origin;

it indicated a temporal limit, not the fact of having been born to the earth.[53] Virgil's *Aeneid* is the epic poem of the Roman *origo*, its *monumentum*.

8 The theological–political charter of the *ger*

The Jewish landscape is inhabited by figures of peerless unfamiliarity, unique and atypical for the Western tradition, which has attempted in vain to domesticate them. The lead character, the foreigner knocking at the door, is the *ger.* And it is the *ezrakh*, the citizen, who opens the door to her. But unfamiliarity is also spoken in other ways, and next to the *ger* there appear the terms *nokerì* and *zar*. Such a diverse terminology corresponds to a complex constellation. Read in translation, these three terms, which cannot simply be swapped for one another, can be misunderstood and give rise to improper generalizations. The gravest risk is that of abstracting them from the political context in which they developed – which is to say, by overlooking the Biblical City. This is what happens in the most widespread hermeneutics (be they Christian or Jewish), which, moved by religious inspiration, tends to erase this political pedigree. It is tacitly assumed that, since the Jewish people is 'errant' and thus evanescent, it does not represent a political entity, and nor, therefore, does a Jewish City exist. In the rare cases in which this is indeed recognized, it assumes the darkest hues of violent theocracy, of tribal ethnicity or of nationalist particularism. The opposite outcome, which also emerged in the Jewish philosophy of the last century, is a spiritually inspired interpretation that reads the Biblical passages on the 'foreigner' in a purely moral key, exalting Judaism's ethics of the other.

Nonetheless, the Biblical City does indeed exist, with all its virtues and vices. It is against this backdrop, characterized not only by an ethics but also by a constitutional right and a public law, that the question of the foreigner ought to be delineated in its full political significance.

The constitution of the Torah is shot through with – and almost sustained by – an outright charter of the 'resident foreigner', the immigrant who lives ameong the people of Israel. What is her condition? What are her rights? How is the relationship between *ger* and *ezrakh*, between foreigner and citizen, configured?

If one moves directly from Athens or Rome to Jerusalem, as indeed is often the case, one will end up projecting Greek and Roman concepts onto a Jewish landscape. If *ger* is translated as 'foreigner', then many translations – even the rabbinical one

– render *ezrakh*, taken as an antithetical pole, as 'autochthonous' or even 'indigenous'. In this is concealed the decisive error that so prejudices all the hermeneutics of the roles of the foreigner and of extraneousness within Judaism. Having become established over the centuries, the supposed antithesis between *ger* and *ezhrakh* not only reproposes the tension internal to the *pólis*, but also retraces the well-known Pauline dichotomy between universal and particular. In this perspective, then, on the one hand would stand the *ezrakh*, the autochthonous, who impersonates Jewish particularism, and on the other the *ger*, the foreigner, called on to disclose the universal.[54]

To start out from this antithesis between the autochthonous and the foreigner is already to presume that there does not exist a Biblical City with its own peculiarities. The *ezrakh*, deprived of her political context, would then dominate the Jewish landscape. If Athens is the *pólis* with its laws and its institutions, Jerusalem would not be similarly recognized. And even if autochthony was the sacred foundation of citizenship, given that the Athenian proclaimed himself the son of the soil, the Athenians spoke of *politaî*, of citizens, not of *autochthones*. On the contrary, the *ezrakhîm*, seen as the exponents of an ethnic tribalism, are simply called 'autochthonous'.

But how did things work in the Biblical City? Who is the *ezrakh* and who is the *ger*? As soon as the threshold of this political space has been crossed, there emerges the need to overturn the commonplace vision and arrive at a hermeneutics that recovers the Hebrew textual tradition.

The word *ger* itself has the first surprise in store. It contains a paradox which is bound to explode many schemas. The Hebrew language in fact turns to one same root to designate both inhabitation and extraneousness. The *ger* derives her name from *gur*, which means 'to inhabit'. Through this immediate linguistic connection, the foreigner is tied to inhabitation, and inhabitation to the foreigner. This contradicts any economy of the earth and any logic of autochthony. Indeed, from a Greek point of view, this seems a contradiction in terms, as if the semantics of *ger* combined two concepts that mutually exclude one another. For, usually, the foreigner is she who comes from the outside, who is not yet resident, who does not belong to the sphere of habitation, which is instead devoted to the inhabitant – or, better, to the autochthonous. The meaning of *ger* instead suggests a reciprocal link between the foreigner and habitation, which promises to modify both these terms.

Literally, *ger* means 'he who inhabits'. The foreigner – a term which in the Biblical text indicates whoever arrives from the outside and is conjugated with Israel as a guest or as a proselyte, in what is, therefore, a very broad meaning – is at the same time the inhabitant. The short circuit produced by the semantics of the *ger* casts a new light on the foreigner and on habitation. Extraneousness cannot be reified or made absolute; on the contrary, it indicates a temporary, passing condition. The foreigner is always in-passing. Hence the difference that distinguishes her and marks her extraneousness is not an identitarian difference, but rather a multiple and individual one. Each foreigner is different on account of her own singular path. Her fleeting and hybrid figure helps to dig out an empty space wihin identity, to make it different, to keep it in movement. This, precisely because the unfamiliarity which she incarnates and introduces into the abode is not without effects on this latter. The *ger* is testament to the fact that another habitation is possible; she attests to another relationship with the Earth and corresponds to another way of being in the world. If the foreigner is always also an inhabitant, an inhabitant is always a foreigner. To inhabit means to remain as foreigners. The presence of those who inhabit the city never appears complete – there always remains a fundamental absence. Habitation is not, therefore, possession and appropriation, it is not being at one with the soil, it is not the rootedness of autochthony; rather, it is fulfilled through the passage itself. One can stay without sinking roots, one can reside while remaining separate from the land. If it is the opposite of familiarity – with respect to which it is continually antithetical – unfamiliarity does not stand opposed to habitation, but rather inflects it.

The foreigner reminds the inhabitant that she has forgotten that she is herself a foreigner. The *ger* points back to her own past the Jew who, having come from elsewhere – as the etymology of *ivrì* [which is etymologically connected to Hebrew] itself tells us – cannot be of this place. The sun sets on the illusion of belonging to a place, for the Jew no less than for the *ger*. The inhabitant, the *ger*, may have erased her own constitutive *gerùt*, her 'extraneousness', and thus imagined that she is indigenous. But in her relationship with Israel, in this proximity, she rediscovers the fact that she is a foreigner.

In this complex game of mirrors, in which roles are swapped and the sides reversed, each supposed autochthonous person is compelled to see her own extraneousness in the other. Each person has to recognize that they are inhabitants but also foreigners.

This sums up the decisive role of the *ger* who inhabits among the people of Israel. The foreigner, *qua* inhabitant, does not stand opposed to the *ezrakh*, whose citizenship is not founded on autochthony. She who knocks on the door does not clash with a telluric ethnicity, with a rooted particularism. Just as the City is built on the Law, thus the *ger* comes to make up part of the community by way of the bond that the Law provides. This is an entrance into the universe of covenant and right. To become part of this universe does not mean to identify. The foreigner maintains her extraneousness, but at the same time her rights are recognized.

There exists no special status for the foreigner, because extraneousness is inscribed in the heart of Jewish citizenship. Both – the citizen as much as the inhabitant, the *ezrakh* as much as the *ger* – find themselves under the aegis of one same constitution. Thus it is said that 'The same law applies both to the native-born [*ezrakh*] and to the foreigner [*ger*] residing [*gar*] among you.'[55] Often they are placed on an equal footing with regard to rights that they share – they are members of the political community that celebrates Pesach, the feast of citizenship – and in terms of the recurrent injunctions directed at both: 'But you must keep my decrees and my laws. The native-born and the foreigners residing among you must not do any of these detestable things.'[56] In short: the *ger* and the Jew have one and the same status. What goes for the foreigner goes for all Israel in its constitutive extraneousness. Rather than joining up with the covenant of Abraham from the outside, the *ger* is always-already part of it.

This is not to deny that the Torah also contains a veritable charter for the 'resident foreigner' – indeed one which is aimed to protect her, considering her fragility, the possibility of her being isolated, and her poverty. These appeals are directed to the Jewish people which accommodates the *ger* and, for this reason, has further duties towards her. Here, there is no question of whether to admit the foreigner or turn her away. Rather, this is a matter of prescribing what behaviour ought to be kept up in her regard: 'You must not exploit or oppress a foreign resident [*ger*], for you yourselves were foreigners [*gerim*] in the land of Egypt'; 'Do not oppress a foreigner [*ger*]; you yourselves know how it feels [*néfesh*] to be foreigners, because you were foreigners in Egypt.'[57]

The appeals that point the Jewish people back to its own *gerùt*, to its own foreign condition, in order thus to understand the condition of the *ger*, do not stop at suggesting a certain ethical disposition, an attitude based on empathy. They soon become concrete. They are commanded 'do not take advantage', 'do not oppress', because the foreigner runs the risk of being exploited. She is the hired labourer, the wage earner who depends on that payment to live, lacking in other resources, defenceless and exposed to abuses:

Do not take advantage of a hired worker [*sakhìr*] who is poor and needy, whether that worker is a fellow Israelite or a foreigner residing in one of your towns. Pay them their wages [*sakhar*] each day before sunset, because they are poor and are counting on it. Otherwise they may cry to the Lord against you, and you will be guilty of sin.[58]

In the code of the covenant, 'your foreigner' is put on the same footing as 'your brother', not only in terms of the right of residency but also rights at work. Indeed, the *ger*, too, celebrates the Shabbat and rests on the seventh day, participating in that day without work which brings to the surface the community of equals.[59] This oft-reasserted equivalence also applies when the citizen or the *ger* has committed some wrong.[60] Even in that case, for whoever struck a fatal blow without premeditation and without hatred – even if she is a foreigner – the gates of the refuge-city offer sanctuary from the anger of the dead person's relatives.[61] However, to put them on an equal footing is not only a matter of providing access to the same rights, but also of balancing unjust conditions. The *ger* is constantly compared to the widow and the orphan, to those who have neither family nor land to cultivate, and thus require particular protection:

Do not deprive the foreigner or the fatherless of justice, or take the cloak of the widow as a pledge.
Remember that you were slaves in Egypt and the Lord your God redeemed you from there. That is why I command you to do this.
When you are harvesting in your field and you overlook a sheaf, do not go back to get it. Leave it for the foreigner, the fatherless and the widow, so that the Lord your God may bless you in all the work of your hands.
When you beat the olives from your trees, do not go over the branches a second time. Leave what remains for the foreigner, the fatherless and the widow.
When you harvest the grapes in your vineyard, do not go over the vines again. Leave what remains for the foreigner, the fatherless and the widow.
Remember that you were slaves in Egypt. That is why I command you to do this.[62]

The norms that allow the gathering of the harvest are combined with numerous tithes – the triennial tithe, the tithe of the sabbatical year, as well as a share in the offerings that are assigned to the needy. Hospitality first of all guarantees lodging and sustenance.

The connection that links to the foreigner to the weakest, to those who are isolated and lack a family, thus seems obvious.

Rather less clear is the insistence with which the *gerîm* are compared to the Levites. But the answer lies in the condition of the Levite, who has 'no allotment or inheritance'.[63] Both the *gerîm* and the Levites, therefore, are separate from the body of the people and dispersed within its ranks. The difference is that the Levites are a tribe, one among the twelve tribes of Israel, and the only one called on to maintain the void of absence within the community and to serve as a reminder – in its expropriated condition – of extraneousness and exile. Analogous is the calling of the *gerîm*, who are horizontally distributed among all the twelve tribes, including among the Levites.[64] Thus, across the board, among each tribe there inhabit members who are separate and unfamiliar on account of their two forms of extraneousness. The separation of the Levite is tribal and religious, whereas that of the *ger* is extra-tribal and political. And whereas the former 'remains tribal, the other is global'.[65] Thus the Levites and the *gerîm*, who only reside in the urban territory, inscribe the void of separation within the City in two different ways. Hence the unexpected and disconcerting comparison that the Talmud ventures between the *cohen* and the *ger*, between the priest who belongs to the *cohanîm* – themselves internal to but distinct from the Levites – and the foreigner who has joined onto the people of Israel, whose merit, not acquired through birth, is all the greater in that she marks a separation.[66]

9 Jerusalem, the City of foreigners

The architecture of the Biblical City is not uniform and unitary. Nor is its political identity. Following in line with the split, there are always two entities, two sides, two figures that emerge and rival one another – also in and through their extraneousness. The City faithfully retraces this duplication, which is a structural principle of Judaism. This explains why citizenship itself is divided in two: on the one hand, the *ezrakh*; on the other, the *ger*. Though they stand under the aegis of one same constitution, citizenship is not single and unitary, but rather split between the *ezrakh*, the citizen, and the *ger*, the foreigner who lives within the gates but whose presence always points back to the void of absence. The citizen could otherwise get used to familiarity and bed down in uniformity. Decisive, therefore, is the role of the *ger* who opens up citizenship, taking it outside its boundaries and upholding it as the realm of the Law. The *ger* is the abode of the people of Israel. As she inhabits the city, she displays a different relationship with the world, which is not the opposite of the sovereignty on which citizenship depends, but rather a wholly other sovereignty.

A foreign woman embodies this role, or, rather, serves as its archetype: namely, Ruth the Moabite. But who is this poor woman, this widow who has left her own country? Ruth comes from the king of Moab and from a people who are the offspring of Lot's incest with his daughters. These latter survived the destruction of Sodom in virtue of their hospitality; and, convinced that there was no other life, they got their father drunk in order to procreate with him and give the human race a future. Ruth represents the height of the extraneousness that comes to make up part of the Hebrew people. Excluded from the excluded, the bastard daughter of bastard daughters, she is the hope of Israel, to the point of becoming the 'mother of royalty' because it is from her that the Davidian-Messianic dynasty derives. Hence why *gerùt*, 'extraneousness', is the source of Hebrew sovereignty.[67]

In the Biblical City, extraneousness reigns sovereign. In this sense, it distinguishes itself from the Greek *pólis*, for it is not situated in a cosmic order but rather founded on the presence-absence of God. The schema on which the City is built is that of the camp in the desert, which – as is made clear at the beginning of the Book of Numbers – is set up on each occasion around the 'tent of meeting', the tent of encounters, in which one welcomes and is welcomed. Empty and vacant spaces criss-cross this community's place of residence, and cause breaks in its fullness. The being-together unfolds around the empty space that is left open for extraneousness. If that void were not there, it would not be possible to allow the guest to enter, and nor would the abode survive. The community is constantly put to the test of extraneousness, as if deep down in the self there were always an other. The architecture of the abode, gathered around the empty space, corresponds to the community of the people, which is always such thanks to the withdrawal of one part. Here there is not compactness or completeness or autochthony. At the bottom, at the foundation, there is extraneousness.

To withdraw in order to make space for the other is the model of creation. It was thus that God, as he retreated and withdrew, left that void from which man and the world emerged. The void is the source of life. And it must be protected, in a world which is not complete, on account of God's exile. In turn, the human being is called on to reiterate this withdrawal, to preserve the void, by way of separation – first of all, through her separation from her self. Hence her constitutive extraneousness.

In the suggestive tale of the Gan Eden, the chosen site of human residency on the Earth, this extraneousness unmistakably resonates.

Taken from the Earth, *adamà*, man, *adàm*, who has been inspired with a vital breath, is 'placed' in the garden of Eden so that he will cultivate and protect it.[68] Planted by God in the village of Kédem, to the East, the garden rich in trees and fruit is a sanctuary within the world, a site of intimacy. The expulsion from Gan Eden is an exile on *adamà*, a strange existential exile that sends the human being tumbling down to Earth, of which he is part, but which is not, and cannot be, the site of his fulfilment. To recall Gan Eden is to remain separate from the Earth on which one is exiled. The Biblical City is erected in order to provide the place where the memory of the lost garden is inscribed on the Earth. This separation from the Earth, which is at the very basis of the Biblical City, renders hollow any notion of autochthony.

Here one can measure the distance between the autochthonous and the Jew. Considered 'foreign', the Jew resides in the Gan Eden in separation from the 'rooted', those who are prisoners of *adamà*. Egypt indicates not only slavery, but the tie to the Earth. In her extraneousness, the Jew stands counterposed to the illusion of autochthony. In this light, the *ger* is the inhabitant who had remained under the illusion of being autochthonous but who, upon entering the City of foreigners and taking up citizenship there, becomes de-naturalized – as opposed to naturalized – as she breaks out of the prison of the bond to the land.

But where does the *ger* come from? Perhaps they were members of the tribes of the North who have now moved in among the Southern tribes? Or perhaps they were the inhabitants of Canaan, who remained on the same territory but along with Israel passed over to the condition of foreigners? More plausible, given their political status, is that the *ger* is a descendant of the *erev rav*, the 'great multitude' which united with Israel on the way out of Egypt.[69] The presence of the *gerîm* confers a universal significance upon the exodus.

Foreigners are the former slaves who exploited the gap that opened up in Egypt's totality and fled. The Jewish people's exit not only puts an end to its own oppression but also breaks apart the principle of slavery. From that moment, anyone and everyone knew that they no longer had to be a slave.

The exodus is an arrival: as Israel heads out of Egypt, from within another people, it simultaneously constitutes itself. The foundational scene is a crossing, a passage. The foundation does not have a principle, a beginning. The exit from the other precedes any identity, and this latter will always be marked by that memory. The Jewish people is always-already preceded by another people – and it recognizes this even in the scene of its singular foundation, namely the scene of the exodus. Autochthony remains impossible. The people's emergence, its entrance into history, is an exit. In this unusual and extraordinary reversal of the within and the outside, openness will remain engraved in the abode itself.

The *gerîm* play an ambivalent role in this inside-outside which marks the inhabitation of Israel. On the one hand, they perpetuate nostalgia for Egypt, the temptation of idolatry, the lament for the past, while on the other hand, they constitute the need to achieve emancipation, the impossibility of standing still, the gaze directed towards the future. If, on the one hand, the *erev rav*, the great multitude, attests to the void left behind in Egypt, on the other hand, it preserves the mark of exile within Israel itself; it prevents it becoming rooted and prompts a further and permanent exit, that of the Hebrew people. In a game of mirrors, the *erev rav* is another Israel within Israel: its gloomiest and most bankrupt side, the immobile ipseity to which it could regress, and at the same time the chosen otherness to which Israel is called, that void to be protected among the nations.

The *ger*'s political status refers to a temporary condition. Even as the individual *ger* is inserted within the people, the *gerùt* itself – the extraneousness that stands as testament to exile – does not itself disappear. But this insertion is a denaturalization. For the *ger* is the inhabitant who, in leaving behind any illusion of becoming at one with the soil and 'being of this place', becomes a foreigner among foreigners and thus accesses a Sinaitic citizenship. After all, she is the resident in the Biblical City who does not forget that she has come from elsewhere.

This is possible because the *ger* is considered foreign only with respect to the place where she is staying. The term does not entail any other meaning.[70] So, here, there does not exist the counterposition that was made between Greeks and barbarians – perhaps the most developed one in the ancient world – where the stigma focused on these latter's way of speaking. Indeed, *oi barbaroi* are those who talk gibberish and do not even speak a language; this definition thus did little to conceal the unbridgeable ethnic divide. On the contrary, it is only the relationship with Divinity that distinguishes the nations of Israel from the *goy kadosh*, the 'separate/holy nation', called on only in order to bring separation into the world. For this reason, Sinaitic citizenship could not be anything like Athenian citizenship.

In the Biblical terminology, alongside the *ger* there appears the *nokerì*, of whom it is said in Deutoronomy: 'he is not your brother'.[71] Yet the *ger* are often referred to as 'your *ger*', for they are inhabitants heading along the way together with Israel.

The word *nokerì* suggests less 'foreigner' than the 'estranged', the 'alienated' – indeed, *nikur* means alienation. He is, therefore, the radically autochthonous who, proud of sinking his roots in the ancestral soil, refuses to pass to *ezrakhùt*, to the citizenship which relies precisely on separation from the land. In this sense, the *nokerì* does not inhabit, for he is rooted; he is termed outside of the Law, and for this reason connected back to the foreign divinities *eloheinekar*. Close to the root *makar*, which means 'to sell', the *nokerì* is the tragic representation of the autochthonous person who remains entrenched in his certainties, of the proprietor who defends and lays claim to his property. He is trapped in the relations of measurement, a prisoner to exchange.

Alienation is also called *zarùt*, which for good reason is also a quality of the *nokerì*. Again, this is a concept very different from the openly embraced extraneousness of the *ger*. Just as *nokerì* is the antithesis of the *ezrakh*, so, too, is *zar* the antithesis of *kadòsh*. *Zar* was the term for whoever did not want to separate himself, first of all, from his own self – thus running into an extraneous idolatry, *avodà zarà,* the idolatry of he who sacralizes his own rooted identity. The verse 'there is no *zar* with us in the house' has a double meaning: it means not only that in the house there is no one who is a *zar*, but also that there is no home where there is a *zar*.[72]

The importance of the *ger*, the foreigner who has come from elsewhere and resides in the Biblical City thus becomes all the more evident. It is, in fact the *ger* who holds up the keystone of the City. For, without her presence, the void of absence would shrink and the city would end up being a metropolis full of lights, which lacked in places to offer sanctuary and to give refuge. Far from being a pariah, the foreigner constitutes another way of inhabiting the city, another citizenship, another sovereignty.

The idolatry of rootedness has the immediate effect of war, whether that means a war to defend the land or to conquer it. In an overly full world in which there is no 'retreat', war becomes the primary way of relating to the world. The *ger*, standing in between the full and occupied spaces, pulls apart the simulacrum of autochthony and instead exhibits the empty space intolerable to power, which is unable to assimilate this space to its empire. She is thus the privileged victim of war and the way of being that is upheld by war. The antithesis between war and *gerùt* could not be sharper.

In the charter of the 'resident foreigner', the fundamental principle is that which calls for her to be welcomed as a citizen. For the *ger* reminds the Hebrew people, who came out of Egypt, that it was itself foreign, and pushes it to preserve exile within this abode: 'The foreigner [*ger*] residing among you must be treated as your native-born [*ezrakh*]. Love them as yourself, for you were foreigners [*gerîm*] in Egypt.'[73]

The figure of the foreigner shakes up inhabitation, estranges it and uproots it from the land. This figure tears it away from possession, from belonging, from having, and transfers it to being. It relates it back to that existence-in-the-world which is but a temporary stay. According to the political constitution that appears in the Torah, all citizens are foreigners and all inhabitants are both guests and hosts. The concept of hospitality widens and deepens, to the point of conciding with the concept of citizenship. No longer can the clump of earth, the soil, property, be the foundation of this dual right legitimized in inhabitation: 'The land must not be sold permanently, because the land is mine and you reside in my land as foreigners and strangers.'[74]

From the inalienability of the Earth, proclaimed in no mistaken terms, descends the political–existential condition of the inhabitant who is *at the same time* a foreigner and resident. The contradiction is a striking one: a foreigner cannot be resident and, on the other hand, a resident cannot be foreign.[75] Except that the contradiction wrapped up in the semantics of the verb *gur* is here explicated. Thus, next to the term *ger* appears *toshav*, which means 'temporary resident' but also 'guest'. The inhabitants of the Earth, to which the Earth does not belong and who do not belong to the Earth, are *gerîm vetoshavîm*, foreigners and temporary residents. Precisely insofar as they are foreigners, it is possible for them to be residents, and, vice versa, precisely insofar as they are residents, they cannot but be foreigners.

The status of the *ger toshav*, of the resident foreigner, is solely based on the injunction to remember extraneousness – an extraneousness which is itself sustained by memory. It renders exile ineluctable. It makes it not only a theological category, but also an existential and political one.

10 On return

It would be misleading to believe that the resident foreigner is fated to mere errancy. As if she could not make a return. But what does a 'return' mean? Philosophy has never posed this question. Doubtless because 'return' is considered self-evident, when understood simply to mean a return to the origin, coming back, repatriation. An unreserved priority is, instead, placed on errancy, to which so many enthusiastic paeans have been written.

In this regard, Heidegger constitutes the exception. In his reflection on the sojourn and on migration, he steers clear of making any easy encomium to errancy, as any 'adventurer' would do, and instead follows in the wake of the navigators who, without losing their route, keep vigil in awaiting their return, even when they are out on the open sea. That 'return' is not only a poetic word taken from Hölderlin's hymns, but rises to the level of a philosophical concept, is attested by the entire phenomenology of inhabitation. Especially where Heidegger indicates the double trick which is also a double danger: the naïve permanency of those who believe themselves solidly rooted in the native soil, and the planetary errancy promoted by technological mobility.

Migrating does not, as many hastily assume, mean the same thing as errancy. This journey is a making-oneself-at-home which always entails a return. In Heidegger's landscape, a wooded road, where the path has more of a vertical depth than an open horizon-tality, proceeds from the elsewhere to home. But home is never reached. Heidegger warns against the risk of taking the arrival for a return. The impervious slow path that leads towards home is an incessant approach. As home gets farther away, so, too, does the return.

Introduced as a philosophical concept in a phenomenology of habitation and migration that marks a decisive turning point, the return nonetheless disappears into an immemorial elsewhere. Even Heidegger seems to give in to the idea that the return is a simple repatriation. Perhaps, therefore, it would be necessary to contravene his warning and embrace the risk of the arrival. At a certain point, the navigator will have to arrive, will have to reach the shore (and in Italian this is suggested by the etymology: shore = *riva*). What happens to return, then? Is another return possible?

The instant at which, after being exiled, one reaches the shore, is perhaps the most difficult. Those who arrive may be driven to believe that the land she has reached is her property, and may regress into a spatial immanence from which exile had earlier liberated her, deluding herself that she has overcome her condition as a foreigner, and that her extraneousness has been revoked as she adopts a new, rooted identity. Once again, she imagines that she can sink roots in the soil, become at one with the earth. As if she had not already glimpsed the void which all of us inhabit. As if she had never experi-enced exile. The temptation is to erase it. The allure of possession, the flattery of stability may prevail. In this incipient sedentary life, in which she fantasizes about being set up and stable in a place that belongs to her, and to which she belongs, of being, rather, always-already autochthonous, she casts out glances of threatening and obstinate hostility. And it is in the very moment of her arrival that the violence is prepared.

Ought one then to avoid the return, find a way around it? Not least given that there is no original place to which to return, given that the abode is lost, and the root broken? On the contrary, it is indispensable to ask oneself whether another return which does not erase exile is, instead, possible. One ought not, indeed, to give up on the return which constitutes the cardinal difference, for it distinguishes exile from both uprootedness and errancy. The uprooted person wants to return to the starting point, following the chimera of that origin; the wanderer is condemned to a tragic errancy without a beginning or a destination.

Within exile, the return entails a turning point, a moment of inversion. The re-turn involves a turn. Just as the immigrant does not renege on her emigration, the exile is marked by the wound of exile itself, which becomes an unexpected crossing, an unsuspected opening. It is in return that exile can manifest its liberatory charge. If it is not abolished, if it is not cancelled out with the pretence of rootedness in the identical, it reveals itself to be the matrix of a rebirth. The return takes on a new value; its semantics dilate in an unprecedented direction and hint at a divergent interpretation. On the one hand, the return is decisive to exile, which would otherwise be only uprootedness or errancy. On the other hand, exile is decisive for the return. It is necessary to preserve its memory and bear witness to its unfillable fault-line. It is exile that keeps open the prospect of return.

When the exile on her diasporic path prepares to return, she has now discovered that the point of departure, illusorily considered an origin, was already a place of exile. If she also re-entered what she considered her native city, she would have to change her thinking, exposing herself to the desolating experience of an unhealable extraneousness. The door from which one sets off is no longer accessible. Just like how, for the sailors who had circumnavigated the globe, Seville was no longer Seville.

In leaving her origins behind, the exile heads out towards a return which can be neither a re-entry nor a repatriation. She sets off in order to return not to the place to which she supposedly originally belonged, but to the place to which she is called by choice – not to that of a rooted being-in-one's-own-place, but that of an elective being-at-the-other's-place. This does not mean that the return is ephemeral or fictitious. The land of the return is a concrete one. But the relationship with the land changes – for, as a promised land, it is no longer appropriable. The promise remains there to forbid rootedness, possession, property.

Even after the return, the exile cannot forget that she is a guest on the land and cannot erase her condition as a resident foreigner. As she learned in exile, she inhabits a separation. The new habitation, which will resist the assault of time, is another way of inhabiting. The place in which she resides does not coincide with the self, or the self with the place. She is extraneous in her abode – and the others are extraneous, too. Migrants in a promised land, all of them guests, who are made to correspond to one another in a welcoming of extraneousness which is the one and only bond of this habitation.

4

LIVING TOGETHER IN THE NEW MILLENNIUM

... for the men, not the walls nor the empty galleys, are
the city.

Thucydides, *History of the Peloponnesian War*, VII, 77

... and I fear seeing them wounded on sharpened points and
barbed wire, I fear seeing them fall. The border-dreamers
often fall from on high. They hid the earth with a force of
inertia by their hopes.

O. Weber, *Frontières*[1]

1 The new age of walls

Die Mauer ist weg! 'The Wall has fallen!' At midnight on 9 November
1989, the border crossings that had divided Berlin for decades were
opened. Between incredulity, surpise and joy, thousands of East
Germans poured out onto the streets of the Western part of the city,
from Kurfürstendamm to Kantstraße. It was the end of an era – the
era of the Cold War. Ever since its construction in 1961, the Berlin
Wall had represented the quintessence of the Iron Curtain, which
was not just a figure of speech but a militarized barrier that had cut
through Europe, separating it into two opposed blocs. Such was its
importance that it earned itself a capital letter: the Wall.

Perhaps no one succeeded in portraying this gloomy desperation
as much as Wim Wenders, with his 1987 film *Wings of Desire*. From
up above in the sky, the angels, condemned to being unable to

communicate with men, observe the day-to-day life of the Berliners imprisoned – in the West as in the East – in an irredeemable solitude. In a political–existential landscape frescoed with the most varied hues of grey, the divided city emerges as a paradigm of the new exile.

As always, the official figures are, if anything, too low: 136 people were killed trying to pass to the other side; more than 5,000 attempts to flee were made; and over 75,000 were arrested. The apogee of exclusion, the Berlin Wall at that time seemed to recapitulate in itself all the walls of the past. As symbols of appropriation, military frontiers and bastions of civilization, walls have studded the human landscape since remotest antiquity, from the Great Wall of China to the Romans' *limes*, from the Maginot Line to the Atlantikwall. But political walls – sovereign walls, erected in order to put sovereignty on show even more than to exercise it with the power of the limit – were a novelty of the twentieth century. These were not simply defensive fortifications, whose ruins have now become protected monuments, but rather offensive walls whose intent was to aggressively dissuade and violently stop.[2] Of all political walls, the Berlin Wall seemed the ultimate hyperbole, after whose fall all the other remnants of the obscurantism which here and there still defaced the Earth would be erased.

This was not the case. One could say that the meaning of the Wall was misunderstood. It did not mark an end but rather a beginning, or a hint – the signal of a transition, from the division between East and West to the division between North and South. After the Berlin Wall, the new millennium began with a new age of walls. The ones that existed already have not been removed, but reinforced. Most of them concern 'conflicted borders', from the wall between the two Koreas to the 'green line' that cuts Cyprus in two, between a Greek and a Turkish part, the walls between India and Pakistan, or indeed the sand wall through the Western Sahara, constructed by Morocco in several phases and completed in 1987, which extends for over 1,696 miles and is defended by ditches and over 6,000 anti-personnel mines. In the areas of the planet subject to greatest tensions, the barriers have multiplied. The former borders of the Soviet Empire, now become uncertain and controversial, have been marked and re-marked by walls and barbed wire, from Uzbekistan to Kyrgyzstan, from Turkmenistan to Abkhazia, from Georgia to Ossetia, and from the Caspian Sea to the Black Sea – not to forget Ukraine. And that is to look past the entire Middle East, where wars and invasions have, among other things, had the effect of putting up walls, barriers and trenches of all kinds in Iraq, Saudi Arabia, Kuwait, Qatar, Yemen and Jordan. Standing out above all of them is the wall erected by Israel in the West Bank and around the Gaza Strip after the Second Intifada and the traumatic repetition of violent attacks. This is the first great anti-terrorism wall, though its goal – as is especially clearly apparent in the territories to the East – is also to protect, if not even extend, Israel's borders. Hybrid walls, put up with one aim and used for another, are destined to multiply.

But the novelty *par excellence* are the walls against 'clandestine immigration'. The most famous is 'Bush's wall' at the border between the United States and Mexico. The tortilla border, the longest barrier in the world, which snakes 1,952 miles from the Atlantic to the Pacific, was built in order to manage, govern and, ultimately, impede entry by the *migrantes*. As composite, intricate and multiform as the history of 'Hispanic' immigration into the United States, patterned by exploitation, violence and purposeful illegality, the border is a sort of construction site, a project-in-progress that Trump has promised to complete in order to seal the Line once and for all. In the meantime, the border is crossed legally by over a million people every day, who pass through thirty-six checkpoints; the number of cars and trucks is not even counted. Still less is it possible to calculate the volume of illegal traffic. The border is studded by ten cities, starting with Tijuana, the principal crossing, situated on the Pacific Coast. In the central part, around El Paso – Ciudad Juarez, the border area on both banks of the Rio Grande is so vast that it is called *Tercera Nación* or even 'Mexicamerica'. The name belies the border and the possibility of closing it forever. Strengthened in accordance with the Patriot Act – the anti-terrorism law which after the 2001 attacks also issued directives on border protection – and reconstructed along over 680 miles after the Secure Fence Act of 2006, the wall is much more heteroclite than might be imagined. Metal barriers, anti-vehicle ditches, cement palisades, rudimentary wire fences, steel tubes, and even 'Czech hedgehogs' – crossed metal bars – follow one after another along the path traced out by the border. Especially in the desert, from Arizona to Texas and New Mexico, there are confrontations between Border Patrol guards flanked by far-Right militiamen like the Minutemen and, on the other side, the *migrantes*, who pay the *coyotes* in order to get across, and are often aided by humanitarian organizations such as No More Death – No más muertes or Human Borders. The wall currently being built is meant to be more homogeneous, a sort of tower system composed of 100-foot-high metal pillars fitted out with a highly sophisticated electronic apparatus consisting of infrared and thermo-acoustic sensors. It remains to be seen whether this will be sufficient to stop the *migrantes*, whose tragic history has already become a subject for literature and cinema.

Europe, which had sharply criticized 'Bush's wall', has not hesitated in itself setting up all kinds of barriers, starting with the ones in the enclaves of Ceuta and Melilla, in order to defend the Schengen area.[3] The debate on these barriers and on political walls is very heated. There are those who condemn them in no uncertain terms and others who, perhaps avoiding the use of the word 'wall' – which seems illegitimate after the Berlin Wall – invoke an emergency in order to justify some sort of 'line of protection'.

The properly philosophical question concerns the meaning of the wall – an emblem, as Wendy Brown has emphasized, of a sovereignty in decline which needs to be theatricized in order to assert itself.[4] It is not difficult, therefore, to recognize the terms of a question that is repeatedly proposed anew in a different aspect. A psychopolitics of walls points back to the tragic character of a segregation which, despite any apparent sense of security, is always also a self-segregation. Whoever chooses to build a wall out of fear of the other, out of the need to protect themselves from everything unfamiliar, ends up suffering the consequences of this. A geopolitics of walls cannot fail to acknowledge the impasse of globalization, the block in reaction against accelerated mobility. The anti-immigration wall sought by the nation-state is not, however, just the icon of its erosion. It also marks on the map the trace of a new clash: namely, the one between North and South. This is a new clash because – however one understands these cardinal points on a globe that could also be turned on its head – it not only emerges from a profound imbalance, or, rather, from what seems like an unbridgeable gap, but is made more acute, exacerbated, by a hostility that had perhaps previously remained hidden under the surface. No compassion, no indulgence, no solidarity. For the North, the South is now nothing other than a threat. The new border is that of a North which is still hesitant – and embarrassed to admit it – but nonetheless determined to contain the drive of immigration coming from the South, even at the cost of walling up democracy and erasing human rights.

2 Lampedusa: of what border is it the name?

Perhaps it is a certain myth of globalization that makes people believe that a world without borders is close in the future. On the contrary, these traditional lines of division, which seemed to have been overcome, have everywhere multiplied and strengthened wherever there are states, no states, semi-states, phantom states, failed states or failing states. Anything but abolished, borders remain the foundations of the geopolitical alphabet. As if by way of reaction to the steamroller of globalization and the *horror vacui* prompted by the planetary disorientation, it has become indispensable to resort to old and trusted excuses. Thus, the borders – the epiphany of an eroded and endangered sovereignty, which needs walls under surveillance – have returned to assume a present-day relevance alongside many other types of barriers. Such is the revenge of the local, or what some call the 'glocal'. This is a nationalist, petty-bourgeois, particularist revanchism. The old cosmopolitan dream – once dreamt of by that inter-national class, the proletariat, which unlike the bourgeoisie could never have recognized itself in national interests or given up on the ideals of a global justice – has now crashed up against its rocks.

In the rough and conflict-ridden landscape of the new millennium, the expert geographer Michel Foucher has ascertained, counted, listed an ever higher quantity of political borders – at least 332 – on the surface of the globe, amounting to the truly disconcerting total length of over 154,000 miles.[5] In this regard, it is worth noting that borders arose together with the geographical maps that documented and ratified the human occupation of the Earth. As is well known, it was the Europeans who exported cartographic culture with their conquests, together with the idea that it was legitimate – or, rather, opportune – to accurately relate the boundaries of the partitioned territories. The map became the condition for the political existence of nation-states.

Often, mountains, rivers, valleys and coasts are taken as a pretext, in order to give a 'natural' licence to these artificial limits.[6] Perhaps also for this reason, it seems so difficult to say goodbye to the concept of the border that, for a peninsula such as Italy, for example, it seems almost self-evident. To the North there is the chain of the Alps, and the sea all around. With the opening of the Schengen area, these borders have transformed into Europe's closed ports. On the other side is Africa. The Mediterranean, the sea which twenty-six different countries face onto, has become one of the world's deepest faultlines, and at the same time the passage most crossed by migrant boats.

Lampedusa, Italy. Far to the South: latitude 35°30'N. Farther south than either Tunis or Algiers. In geographical terms, the island ought not to be Italian territory, for it is situated on the 'African plate', unlike Linosa, which makes up part of the Pelagian archipelago. The distances speak clearly: 205 km from Sicily and 113 km from Tunisia. Lampedusa and Lampione are African islands in Italy – or, rather, in Europe.

The Greeks called it Lutadússa; the Romans, Lompadusa. The name comes from a root which means 'light, flame'. A luminous island, a warm one, with its rocks of dolomite, its crumbling walls, its jagged cliffs, its deep coves, its mysterious grottoes, and its wide-open bays. The most famous is the beach on the islet of Conigli: nothing to do with bunnies [*conigli* = Italian for 'rabbits'] but, instead, the domain of turtles and seagulls.

Lampedusa, Europe. The most important site on the island is the lighthouse of Capo Grecale. For years, now, since the first landing in October 1992, it has guided migrants' route. When they glimpse it from a distance, they know that the Italian coast is just a short stretch away. The lighthouse at Capo Grecale is the contemporary version of a Statue of Liberty for the whole of Europe, albeit a faceless one which does not exist in the memory, neither underpinned by poetic verses nor by words of indignation, hope or welcome. Those who challenge the sea after challenging the desert are, indeed, not welcome. Sharp and slimy rocks lie in wait for them.

Yet history tells of an incessant back-and-forth of different peoples: Phoenicians, Greeks, Romans, Arabs and then, still after that, the French, the Maltese and the British. Even the Russians wanted to establish themselves there. Certainly, there were also bands of pirates. But, for a long time, Lampedusa remained open and hospitable. In the nineteenth century, like all the lands of Southern Italy, it passed from the Bourbons to the Kingdom of Italy. Here, already, contours and connotations changed, for a penal colony was built on the island. Chosen as a strategic stronghold for the defence of the Axis, between the two world wars it became a base for naval and anti-aircraft batteries, up till the point of the Allied landings. In the Italian imaginary of the postwar period, it was the island of thyme and oregano, of crystal-clear waters and white sand, of sunkissed holidays and the Mediterranean scrubland lightly brushed by different winds – the Maestrale, the Scirocco and the Grecale, respectful enough never to clash with each others' paths.

The *Gate of Europe* is a sculpture begun on 28 June 2008 on a piece of high ground not far from the port, on the southernmost promontory. 15 feet high and 9 wide, constructed with a special ceramic that absorbs and reflects light – including moonlight – it is a monument to migrants and, at the same time, a symbolic lighthouse. Numbers, shoes and bowls are sculpted in bas-relief.[7]

Despite difficulties, obstacles and contradictions of all kinds, sometimes running into legal troubles, the fishermen and the inhabitants of the island have rescued the shipwrecked and welcomed migrants, inspired by an ancient and sacred Mediterranean hospitality which would be impossible to break.[8] Thousands arrived and then set off again; thousands never made it. Lampedusa has dug graves for the bodies returned by the sea, in the old cemetery as in the new one. At first the gravestones had brief, almost hurried inscriptions, as if this was all just a passing emergency:

29 September 2000
Here lies
An unidentified migrant

In the white cemetery, among the graves of the islanders, the stones for the migrants then took on a narrative tone:

On 1 August 2011
Two Coast Guard naval units reached a 15-metre vessel that had come from Libya and followed its journey as far as Lampedusa. Here the engine ran into trouble and the shipwrecked were transferred onto patrol vessels. 271 people, including 36 women and 21 children, were saved. The bodies of 25 people who had died of asphyxia during the crossing were found in the hold of the trawler.
Six of them lie here.

There are also small signs and pieces of card. These were periods in which the number of landings multiplied and there were a great many bodies to bury. But the gravestones that record the manner, the time and the place of the shipwreck are a contribution to the unwritten history of the immense tragedy of emigration in the new millennium.

17 March 2012

The Port Authority and Guardia di Finanza, following an
alarm raised at dawn by satellite telephone, came in aid
of a boat in danger in the Strait of Sicily, 70 miles from
Lampedusa in international waters. On the broken-down
vessel were found 52 people exhausted by their long stay out
at sea. On board there were also the lifeless bodies of five
persons who had died of the hardships suffered during the
crossing. Three were men and two were women, one of whom
was pregnant. Their name, age or provenance are unknown.
Here lie
A man of between 25 and 30 years of age of probable
sub-Saharan origin

A man presumably below 18 years of age of probable
sub-Saharan origin
A man of around 30 years of age of probable sub-Saharan
origin
A woman of around 20 to 25 years of age, pregnant, of
probable sub-Saharan origin
A woman of around 20 to 25 years of age of probable
sub-Saharan origin

In Lampedusa there is also a cemetery for boats. They look like
they have been scattered there haphazardly waiting to take to sea
again. Yet under the red, blue and green paint marked by writing
in Arabic, one sees the wood rotting. These are the migrant boats
– bigger ones, smaller ones, others very small indeed – which did
manage to get the better of the waves. Here and there, there are
dinghies – it is said that only the ones less than thirty years old go
out into the sea.

Nothing seems more distant from Europe, and from the European
Union that is in fact not a union. Thus, over the years, Lampedusa
has been 'abandoned', as many say, left to itself, isolated – more
an island than ever. Yet this is only partly true. For Europe's
'immigration policy' lies precisely in this deliberate desertion, which
is far from a chance happening. If migrants drown, this tribute to
victims will serve to 'stop the flows' and will in any case be put down
to the 'smugglers', promoted in the meantime to 'human traffickers'.
Whoever might set out along the way should understand that she
has already been rejected upon departure.

If, therefore, one were to pose a question paraphrasing the title
of a book by Alain Badiou[9] and ask what border Lampedusa is
the name of, the answer would be that it is the name of a trench,
of a barricade, of a fortification. Lampedusa is the outpost where
Europe, after transforming the coastal nations into border guards,
fights its undeclared war against the migrants, peddled as a 'fight
against traffickers'.

Its allies are the African states, armed and supported – even
if they are violent regimes – so that they will maintain a careful
surveillance over the coasts, so that they will not allow the migrants
to move, processing them through 'prisons', internment camps or
refugee camps. The border needs back-up. Complicating things are
the NGOs, from Médécins sans Frontières to Proactiva Open Arms,
SOS Méditerranée, MOAS, Save the Children, Jugend Rettet, Sea
Watch, Sea Eye, and Life Boat. Arraigned against these NGOs is a
firing squad that seeks to neutralize them. In stretches of open sea,
in the spaces between borders, act all those who still fly the flag of

justice, who believe in humanity, whatever form and colour it may have. For this, they are called 'humanitarians'.

3 Condemned to immobility

Borders are not only political; they can have other functions and some other scope. Real or symbolic, they belong to the variegated spatial alphabet of delimitation and exclusion. To understand the ambivalence that criss-crosses and permeates the border – the *frontier*, the *frontière* – it is worth reflecting on its etymology and thus distinguishing it from the confine and the limit – terms which have become synonymous. The 'confine' is the line that marks the end of two territories, a *fine* [end] which, as the *con* suggests, is shared and recognized by both sides.[10] On the other hand, the limit – itself a word of Latin provenance – is the unilaterally established *limes*. The most famous *limes* is the one between the Roman Empire and the Germanic lands. Outside of the Latin languages, the semantics of limits changes. If 'boundary' refers to binding, the German *Grenze*, a Slavic loan word (as Grimm's *Wörterbuch* emphasizes), indicates the end of a space, the line of separation.[11] The word 'frontier' immediately betrays its origins in a military lexicon, indicating the front, the confrontation. The whole image of the frontier also entails a clash between fronts, a face-to-face that opens up to a confrontation that is not necessarily a matter of war.

Contrary to what is generally believed, the frontier is not a line, but a place – a site of contact and conflict, of encounter and tension, between the self and the other. Seen in a political light, the frontier reproduces a power balance, represents an asymmetrical relationship and constitutes a complex *dispositif*. If, on the one hand, all the power of the state is offloaded on the frontier, thus allowing the state to exercise its sovereignty even at the cost of being violent towards non-citizens, on the other hand, the *dispositif* of the frontier is global capitalism's preferred passage, one able to regulate market flows. These two forces are not always in harmony and they can, conversely, even pursue divergent interests. Protectionism – including in its most recent forms, from Trump's policy in the United States to Brexit – clearly demonstrates this. But this also comes to light in a troubling and yet oft-unremarked phenomenon: namely, the widespread privatization of frontiers, control over which is entrusted to special surveillance firms and agencies able to manage sophisticated technological mechanisms. If the individual citizen armed with a passport is ever more abandoned to the complex border system, the migrant, who is utterly without defences, may remain a prisoner caught in the netting, and may even lose her life.

The frontiers are not equal for everyone. The world without frontiers is the materialization of what Paul Virilio calls the 'virtual meta-city', the homogeneous globality favoured by the acceleration of technology, of the market and of understanding. It is the new planetary mobility. It is especially enjoyed by the new luxury nomads, these hypersedentarists endowed with the best passports, multiple titles and a lot of money, who move in a standardized space from one office to another without ever having the impression that they have passed through any frontier.[12] Yet, as power and wealth lessen, the planet divides, fragments and displays its rugged visage. For the citizens of Europe, the United States and Canada, whose digital passports almost everywhere open up a passage and rarely require a visa, the world without frontiers is an everyday reality. For all those who come from less powerful states, the globe is anything but homogeneous. The world-cities, the global metropoles, are testament to the countless inequalities, the striking differences.[13] But it is, above all, for migrants that the frontiers rise up as insuperable barriers.

The comparison with tourists shows the whole ambivalence that the frontier has in store. A figure who represents the mirror-image of the migrant, the tourist, far from the ancient idea of travel that now lies in ruins, moves under the impulse of both the need to consume – the consumption of sites, of landscapes, of museums, etc. – and the need for comfort, racking up new destinations, all in expectation of the much-deserved return. She enjoys an extra-territoriality, in an inverse sense to the migrant's. She sojourns in a big resort or a tourist village, in the objective of preserving herself from any risk; the other does not interest her and nor does she intend to put her own identity in jeopardy. She travels but it is as if she were not travelling, for she does not take any step outside her own self.[14] The frontiers open up readily for the tourist, who spends in order to travel and travels in order to spend. The opposite happens in the case of the migrant, who earns in order to travel and travels in order to earn. The frontiers close to her.

In this as in other cases, this is not, then, a matter of being for or against. The bizarre *In Praise of Borders* written by Régis Debray, which well reflects the degeneration of a progressivism that has ended up marrying the cause of the national border, not only confuses the unlimited with the borderless but fails to grasp the significance of a *dispositif* that functions alternatively either to stop or to drive circulation.[15]

In the globalized world, in which success is measured by the possibility of moving freely, the frontier can become a means of exclusion. This is not, moreover, the first time in history that the restriction of space has become a trademark of discrimination – one need only think of the ghetto, the prison and the madhouse.

Thus, the migrants who have dared to get moving, challenging the frontiers, are condemned to immobility – a ruling against which they have no right to appeal. In this verdict, which makes up a pair with the condemnation of the migrant to invisibility, one should be able to recognize a treatment designed to get rid of these human – or inhuman – 'scum' of globalization.

4 The world of the camps

Here one arrives at the question of the camps, these transit areas where many migrants' journey in fact comes to an end. Just as philosophy, with the exception of Agamben's work, has avoided the theme of migration, it has also steered well clear of the world of the camps.[16] It has, above all, been historians, legal scholars, sociologists and anthropologists who have examined this phenomenon. Among these latter, it is worth mentioning Michel Agier, who is to be thanked for his penetrating research, and in particular the detailed landscape he provides of the camps that pockmark the globe – a geopolitical map.[17]

The world of the camps raises many philosophical and political questions, including in terms of its side-effects on the city. These questions need to be addressed in an overall study. To offer just one example, there does not yet exist a phenomenology of life in the camps, or a reflection on the wait therein.[18]

Though some have advanced the hypothesis of a 'return of the camps', what ought instead to be recognized is a troubling continunity. In their retrospective on the twentieth century, defined as the 'century of the camps', Joël Kotek and Pierre Rigoulot delineated the different forms of concentration camp, bringing to light the similarities and differences between them. What thread links together the *campos de concentraciones* which the Spanish established in Cuba in order to repress the popular uprising, or the *concentration camps* in which the British massed together the South African Boers, with the Nazi *lagers*, the Soviet *gulags*, the camps in China and North Korea, or even the ones in former Yugoslavia? And what links these camps to the 'centres' for foreigners, where 'reception' becomes a pretext for internment and where humanitarian protection and police controls end up welded together?

The history of the concentrationary system as reconstructed by Kotek and Rigoulot follows the pioneering studies by Arendt, whose typology they adopt while also adding one further distinction. In the schema first elaborated by Arendt, a distinction is drawn between three different camps, which correspond to the three images of life in the afterworld: Hades, Purgatory and Hell. The intention is to underline the senselessness that envelops all these forms, and, not by coincidence, ends up in outright unreality. Seen from the outside, Arendt writes, the camps, and what happens within them, can be described as 'images drawn from a life after death, that is, a life removed from earthly purposes'.[19] Each of these symbolic denominations corresponds to a different type of camp: Hades to the internment camp, Purgatory to the labour camp, and Hell to the concentration and extermination camps. To indicate this latter, Kotek and Rigoulot also add the Jewish image of Gehenna. They specify that by this they mean 'the world of the six Nazi centres of immediate death, where there is no history or heroism but only an abrupt death in the most absolute anonymity'.[20] Gehenna thus indicates the camps that the Germans called *Vernichtungslager*, where mortality surpassed 99 per cent because the immediate goal was outright annihilation. Other than Auschwitz – half extermination camp, half concentration camp, from which a majority in fact returned as survivors – these centres of death, of which we still know little, were Chełmno, Bełżec, Majdanek, Sobibór and Treblinka.

Despite the profound differences between one type and another, Arendt identifies a continuum that makes such a typology plausible. Here, one can speak of family resemblances, which also contribute to clarifying the occasional mixing of these different types. The criterion for distinguishing between them is the function of the camp – that is, the question of what happens within it. Contrary to what is generally believed, forced labour is not necessarily part of the camp. Moreover, the concentrationary logic does not respond either to utility or – still less – to economics. The only economic use it has, at the very most, is to finance the surveillance apparatus.

At the basis of this typology is the 'camp', a normally hermetically sealed terrain that is summarily and temporarily fitted out in order to intern 'undesirable' individuals, without any respect for their human rights. A peculiarity of the camp is administrative detention. Its primary aim is elimination, understood in the etymological sense, from the Latin *eliminare* which means 'push out', 'send away', out of the *limes*, beyond the threshold, outside the confines. E-limination can happen in different forms, ranging from expulsion to physical annihilation.

A 'gentle' form of concentration, Hades begins the typology because – precisely in the sense in which Plato narrated this realm beyond the grave, which lies in darkness, closed off to the gaze of the living – being non-existent and invisible to others is the fate that strikes all those interned therein. Arendt was convinced that Hades was the first stage in the concentrationary universe. She spoke out of experience, given that in 1941 she had herself been interned in the French camp at Gurs, one of the many across Europe that operated as collection centres for foreigners.

Moreover, already in 1905, the Aliens Act had been passed in the United Kingdom – a law in which there found expression for the first time, through the Migration Police, the principle that it was legitimate to stop foreigners at the borders and filter them. At root was the idea that those who came from outside represented a threat to internal stability. The Jews who had come from Eastern Europe, fleeing the pogroms, were especially the victims of this law, which sanctioned the possibility of rejecting, on the basis of wholly arbitrary criteria, foreigners in need of hospitality.

For Arendt, it was already clear that the camps did not constitute a 'totalitarian invention'. They had emerged even prior to totalitarianism, and in her prediction they would persist even in democratic societies in order to offer a makeshift solution to the problem of overpopulation and the economically superfluous. This prophecy was proven correct. The camp is not a spectre from the past – rather, it is a phenomenon which, as Agamben has explained, represents the 'hidden matrix', the 'nomos of the political space in which we are still living'.[21]

If it now seems almost self-evident that even foreigners who have not committed any crime should be interned and processed, it ought to be remembered that this apparently obvious proposition is itself part of the concentrationary universe. For all their variety, camps for foreigners are waiting areas where the transitory becomes permanent. These are forced pauses where excess humanity is captured and held outside. This excess sanctions the out-of-placeness of the foreigners, the excluded and interned, the expulsed and processed, as waste to be removed. Here power acts on the human flows of migration, controls mobility and manages the undesirables.

The camps which stud Europe's frontiers attest not only to the missed promise of the 'never again' – what ought not to have again repeated itself on European territory.[22] They are a *dispositif* of confinement, in the broadest sense of the world, because they are at the confines, because they confine, and – evoking the spectre of the transgressed limit – they swallow an undeclared belligerence, the tacit war against the migrants.

5 The passport: a paradoxical document

Does it serve to pass some confine, or to identify oneself? Or both? And, if this is so, why on earth should one need to demonstrate one's own identity in order to cross a border? In the invention of the passport, and through its twists and turns, it is possible to read the history of migration as if through a kaleidoscope. Yet there has been very little reflection on this highly paradoxical document.

Foucault does not mention it in his lectures, even though the passport has been a security *dispositif* decisive for population control and in the administration of power.[23] Moreover, this document is closely linked to the birth of the state and to its monopoly of violence. More than attesting the identity of the individual, the passport certifies her belonging to a state. Whoever does not have a passport does not have citizenship and does not have identity.

'Your papers!' In today's era, this demand seems a self-evident one. Usually it is the police who demand one's details. The arriving foreigner is identified at the frontier. 'Why are you here?' 'For how long?' 'Name and address of the hotel you'll be staying in?' And there is no certainty that she will not be stopped or even rejected. On closer inspection, the demand, which itself fundamentally undermines any sense of hospitality, is the confirmation that whoever travels is 'out of place', not where she had been assigned to be.[24] This does not constitute a problem if this is a temporary move, as in the case of a tourist, a manager or a student. But for the migrant it becomes an insurmountable difficulty.

Nonetheless, the idea that to move is to be 'out of place' is by no means self-evident, and in fact it is relatively recent. In the premodern landscape, it would thus have been unimaginable to have asked for documents attesting to someone's identity. Rather, papers of this kind did not exist. For the most part, life unfolded within the confines of a village or a small town where mutual acquaintance and trust moulded relations, and in which the iron social hierarchy which delimited social layers, classes and ranks attributed an unchangeable place to each person. It seems that it was the Longobard King Rachi (or Ratchis) who issued the first edict that allowed subjects to leave his realm only with written authorization, in a decree he made in 746. Throughout the Middle Ages, to make a journey was exceptional. Only few moved around: merchants, artists, knights, or indeed pilgrims, beggars and marauders. Given the uncertainties involved, a safe-conduct was used: first, an escort that accompanied the voyager through unknown territory, and then security papers that were supposed to protect whoever exhibited them. In this second form of safe-conduct, one ought to detect the forerunner of the passport; on the one hand, it attested to the person's identity, and, on the other, it contained the seal of the authority that had issued it, thus guaranteeing protection. A legendary document, often the protagonist of novellas and novels on account of the adventurous exchanges of identity, the safe-conduct was above all conceived as a permission for passage that temporarily justified the fact that the person carrying it with her was 'out of place'.[25] The turning point came in 1503, when Catholic Spain banned Jews and *conversos* from leaving the country in order to reach the New World. These measures, which were subsequently strengthened, decreed a – also discriminatory – sense of belonging, on whose basis administrative means were used to impede movement. From this point, the function of the passport changed. Not only did it identify the foreigner, but it now also served to control the domestic population. Registers helped make it easier to establish such controls. In its varied developments, the French Revolution represented a significant parenthesis. In a *cité* in which all were to be 'friends, guests, brothers', in which public hospitality was the revolution itself, the 'slavery of passports' was abolished.[26] Everything changed when the king tried to leave the country, and in particular when the enemies of France dispatched their agents, who hid behind the mask of being potential revolutionaries. The sovereignty of the state imposed itself as it closed the borders and restored the passport for foreigners. The war then prescribed the introduction of an état civil for each person; from this moment, one could be a citizen only if one was registered by the municipal authorities. The passport served not only to control the foreigner's comings and goings but also to certify the identity of the citizen.

Linked to the nation-state, the passport followed its peripeties as it became a powerful tool, which reached its apogee in the Third Reich and in the elaborate legislation, from the Nuremburg laws onwards, which sought to 'protect German blood'. On 5 October 1938, the 'Law on Jews' Passports' was issued, compelling the Jews to return their identity documents – cancelled at a stroke – to the German authorities. They received new papers on which a large J, for *Jude*, was imprinted. This was a route map sending them to the *lager*.

In the new century, in which mobility has become a mass phenomenon, the passport has acquired decisive importance, as it has taken on further and ever more sophisticated functions. After 11 September 2001, states' need to hold information on foreigners who enter their territory, no less than on their own citizens, has increased enormously. The digital passport has been combined with biometric identification, which is to say the inspection of those characteristics – the photograph of the face, the fingerprints, the iris of the eye – which make a person unique. If the classic registrar data – name, surname, date of birth, residence and nationality – were still open to manipulation, biometric data have definitively eliminated the centuries-old gap between a person and their documents. The microchip registration of these data in the biometric passport sparks a great deal of perplexity. One can imagine that, in a none-too-distant future, the document will be wholly eliminated, as the body itself, with its biometric characteristics, is destined to become simultaneously both the certain proof of identity and the moving frontier that each person brings with them before they arrive at any static border. The control exercised by the state thus appears unlimited – especially, and above all, its power over those bodies not registered by a microchip, and who can thus always be rejected.

6 'To each their own home!' Crypto-racism and the new Hitlerism

First of all comes the denial – the self-denial. 'I'm not a racist, but …' It seems that the racist no longer has the courage to declare himself publicly. He is ashamed of himself and, above all, fears that condemnation that was supposed to have become universal after Nuremburg. He seeks to dissemble; he muddies the waters, confuses, derails. Thus, the new racist of the post-Nazi era resorts to subterfuge and expedients, carefully chooses his words, and plays on ambiguity, in the attempt to get around the censure put up by anti-racism. One can call him a crypto-racist, for a racist he remains, and there is little use hiding it. His own 'but' is, in part, an admission: 'I am not a racist, but …' It is not difficult to provide a sample of these kinds of expression, particularly abundant on the Internet:

> I'm not a racist but I can't stand these gypsies. I'm not a racist but these blacks shouldn't hang around in the carpark. I'm not a racist but I don't like immigrants. I'm not a racist, but when they come here they bring diseases. I'm not a racist, but you've brought a plague to Europe. I'm not a racist, but enough of these non-Europeans [*extracomunitari*]. I'm not a racist, but everyone should stick to their own home.[27]

The crypto-racist is a species that surprises the perspective of progress readying to celebrate the beginning of the new era. Stripped of any scientific foundation and sanctioned and punished by history, racism was not meant to exist anymore. If it did still crop up here and there, this could be explained as just a grotesque exhibition of idiosyncrasy or the superstitions of a few nostalgics. It would, then, only be a matter of time for history to do its work and definitively erase these traces of the past. The optimist who thought along these lines, trusting in the final victory of 'culture' (as if the Nazis were 'uncultured') reduced anti-racism to the work of pointing out racism wherever it existed. This was a thankless and indeed annoying responsibility, for each time this task seemed complete, it was necessary to start again. And there is more: for the optimist convinced that the phenomenon was confined to a few peripheral fascists, to a few irrelevant neo-Nazi sects, would end up having to rethink. What, indeed, ought to be said about the hatred towards immigrants, the rampant xenophobia, the countless episodes of discrimination? How should they be defined? What words should be used?

With his dissimulation, his verbal twists, his logical–grammatical somersaults, the crypto-racist manages to raise question marks over the definition of racism. What on Earth is it? If it can be agreed on the basis of canonical criteria that it is the ideology of 'race', according to which there exist different 'races' of humans and there is a necessary hierarchy between them, then racism did indeed disappear some time ago, and there is nothing to be discussed. For it has now been scientifically demonstrated that 'races' do not exist – that they are an invention. The crypto-racist seeks refuge behind the disappearance of 'races'; but this is like hiding behind one's own finger. Nonetheless, it is paradoxical that, after the sun has set on 'races', racism has still remained.[28] Faced with this paradox, the anti-racist seems disarmed, and ends up in an impasse. She has involuntarily contributed to making racism vanish from the contemporary horizon. Therefore, she is often compelled to take recourse to legal avenues – which can, however, come back on her like a boomerang – almost as if to reassert the gravity of racism. Thanks to its syncretic masks, from unprecedented forms of sovereigntism to the various conjugations of the 'clash of civilizations', neo-racism evades examination and eludes condemnation.

There remains the problem of the definition on which the crypto-racist himself plays. In order to avoid the shifting sands of racism and, indeed, any wish to rigidly define it, what needs to be done is to catch it *in flagrante* in the ancestral deed which, for Claude Lévi-Strauss, marks the savage mind. This is the act through which the savage – that is, the racist – separates the 'we' from the 'not we', the civilized from the savages, the humans from the inhuman. The separation is a hiatus; it places its own self at the centre and rejects the other into a dangerous margin. This act, which does not necessarily establish a divide between different 'races', but can also distinguish between two cultures, crystallized in rigid schemas, marks an immutable discrimination, a permanent exclusion.

If this is an ancestral act, racism – this Western invention which later became universal – nonetheless has a certain history, and even a birth certificate dating back to the dawn of modernity. This latter was the *estatutos de limpieza de sangre* stipulated in Toledo on 5 June 1449, with which the converted Jews were stigmatized, as they were distinguished from 'Christians of pure Christian origin'. This indicated, for the first time, the immutable, metaphysical Jewish essence from which no baptismal water could offer refuge. This schema was destined to repeat itself according to different forms and modalities, ultimately culminating in the myth of the 'pure blood' which had to be protected from any contamination. The unity of humanity, as taught by the Bible, broke apart, while an evolutionist vision, in which there emerged 'species' classified in a hierarchy, gave rise to a dehumanization of the 'irrecoverable', the beast-like subhumans whom it would be legitimate to term 'monkeys', 'rats', 'lice', 'parasites', etc., following a dark list of metaphors that has constantly kept growing. Nature and culture make up a single whole, to determine the place of the 'subhumans' whose inferiority is without remedy, and who are destined in each moment to be definitively separated from the consortium of humans – in the name of purity.

But the discriminating act can play not only on blood but also on soil. From here emerges the need for rootedness, and the aspiration to make everyone stay in their own place. Mobility is, in fact, seen as a dangerous source of mixing and contamination.[29]

One can only recognize what one knows. And, all too often, there is continued ignorance over the fact that this conception of rootedness in the soil is a direct legacy of Hitlerism, which, in its novel versions in the new millennium, not by chance insists more on the soil than on the blood, a myth that has been partly obfuscated. 'Everyone in their own country!' Nazism was the first project for the biopolitical remodelling of the planet that proffered stable criteria for, and modes of, cohabitation – to the point of deciding that an entire people, the Jewish people, no longer had the right to inhabit the planet.

In the post-Nazi worldview, there has held firm the idea that it is legitimate to decide with whom to cohabit. The new Hitlerism here finds its point of strength, and neo-racism its trampoline. The fear for one's own presumed identity, put under threat by the unknown and repugnant other, foments hatred towards the 'clandestine', the 'migrant'; it sparks dread of the loss of class position that spreads among the poorer layers and enflames xenophobic populism.

The neo-racist says that 'everyone should live in their own country'. He has no need to come out, point-blank, with phrases such as 'let's let these niggers die in the sea'. He preaches rejection and applauds repatriations. He equates immigration to an 'invasion'. He argues that migrants are suspect, that they carry diseases, that they steal jobs, that they cost too much. He says that he is fighting against the 'immigration business', but, in reality, what he does not tolerate is immigration itself. He curses the 'gypsy' and whips up anger against the 'traveller'. He indulges conspiracy theories, deviously referring to migration as the 'deportation of slaves', as if the migrants were unable to have intentions and will, as if they were not humans.

7 Hospitality: in the impasse between ethics and politics

Hospitality seems to have disappeared from both the contemporary landscape and the political vocabulary. The question – and this is continually repeated – is reduced to a matter of how to 'govern' the 'influxes of migrants'. The rejection of hospitality – which is judged wholly unacceptable and out of place – ensures that all the tensions explode at the frontiers themselves: the tensions between state sovereignty and individual liberty, between law and justice, between institutions and compassion, between political governance and ethical imperatives. The practice of hospitality, as ancient as the origins of civilization, has always been accompanied by tensions. Yet the ones that imbue and excite everyday politics in the present era have their own particular drives.

Anachronistic, out of place, inopportune – for many the act of hospitality seems absurd, and they go so far as to stigmatize it, scoff at it, attack it. For them, this is the deed of beautiful souls, of humanitarians, of those naïve types that show off their benevolence towards migrants and purport to offer hospitality to foreigners who ought instead to be treated as enemies. This act is, at most, tolerated in the restricted margins of religious charity or the likewise circumscribed margins of ethical engagement. In short, hospitality is relegated to a supra- or infra-political – if not extra-political – sphere. It depends on one's point of view. But it in any case remains outside of politics, which certainly cannot govern by handing itself over to the impulses of the heart, to the fervour of faith, to ethical obligations.

Before hospitality must come being – or rather, wellbeing, welfare.

Welfare chauvinism combines with the new and impetuous nationalism of the post-national era to reassert the empire of law.
Hospitality, with its call for justice, with its extra dispensation,
its surplus of humanity, continually challenges right, its laws,
its regularity. Daring and incautious, it gravely jeopardizes the
political–juridical order, to the point that it appears irritatingly
superfluous. The prudency of the rule and the virtue of the
exception, institutional will and the wait for the event, cleverness in
calculation and the instinct of charity – the conflict between them
could not be more acute. For what clashes with hospitality is, most
importantly, liberal morality with its egalitarian principles – or,
rather, its abstractly egalitarian ones, and its need to sift through
the countless conditions that would allow the reception of those
who deserve hospitality. On the opposite front stands the Judeo-
Christian morality based on the model of the Good Samaritan,
which simply aids the wounded person it finds on the street, without
questioning the whys and the wherefores. This immediacy towards
one's neighbour finds an echo in Paul of Tarsus and his Epistle to
the Ephesians: 'So then ye are no more strangers and sojourners,
but ye are fellow-citizens with the saints, and of the household of
God.'[30] Intolerant of this practice, which it accuses of being partial,
liberal modernity tends to neutralize it. It is no chance thing that
the theorists of liberalism have dedicated extensive comments to the
parable of the Good Samaritan, with the intent of invalidating its
content, which is judged impracticable.

Is it necessary, then, to recognize the end of hospitality? Precisely
because it appears so profoundly anti-modern, even having exceeded
modernity – which makes it so decidedly out of step with the
present – and having preserved a tight connection with the ancient
horizon and with the sacred sphere, from which it comes, hospitality
maintains its power of attraction and its oppositional potential. It
rises to the level of a critical instance of politics; it opens the gap
which also allows another perspective on the flat and cynical world
of liberal governance.

An extra-political, ethical instance, hospitality is also a philosophical instance. And in the recent past it has been linked to the
name of Jacques Derrida, who had the merit of introducing it back
into the debate. In this regard, it is worth remembering the developments that contributed to the revival of this theme. Known for
his deconstruction, from the mid-1980s onwards Derrida increasingly concentrated on openly political questions, as attested by the
themes of his seminars. Many recognize his 1994 essay *Force de
loi* as marking a political turning-point in his thought. However,
Derrida himself denied that there was any turning-point, as he

insisted on the political engagement that had always-already characterized deconstruction.[31] The concern to assert this continuity was
articulated with the need to respond to the attacks coming from
Habermas, and to all those, from Luc Ferry to Alain Renaut, who
accused him of being an apolitical and irresponsible philosopher.
For Derrida, *La déconstruction est la justice* – deconstruction is
justice.[32] This phrase, destined to be the pivot of his reflection,
marked a turning-point within a wider continuity. His thinking on
justice developed in a series of – sometimes even very short – texts,
often written in the urgency of the political moment. And from 1990
onwards, the political emergency that excited polemic in France was
the question of the *sans-papiers*. The apogee of the tension was
reached in 1996, when a group of *sans-papiers* occupied the churches
of Saint Ambroise and Saint Bernard in Paris in order to protest
against immigration laws and the supposed 'crime of hospitality'
that lay down penalties for whoever took in unregularized migrants.
Intellectuals also mobilized. In October 1997, the 'Appeal of the 17'
was published, and Derrida subsequently signed up to it with his
own open letter. His interest in hospitality, however, dates back to
years previously, as attested not only by his involvement in activist
causes but also by his deconstructivist reading of Kant's texts on
cosmopolitanism.[33] Already in 1991, Derrida had given a talk on this
question at UNESCO.[34] Among his public interventions, alongside
his seminars and lectures, it is worth mentioning the speech he sent
to the International Writers' Parliament held in Strasbourg between
21 and 22 March 1996, with the intention of establishing a network
of refuge-cities to take in persecuted writers. The title chosen by
Derrida was programmatic: *Cosmopolites de tous les pays, encore un
effort!* – Cosmopolitans of all lands, one more push![35]

From the outset, even where it seemed to be limited to the deconstruction of classic texts of philosophy and literature, Derrida
embraced the cause of hospitality in all its alternative hues, its
ethical values, and its symbolism – which is so political as to be
extra-political, as to be able to challenge governmental realism
and its inhospitable laws on immigration. There was to be no
compromise; no attempt to delineate – like the American philosophers – normative theories on the community or on the frontier;
no concern to invent new moral criteria. Rather, hospitality was
mobilized in all its anachronic potential, as an immemorial law
which boasts a complex and fascinating history. This, even to the
point that hospitality becomes a utopian instance, the beyond from
which to observe law and politics in a new way.

Derrida turned to the ancient Jewish landscape traversed by
the Good Samaritan and inhabited by Abraham and by all those

figures who, with disconcerting simplicity, welcomed and hosted those who arrived. *Arrivant* is the absolute arriving person who turns up unexpected, without being invited, and whose sudden appearance explodes any frontier, any limit, any threshold. There is no calculation that holds, no foresight, no control.[36] Hospitality is pure openness to the arriving person, it is unconditional hospitality, which in this hyperbole coincides with a justice that is always a coming future, also called 'a messianic without messianism'.[37]

Derrida repeatedly recognized his debt to Emmanuel Lévinas, in particular in the famous conference held in December 1996, a year after the latter's death, tellingly entitled 'Le mot d'accueil' – The word 'welcome'. The text was driven by Derrida's aspiration to reread Lévinas's work, seeking the timbre that harmonized it and was also the note of the accord between them. 'Although the word is neither frequently used nor emphasized within it, *Totality and Infinity* bequeaths to us an immense treatise of hospitality.'[38] Thus Derrida wrote that he had identified the inaugural act of Lévinas's thought precisely in *reception*. This move was not, however, followed by a philosophy of reception. One would thus search in vain for a treatise on hospitality. It may, therefore, seem all the more surprising that Derrida should have explicitly invoked this act. But the point is that, for Lévinas, reception is not an ethical or political theme. Nor was it a matter of questioning the possibility of reception – which would itself mean reducing it to a specific moral problem – or of establishing how it could then be extended into the political domain. Lévinas did not propose an ethic of hospitality – rather, he developed an ethic *as* hospitality.

Lévinas's critique is directed against the Western subject, 'a sovereign who is merely concerned to maintain the powers of his sovereignty'.[39] Incapable of exiting from his own self, and driven only by the mania to appropriate the other, to swallow, integrate and assimilate her, this subject follows the chimera of autonomy as proffered by Kant, and chases after the dream of self-coincidence proclaimed by Hegel. Reconciled with the world, as well as with himself, everywhere at home, this full-of-himself subject who has annihilated others' differences on the altar of his own closed sovereignty is the protagonist of the self-centred totalitarianism of which Auschwitz is the logical conclusion. It is, ultimately, necessary to recognize the other's precedence. But this precedence has often been misunderstood, as if Lévinas's discourse were but an edifying sermon on altruism. Lévinas indicates that behind the act of subjugation there stands the act of reception.[40] The world did not begin from the id, which, rather, is always-already convoked and questioned by the other, to whom it is called to respond.

Here lies the id's responsibility, without it having been able to choose – for it constitutes itself as an id only through this turn. The reception of the other founds the id, before it can ask itself how it should behave, whether it should welcome the other or not. Whoever poses themselves these demands still imagines that they are this autonomous, already stably settled subject. But it is not possible to reduce welcome to a further move, accessory to sovereignty. On the contrary, welcome is the fundamental ethical schema that defines the incipit of any future ethic. And vice versa: if there is no welcome, there can be no ethics. Thus, for Lévinas, the paradigm of this ethic which becomes a first philosophy is not Ulysses, whose odyssey was the passage through the unfamiliar with a view to the reappropriation of the self, but rather Abraham, who in his original eccentricity proceeds towards the other.

In its irreducible uniqueness, the face of the other corresponds to the infinite that always exceeds beyond the self and which can never be integrated. When the other comes, this is a troubling event which shakes up the tranquil certainty of the self and belies the supposed self-evidence of being in one's proper place. It is an expulsion of the self, which can react by crying 'invasion', if it is a sovereign self. But it can also respond by feeling shame for being so full of itself – the shame of the host – and can open up a place for the other, reading in this event the moment of its election.

Though he indicated welcome as ethics' inescapable inaugural act, Lévinas pulled back from any ethos of hospitality. What instead prevailed was his resigned messianism: right and politics, insofar as they correspond to hospitality, appear incompatible with the state and are, for this reason, yet to be. On closer inspection, Derrida's position is not much different; indeed, he clearly states that 'Some have said that a certain ethics of Lévinas's seems in contradiction with republican citizenship. I believe that there does indeed exist a certain tension between a certain ethical pluralism (defined by Lévinas) and law.... The passage from pure hospitality to law and politics is a perversion, because conditions are set.'[41]

The gap between hospitality-on-condition and an absolute, or unconditional, hospitality could not be clearer. Derrida would never bridge this divide. There thus comes to light the *aporia* of hospitality, whose realization demands that it is consecrated to a perversion:

> The law of hospitality, the express law that governs the general concept of hospitality, appears as a paradoxical law, pervertible

or perverting. It seems to dictate that absolute hospitality should break with the law of hospitality as right or duty, with the 'pact' of hospitality. To put it in different terms, absolute hospitality requires that I open up my home and that I give not only to the foreigner (provided with a family name, with the social status of being a foreigner, etc.), but to the absolute, unknown, anonymous other, and that I *give place* to them, that I let them come, that I let them arrive, and take place in the place I offer them, without asking of them either reciprocity (entering into a pact) or even their names. The law of absolute hospitality commands a break with hospitality by right, with law or justice as rights. Just hospitality breaks with hospitality by right.[42]

This is an insoluble antinomy: if it is to be put into effect, the law of unconditional hospitality requires the laws of conditional hospitality, in a paradoxical relationship of both collision and collusion. With no other exit route. For the antinomy 'is not dialectizable'.[43] Derrida goes as far as to say that it seems as 'though we were going from impossibility to impossibility'.[44]

Moreover, this antinomy merely exhibits the fundamental tension between justice and right: inseparable from right, which realizes it, justice nonetheless remains irreducible in its purity. Thus, even unconditional hospitality does not manage to translate into political praxis. The word 'impossibility' recurs repeatedly, and points to the tragic character of this translation. This is a radical caesura and can be considered a caesura between an ethical instance – which in its pure irreducibility appears supra- or extra-political – and its political transaction, destined always to be imperfect and unacceptable. The event crashes up against the institution. Even though Derrida did not evade a questioning of the opening and the closedness of the community, it was nonetheless the event, the irruption of the other, that provided the entry point to the horizon of justice and politics, and which is also the point of exit or escape, given that the other always exceeds politics.

And with regard to politics, or 'the political', it ought to be emphasized that Derrida remained caught within the state paradigm.[45] The concern to continually deconstruct sovereignty, very often guided by Schmitt, restricted him to remaining within these limits. Politics appears, therefore, as a matter of state. The attempt to bring out the ghost of its self-foundation drives him to probe the vertical axis of sovereignty. While the *arché* of sovereignty sinks as it retreats, its position radicalizes, and plays on ethics on its absolute purity. Against the power of the sovereign, which mimetically reproduces itself, neturalizing any opposition, it is necessary to await the irruption of the event. Even hospitality, an anti- or supra-political instance, is not the occasion to disclose a horizontality in order to look out at the anarchic other of sovereignty.

Thus, all that remains is to denounce each instance of violence: the violence of the unconditional hospitality that, in failing to discriminate between friend and enemy, allows exposure to mortal risk; and the violence of the conditional violence which discriminates, interrogates, identifies and selects. The antinomy is incurable, even if Derrida – especially in his last interventions – looked with some consternation on the scenario in which the migrant confronts the state.[46]

If hospitality is a 'poetic' event, then its translation seems to be a challenge at the very limits of possibility.[47] Reception does not withstand the test of the foreigner. This is all the more absurd when one considers that Derrida is the philosopher who proposed translation as a political model.[48] But this model does not find an echo in this context, and Derrida remains within the impasse between ethics and politics in large part inherited from Lévinas.

The hiatus has repercussions which even today, at some years' distance, may be called deadly ones. Unfortunately, this backs up the idea that hospitality is not only impossible but circumscribed to ethics, or rather to morality, and is, in short, a moralistic affectation of the do-gooders who wallow in the edifying use of the word 'other'.[49] Given that hospitality is not mobilized in politics, except as an absolute and remote instance, politics in turn remains immune to it and becomes a field of action for whoever has normative designs. Philosophy then ends up indulging the right which stops at state confines.

All those, such as humanitarian organizations, that take responsibility for welcome, which practise it on the margins of infrapolitics, all those who are targeted because they identify with justice, pay the price for this impasse, which has ultimately led to the abandonment of hospitality.

8 Beyond citizenship

Aided by long-distance technologies, accelerated by the spread of planet-wide networks and transnational mechanisms, globalization has provoked a dislocation and an outsourcing that have transformed even the connection between the proximal and the distant, the now and the time of the future. Particularly worth recognizing is the convergence of these disruptive effects with the ones produced

by migration, in particular in the different relationship with place
and locality and in the changed sense of belonging. Migration
would, moreover, be unimaginable without the always convulsive
and contradictory, but doubtless accelerated, technological process.

Everyone can see the side-effects: in unison with the expropriation
of the proper (from identity to filiation and from language to
memory), there advance hybridization, contact, 'contamination'
and the deterritorialization without precedent through which the
here-and-now becomes uncertain and all anchoring seems lost. The
old ghosts of the blood and of the soil now crop up once more. And
even as, in this epoch-defining clash between opposed forces, the
confines between within and outside, familiar and unfamiliar, are
eroded, the ethos of the sojourn seems compromised, inhabitation
threatened and the home precarious and invaded, as it suddenly
becomes something more than 'a house'. For the at-my-place seems
to have disappeared forever in the cold planetary void that no state
frontier is able to master. The instinctive reaction is to withdraw
into a restricted space, into a closed niche, and to retreat as much
as possible into a sanctuary from that shock wave that has hit and
is now undermining the state, sovereignty, the nation and, last but
not least, citizenship.

For good reason, today's citizen has been compared to the citizen
of times of crisis, like the Hellenistic age of the late-imperial era in
Rome, when distance, resentment and disinterest in public affairs
expands the homeland into the universe.

It was the Greek philosophers who proclaimed themselves 'citizens
of the world'. Already Hippias, in a Platonic dialogue, hinted for the
first time towards a citizenship that would surpass the *nómos* of
the city.[50] But the expression 'cosmopolitan', a combination of the
two terms *polítes* and *kósmos*, appears for the first time with the
cynic Diogenes of Sinope. Asked where he was from, he replied, 'I
am a citizen of the world.'[51] He thus maintained his condition as a
polítes and the connection with the *pólis*, while also pointing to the
entire cosmos as his city. This extension also concerned one's links
with others. Zeno of Citium declared all men his 'co-citizens'.[52]
But, lacking in any juridical–political status, this citizenship instead
designated a moral attitude, a way of seeing oneself within the
cosmos and humanity. The 'citizen of the world' felt at home
everywhere and nowhere; but he was no longer bound to a single
homeland. Beyond being an expression of morality, cosmopolitanism was also a political promise.

The turning-point came only in the century of the Enlightenment.
It was Kant who elaborated a 'cosmopolitan right', whose goal was
to guarantee a stable peace, acting so that the foreigner who reached

others' territory would not be treated as an enemy. Kant, too, therefore evaded the question of a global citizenship, which thus remained a vague aspiration, the metaphor for an individual vision that did not necessarily translate politically. Reasserted in the twentieth century by Hans Kelsen, political cosmopolitanism has developed over recent decades, especially in the Anglo-American context, and found its spokespersons in those who consider necessary a reform able to keep pace with economic globalization – that is, a reform capable of establishing supra-national political authorities – in a post-national era.[53] But there is no agreement on the paths to be followed, or even on the ultimate objective. Even less so when political cosmopolitanism resurfaces as the nightmare of a global state. The question of state sovereignty would then be re-proposed on the planetary scale. And this would, moreover, mean a rush towards a centralization of power and the risk evoked, among others, by Hannah Arendt.[54]

This explains why the reflection on a post-national or supra-national politics in general prefers to identify less with cosmopolitanism than, more prudently, with democracy, and to define itself as 'cosmopolitan democracy' – i.e., understood as a gradual democratization of global governance.

Given that the citizen is constituted within the walls of the city to which she belongs, and not in the open space of the world, global citizenship seems like a contradiction in terms. For this reason, it has been seen as a negative concept, a non-citizenship, or as a metaphor. The present tendency is, instead, to think of it as a regulating ideal that nonetheless springs from a concrete need: the transition that is currently being made from national to supra-national forms. This passage also imposes changes on citizenship, which therefore has to be fundamentally rethought.

In this sense, Habermas in particular has sought to critically review the connection between nation and citizenship. In an important essay on this question entitled 'Staatsbürgerschaft und nationale Identität', he pointed to the dangers inherent in a political citizenship which, even within a now post-national horizon in which the modern state is on the way to extinction, still continues to be linked to birth. As its etymology suggests – *natio* – nation comes from the Latin verb *nascere* – 'to be born'. The territorial state takes root and prospers on the basis of a powerful fiction: ethnic homogeneity. The nation, this 'prepolitical' entity, becomes the counterfoil of citizens' political identity and even the source of state sovereignty.[55] The harmful identification between *démos* and *éthnos*, between people and ethnicity, does not, however, make up part either of the concept of democracy or of that of political citizenship. Indeed, it is hard to understand why a community should be sustained by genetic descendancy rather than by the participation of citizens who exercise their rights. It goes without saying that under accusation here are both *ius sanguinis* and *ius soli*, 'right of blood' and 'right of the soil', which is to say the criteria of belonging – and not of participation – inherited from the Greek *pólis*. Habermas outlines in broad terms the two antithetical models of citizenship that have established themselves over time: on the one hand, the 'republican' one introduced by Aristotle in the third book of his *Politics*, and on the other, the 'liberal' one developed by Locke. In the first model, the citizen is integrated in a self-determining collectivity. In the second, conversely, taking up a position that is always a little outside the collective frame, she is the client-citizen who, notwithstanding her own intentions, stipulates a contract and cedes powers to the state, from which, in exchange, she receives certain services. It is not difficult to recognize, in the republican model, what has been predominant in the European context, and in the liberal model the one that has imposed itself in the Anglo-American one. Habermas emphasizes the merit of the former model, which lies in self-determination. Again, today, it needs reasserting that 'political autonomy is an end in itself that can[not] be realized … by the single individual privately pursuing his own interests'.[56] Political autonomy requires community and demands participation. This should not lead us to overlook the inadequacy of the republican model, fossilized in the soil and ossified in blood. It is indispensable to break out of this genetic-nationalist obstinacy, for political citizenship has no need to root itself in a national identity. This would make it open to foreigners, summoned to share not an ethnic tradition, a form of life, or values, but rather a political culture – the only inescapable condition. Habermas concludes by hoping that a democratic citizenship, not closed up in any particularistic sense, can 'prepare the way for that status of cosmopolitan citizenship which is already today taking shape in political communications on a planetary scale'.[57]

Habermas's proposal, the denationalization of citizenship, also understood as 'constitutional patriotism' – because the identity that remained would be constitutionally based – has been taken up by many other authors. These include Seyla Benhabib, who has openly spoken of 'global citizens', consonant with a definitive separation between *démos* and *éthnos*.[58] The sovereignty of the people *qua démos*, democracy can no longer be confined to an *éthnos*, to an ethnic belonging of memory and destiny.

Those who look to global citizenship, within a cosmopolitan horizon – even if with different accents – have considered, and do consider with some interest, all those experiences that exceed the limits of an exclusive or national citizenship.[59] The European citizenship instituted by the 1992 Maastricht Treaty, which repre-sented a decisive step towards EU integration, has itself proven a battlefield. Nonetheless, some have seen the Treaty's ninth article, which makes this citizenship explicit, as a redoubling of the nation, a surplus of nationalism, whereas others have highlighted its declared supranational aspiration, even if this is often only symbolic. Without doubt, it is an ultra-state citizenship that could have had more effective results and opened up new perspectives.

Rather than wager on political forms that go beyond state forms, both Benhabib and Derrida turned their attentions to the city. In a politically haphazard landscape, the city seems like the privileged site in which citizenship is exercised. Benhabib has examined the case of New Haven, where immigrants received an identity card that allowed them access to hospitals, schooling for their children, bank accounts and so on. This simplifies both their lives and that of the town hall itself.[60] This is not a passport granting them US nationality, but a card that provides a civil status and recognizes certain rights which are, in part, also political. For Benhabib, this infra-national experience represents an important precedent, for it shows that new spaces for a global citizenship are opening up precisely within local communities – the communities that are best suited to according rights.

Derrida followed a different path. While in his reflection on cosmopolitanism he re-appraised the autonomy of the city, he moreover looked to a network of refuge-cities that would perhaps be able to take charge of the hospitality that states were shrinking from. Conscious that he was moving on shifting sands, on account of the power of the 'mondialisation' that has deterritorialized politics, he delocalized and dislocated it: 'the political no longer has a location, if I can say that, it no longer has a stable or essential *tópos*'. Derrida asks what 'citizen' could still mean.[61] The answer is marked by caution: 'I say "citizen" rather vaguely, for the moment.' And he continues by insisting that 'this right cannot only be that of the citizen of a state, but also one for "foreigners"'. This comes from 'a new ethic, from a new right, in reality, from a new concept of "hospitality"'.[62] Deconstruction stops here, however, just as it elsewhere stops at the borders of the state, of its tottering and resentful sovereignty, to denounce its obsession with security, the logic of exclusion, hospitality-under-surveillance. Though he recognizes the imperative to think the political beyond the political, Derrida prefers to acknowledge the epochal transition towards other forms that emerge just after the shattering of statehood. The point is that, as Derrida himself repeatedly reasserts, for him the state is a *phármakon*, both poison and remedy – an immunization device which it is not yet possible to do without.

This does not prevent him from considering the new hospitality and the new citizenship that are opening up a path beyond national confines. Situated here is his reflection on cosmopolitanism. This is obviously not a matter of endorsing a global state, but rather of reproposing a citizenship that can no longer be conceived according to the criteria of blood and soil. Derrida's position would, then, seem close to that taken by Habermas. And yet an important difference immediately comes to light: for while, in his cosmopolitan constitutionalism, Habermas seeks to democratize citizenship, unbinding it from the nation, but on the basis of liberal democracy, which simply ought to be extended, Derrida instead shows himself much more critical of both cosmopolitanism and democracy, to the point of resorting to the formula 'to-come' in both cases. The extension must also be a transformation. His gaze turns to migration and international law. Precisely because it is not possible to think about politics as still being linked to the presupposition of place, it is necessary to go 'beyond citizenship'.[63]

9 The limits of cosmopolitanism

Derrida's radicalism emerges when, in order to go beyond the political, he proposes a network of refuge-cities, thus adopting the Biblical example already studied by Lévinas. Moving within the groove of Talmud interpretation, Lévinas aptly grasps refuge-cities as a form of asylum, with all the ambiguity that characterizes this institution.[64] Derrida, conversely, would like to see within them the possibility of another citizenship. Thus, to start out from the city, as counterposed to the state, and imagine a network of 'refuge-cities' which are independent and yet allied among themselves, would be the first step towards reviving the 'ethic of hospitality'. This makes explicit reference to the Hebrew Bible and to the cities where those pursued by a 'blind justice' or blood vendetta, for a 'crime of which they were innocent' or the 'involuntary author', could find safety. Derrida insists on this 'citizen right to immunity and hospitality'.[65]

What goes unacknowledged, however, is that asylum policy proceeds in this way and sanctions the exclusive logic of the exception, putting the foreigner on a similar footing to those who are stained by some crime, pushing hospitality towards immunity. But this way of understanding hospitality on the basis of asylum, almost as a temporary safe haven, an immune and immunizing protection, does not change the ethos of the sojourn, does not leave any scratch on the city, which, rather, the citizens continue to inhabit undisturbed, thanks to this self-immunizing defence. 'Refuge-cities' do not open the doors to another citizenship. Nothing is done here, then, except to remark upon (and re-mark) the metaphysical separation between the within and the outside, to reassert the axiological frontier between citizen and foreigner.[66]

It is, instead, the *ger*, the resident foreigner who – according to these same pages in the Hebrew Bible – crosses this frontier, or rather explodes it, drawing hospitality and citizenship closer together, to the point of making them coincide outright. The model is the Biblical City, where the citizen forgets about being a citizen, residing there, in separation, always as a foreigner. No further step has to be taken in order to be hospitable. For hospitality is inscribed in citizenship.

To go beyond the old concept of citizenship also means to bring out all the limits of cosmopolitanism. In the final analysis this is not a matter of being proclaimed 'citizens' or 'citizens of the world', or of the extension of 'global citizenship'. Rather, it is necessary to go beyond, into the space which humanity must cohabit. This is the important thing: to co-habit. The International as Derrida understands it – as an alliance and sharing that goes beyond the framework of citizenship – moves in this same direction. The protagonists of the International will be the resident foreigners.

In its hollow naïveté, cosmopolitanism does not open up, does not ensure a politics of welcome. Whoever has suffered the torments of war, whoever has put up with hunger and misery, does not ask to circulate freely just wherever – rather, she hopes that at the end of her journey, she will arrive where the world can again be a common one. She makes no pretence to unite with the community of the citizens of the world but does expect to be able to cohabit with others. Cosmopolitanism is a sort of communitarianism, in the sense that it affirms the primacy of the human community over all other institutions. This does not necessarily allow for welcome. Another way of understanding community is possible.

10 Community, immunity, welcome

Traditional political philosophy has evaded the question of welcome. At most, it has referred to it as a problem supposedly posed around the edges of the community – a marginal question. This is no surprise given that for centuries, from Hobbes to Rawls, the dominant paradigm was the contract, aimed at justifying the inclusion in the city of a multitude which, to this end, definitively separated itself from and broke ties with the external. This allowed a 'we' to declare its own existence – a pronoun that can give rise to a collective subject counterposed to others, and make it speak in the first-person plural. The 'we', which simultaneously both includes and excludes, erects itself at the frontier.

It has been noted above that the contract is a powerful fiction – or, better, a double or even triple fiction, that moreover reiterates itself over time. It thus projects into a mythical past the signing of an accord stipulated by neutral and indistinct individuals who supposedly acceded to giving up part of their prerogatives, beginning with freedom, in exchange for civil peace, security and the general will, all guaranteed by the sovereign. Hence the emergence of the Leviathan, the animal of primitive chaos, the sea monster, the tortuous serpent, ready to establish order, to govern in the name of this 'we'. But the fear is more the effect than the cause of this great securitarian Leviathan. The fiction nonetheless goes on, having people believe that other communities have also stipulated this same contract on the basis of their own identical right. Each person finds herself under the banner of order and stability, within her own frontiers, which have to be immutable. Precisely for this reason, it is unnecessary for the contract to be renewed each time around. This would be wasted effort. The descendants of those who make up part of the community – or at most, in exceptional cases, those born on this soil within the frontiers – can say 'we' without having to put down their own signature. The real contract has already been stipulated once and for all, by the so-called 'founding fathers', who through this act have secured citizenship for their children and their descendants. The Athenian model remains the dominant one: the contract is, at the same time, a paternity certificate which founds the fatherland. A fiction within the fiction: birth amounts to a signature. To be born within the community is enough to renew the contract automatically. A truly bizarre idea, though one that has exercised enormous influence. On closer inspection, the artifice lies in an undue reversal: for the contract itself requires and already presupposes the nation and the birthright, limiting itself to making a family community – reproduced by filiation – into the political community *par excellence*. The mythical signers, the founding fathers, presented as isolated invividuals exposed to war and at prey to terror, are in fact already members of a nation summoned to renew itself through the continuity of the generations.

Politics stops at the limits of this community, which is natural and yet fictitious. Questions are confronted in a strictly internal perspective or else evaded. Social justice is circumscribed to the distribution of goods among the members of the community, and the applicability of norms is confined to the deliberation among citizens; the possible admission or else rejection of the foreigner is up to the community, for they concern its self-determination and the legitimacy of its frontiers. In short, contract theory indulges and undergirds the attempt of the community, founded through birth, constantly to immunize itself in order to safeguard its own integrity against all that might threaten it from the outside. As the political body constitutes itself, so, too, are stabilized the principles that guarantee its immunization.

Welcome is one of those questions that barely come into view and are abruptly evaded. It could not have been otherwise, given that traditional political philosophy starts out from the body of the community that it seeks to persevere in its cohesion and strengthen in its power of action. Seen as a threat and a cause of disintegration, welcome is uncoupled from the community. If there is welcome, then there is no community. This idea, too, is destined to a long future.

But what community is being discussed here? And who is talking about it? Which philosophy? For traditional philosophy, which remains within the confines, reception ultimately itself proves to be an unthought. Contemplating is supposedly the task of a – so to speak – impolitical philosophy, capable of questioning this same body but from its margins, as faced with the risk of the confusion that opens up on the outside.

In his work, which above all questions the meaning of community, Roberto Esposito has outlined an impolitical philosophy – or, better, a philosophy 'of the impolitical'.[67] Together with reception, community, too, would seem to be an unthought. Observed in the kaleidoscope of the different interpretations, from the liberal to the communitarian or the communist, it always appears as a property or collective identity. As if the community belonged to a group of individuals, who, thanks to this property, can recognize their own identity within it. Here 'common' means nothing other than 'proper'. The community is semantically pushed towards the values of belonging and identity. But ought it not to mean something utterly different from this? Is 'common' not, perhaps, the opposite of 'proper'?

Before assenting and giving comfort to a dominant interpretation, Esposito chooses the path of etymology. The Latin language suggests that *communitas*, through *cum*, implies sharing; but this is not, however, a matter of sharing something, as in the case of distributing shares of something according to the principle of an equitable co-property. The prefix *cum* refers to the *munus*, a term from which – according to Esposito – there derives the root of *communitas*. What is shared, then, is the *munus* – a complex and difficult-to-translate word that indicates not so much a thing as an absence, a lack of being, which crosses and splits the community, preventing the constitution of a whole body. The *munus* is like a never-repayable debt, like that mutual obligation that ineluctably binds without ever being exhausted in some final pay-off, and which instead increases in tandem with the attempt to be at one with it. The *munus* is beyond measure; it spills over and exceeds. It is not something that can be collectively possessed; on the contrary, it is this shared 'nothing' – the nothing that brings to bear the void on which the community establishes itself. A gaze into this abyss makes it possible to understand that the bind of coresponsibility, with which each is bound to the other, avoids the fall into the precipice.

One can, then, speak of *res communis*, *res nullius*. What is held in common does not belong to anyone – or, more accurately, what is held in common is not property and escapes any appropriation. In this sense, community, considered in the perspective opened up by the *munus*, in that ethic which even as it binds also always leaves an empty space, cannot be understood either as property or as identity. Here, the 'we' is senseless, just as the 'among-us' and the 'our' are; the *munus* requires 'being-within'. Resistant to any possessive grammar, the community does not give rise either to a simple relation, or still less to integration; it does not include or exclude on the basis of an already-stable link. The unprecedented opening of the *munus* is a radical void, the proof of a dispossession, of a continual expropriation.[68]

The literal opposite of the common [*comune*] is the immune. Not the individual. Rather, the individual and the collective are two mirror-image modalities of a regime of immunity, the qualities of a body that has tried to close the wound in order to protect itself, of a replete subjectivity which belongs as a whole and without any remainder. It is proudly identical to itself and displays its pretension to identity in the first person, be it singular or plural.

This immunizing project thus sheds light on the baleful shift that has dragged the common so far that it even appears to indicate a form of belonging; one need only think of the 'communitarian' current. But, in general, as far as modernity is concerned, it is almost self-evident that the common refers to co-belonging. This contradiction has, therefore, paradoxically marked the semantic history and conceptual course of community, which has ended up being understood as immunity. This has itself sanctioned its closedness. For to immunize oneself is to root oneself, with all the fibres of one's being, in the foundation of identity, passing ourselves off as its only proprietors and depositaries, thus guarding ourselves against the risk of contact and of exposure to the other. Philosophy has indulged the immunization of the *cum* in *communitas* and has helped conserve a simple link between individuals, directing this link against the *munus* which instead leaves open the space of the 'co-', of being with others, which will never be able to be filled in. It is in this key that Esposito reads the political and juridical institutions which have been means, instruments, of the project of immunity.[69] Yet, notwithstanding all the attempts to preserve it from the external, the community has not ceased to be traversed within by that void that constitutes the yawning chasm in its foundations.

What does not cross the limit – or, rather, hides the dimension of the common, of being-with in all its potentials – is modernity's already-immunized outlook. Esposito calls 'impolitical' all that which an immunizing politics has expelled, rejecting it outside of its own sphere, such as to be able to constitute itself – everything that has been erased in the attempt to defend the body politic. This list of what lies beyond the confines could be a very long one: from fear to death, from responsibility to brotherhood, from blame to ecstasy. The impolitical is the unthought of political philosophy and is much more political than what this latter wanted to think, for it is everything that relates to the *munus* and the common condition.

Death is the inappropriable object *par excellence*. The foundational immunity of patriotic myth suggests the perpetuation of the body politic above and beyond the death of individual bodies. Hence the sacrifice the individual-become-soldier makes in the name of the community, which erects monuments to these dead and absorbs their remains into the body of the nation. The contract immunizes against the fear of a violent death, which each person would otherwise face abandoned and alone; this contract excites this fear and uses it as an instrument of power. The political community, which is constituted on fear, remains inhabited by it. The more it is threatened from the outside, the more it squeezes individuals within its own internal grip. But the fear of the other culminates in the fear of the violent death. Thus, in the final analysis, what is rejected is otherness itself. If fear is the bond that holds the community together, welcome is impossible. The other is contagion, infection, contamination. The frontier becomes – also symbolically – the indispensable, immunizing defence that protects what is internal and pushes out any otherness, whether that of the other or the absolute otherness of death. In this late-modern context of immunity, in which the threat of the atomic bomb seems, perhaps, to have been reduced, immigration appears as the most worrying threat.[70] The indistinct and dark mass that disembarks and sets foot on the territory awakens fear and again revives the ancestral trauma which the body politic thought it had immunized itself against. And this trauma is the projection of this body's own death.

The foreigner is the intruder. For, from her position at the outside edge, she directly calls into question the immunity of the bond and evokes the *munus* that is hidden within the depths of the body politic. In her placelessness, she hints at that void at the centre of the community, asking for a refuge that cannot be denied if a sense of the common does, indeed, still exist. The foreigner is the opportunity that opens up community again.

Making the world a world in common means, then, to dismantle, to demolish and to deconstruct the immunity around which the political body has long been constructed. For Esposito, this is an 'impolitical' task, for it challenges the habitual use of community and the justification that political philosophy provides for this usage If a politics of welcome seems impossible, unreal, an impolitics of welcome is real and necessary. To this end, it is necessary to reflect on the value of cohabitation and on the meaning of place. Only a responsible sharing of shared places can de-immunize, opening up unprecedented spaces of solidarity and unexpected moments of freedom.

11 When Europe drowned …

It's impossible to pin it to a specific date. It was at dawn, or perhaps at dusk, when the sea by Lampedusa took the lives from another boat and then let the wreckage and the remains drift away. Thus, Europe drowned, just as many times as the shipwrecked themselves did. This, after Europe locked itself down within ever higher walls, within frontiers under CCTV surveillance and nets studded with electronic sensors. In its tasks and in its 'anti-immigration' work, Frontex – the European coast guard and border agency created in 2005, based in Warsaw, Poland – manifestly sums up the victory of immunizing thought.

What can be said of Europe now, after the countless shipwrecks? A veil of grief, mournfulness and melancholy envelops all thought – indeed, even that of those who do not think of the victims and maintain that it is not necessary to take on any burden of responsibility. Beyond the silence of grief can be heard a cacophany of animated voices, an indistinct clamour.

It seems that now it is possible to speak of Europe only in the conditional. What it is today and what it could have been. The future which many had caught a glimpse of has been frustrated, disowned, called off by a present that is as sarcastic as it is gloomy. Even to re-read essays published just a handful of years ago – to mention just a few, the ones by Gadamer, Habermas, Derrida or Brague – has sometimes itself become a sorrowful task. Of course, Europe has always considered itself as being in crisis, simply on account of its enigmatic provenance, its tormented history, its eccentric identity. Yet the Europeans – in this sense distinct from the Greeks who were so proudly authentic and so keenly 'not Europeans' – had always felt themselves to be others and extraneous. For this very reason, many philosophers, writers and intellectuals had trusted in the possibilities contained within this curious European continent, this Asiatic semipeninsula.[71] The expansion of the European Union made it possible to make out a new path. Perhaps new challenges could have been issued from the peripheries, from Rostock and Belfast, from Riga and Palermo. The project itself seemed clear: Europe as the 'home of diversities'.[72]

'Europe' was, then, a proper noun which promised to become not only the unprecedented common term of a rediscovery of politics, but also the laboratory in which new forms of citizenship could be experimented with. These latter would, it seemed, now be unbound from filiation and birth, and heave off the toxic myth of the nation. But Europe simply has not been any of this. When the moment came to make human rights a reality and accommodate those who sought refuge, the homeland of these rights betrayed itself. The predictions, prophecies and prognostics were not realized. The list of things that Europe could have been, and has not been, would be a very long one.

Passing from the conditional to the present indicative, it is necessary to admit that 'Europe' has become the name of a jumble of nations, a haphazard assembly of co-proprietors which, through the blows struck in ephemeral treaties and vacillating compromises, contend for the space in which each can defend its own pretence to identity. There is no sense of the common, no thinking about community. All that is missing, here, is the formal replacement of the European Constitution with a ruling of co-propriety through which each nation could use the EU to immunize itself even further. There is almost no political initiative which is not distorted and overturned. While what had been hoped for was a new 'post-national' form, one that – as Habermas reasoned – was already moving towards a cosmopolitan constitution, instead the nation-state, the guardian of securitarian immunity, which guarantees protection from external threats, starting with migrants, has been reinforced. While what had been imagined was a European citizenship based only on residency, and thus also open to foreigners – or, rather, one able to invent the unprecedented status of the 'European citizen' lacking a nationality internal to Europe – everything ended up in a senseless duplication of belonging, in a double birth privilege. And then there are the confines: the progressive opening up of the Schengen space, which from 1985 onwards was supposed to ease free circulation, has in fact been followed by the obsessive immunization of the frontiers.

Who should be blamed for this reversal? The blame lies with not just the Brussels bureaucracy or the succession of governments, but so, too, the citizens, who have remained distant, passive, indifferent. The events of the last decade, and in particular the great economic–financial crisis, have helped to shipwreck any large-scale project for Europe. Contrary to what the sovereigntists believe, Europe's limitation has not been that it has questioned the individual nation-states' sovereignty, but rather that it has not managed to fundamentally dismantle this old Moloch. Indeed, this latter is today more ghostly and bloodless than ever and for this very reason is all the more determined to lay down the law, and clings all the more tightly. Europe has remained the hostage of nations, which rival each other in a constant, pointless contest within an empty and even ruined institution. There has, therefore, been no attempt to invent new political forms of commonality and cohabitation.

The 'migrant crisis' is the most striking proof of this failure. If the refusal to accommodate migrants can be blamed on individual nations, starting with Hungary, Poland and Slovakia, it must also be recognized that Europe, as a supranational body standing above nations, has not been able to make itself into a refuge, to open itself up to hospitality. And yet, it could have made at least one appeal to human rights and asserted them against the nation. But no – there is no *refugium* for the foreigner; the *ius* of the citizen has won once again. The dark *horror loci* that has tormented Europeans over the centuries has prevailed once more.

Finis terrae, Europe has always been a border territory, a port at the beginning of the journey towards new discoveries and new visions, or better, new horizons – and indeed, in Greek, 'horizon' means 'confine'. Even though it is enigmatic, the name 'Europe' did not have to designate a name, as in the ancient way, but rather a direction in the sky, the direction of the sun sinking into the sea to then rise again. That was how the Greeks looked at that Western shore of the Aegean, always rather observing the dimming penumbra of the evening, where, however, the light in the distance shone even brighter.

And a horizon it remains. One that it does not seem possible to glimpse anywhere else. The horizon of a community dissociated from the nation, from birth, from filiation; one mindful of crimes perpetrated in the name of blood, of wars unleashed in the name of the soil, conscious of exile, open to hospitality, capable of providing space for political forms in which the immune loses its precedence over the common.

12 The power of place

A self-immunizing 'good sense' sees the migrants' arrival as a threat. This good sense constantly separates itself from the common sense, raising economic, cultural and religious questions as well as questions of identity. If, on the one hand, these questions have the air of being very 'realistic', on the other hand they are also immunizing barriers. Hostility revokes hospitality, *a priori*. The demands follow one after another, and they are all of the same tenor. 'Yes, that would be very generous of us. But how can we take them in if we don't have the means to do so?' 'What can we do about it, if there's no jobs and housing for us either?' 'And then, how would we integrate them?' This immunizing good sense, which abandons any ethics, can even reach the perverse level of passing off the refusal to allow entry as a form of concern, and expulsion as a gesture of regard towards the migrant. The political purpose of this self-immunizing good sense is, however, very clear: to defend the state's territory, understood as the closed space of a collective property.

But the migrant who arrives does not lay claim to a place in the sun – she only asks for some place at all. This is a decisive difference. The immunitiarian politics of rejection plays on a rather more dubious assertion. To conquer a 'place in the sun' is to make it in life, to have success in one's work, to reach a prestigious position, and, above all, to occupy the place on the Earth that allows an undisturbed wellbeing. It is telling that, from Pascal onwards, it has been philosophers who have denounced the nefarious effects of the 'place in the sun', interpreting it as the principle of the appropriation of what ought instead to remain in common – a principle from which all conflicts originate. As Pascal writes: '"This is my dog", said these poor children. "That is my place in the sun." There is the origin and image of universal usurpation.'[73]

Very different is the simple request for some spot or better place in which to exist in the community. This community has a void within it – however much it is erased – and it is not, therefore, possible not to leave space for others. It is enough just to move aside a little, to give up on prioritizing one's own ego, at least for a moment. Accommodation is nothing but this. And because she is conceded a place in which to exist, she who arrives can, subsequently,

participate in the common life, sharing in its goods and its obligations. But precisely because this will only come *subsequently*, it
cannot be foreseen or determined in advance and has nothing to
do with the accommodating gesture that makes space for the other.

Proximity with the unfamiliar is always a challenging task,
because it first of all starts out from the concession of space. There
are various versions in circulation of an exemplary short story that
sparks reflection in this regard.[74]

In a train compartment, two passengers are travelling comfortably.
After having stowed their suitcases, they have gradually taken over
possession of the unoccupied seats, leaving newspapers, coats and
bags dispersed here and there. Suddenly, though, the door opens
and two new passengers enter. For the others, their arrival is a
troublesome and unforeseen setback, an annoyance that they had
hoped to avoid. They are forced to free up the seats, to reorder
their things. In short, they have to divide up the available space – a
space that they had, until a few moments previously, considered as
their own territory. Even if they do not know it, the two original
passengers appear bound by a singular sense of solidarity. Faced
with the newcomers, they are like a compact group. They already
have the airs of the autochthonous who demand all the space
for themselves. The tension is palpable. The newcomers sheep-
ishly murmur their apologies; the others respond with affected
movements and a few sideways glances. The railway code and the
written and unwritten norms of civility prevail over the territorial
instinct. Habit contributes to them accepting the two intruders,
though these latter will remain under a cloud. Yet, after a little
while, the door opens, and two new passengers enter. The situation
changes instantly. Those who had previously been outsiders now
in turn feel themselves to be co-proprietors of the compartment
together with the two passengers who had been on the train from
the start. Though they have nothing much in common, they tacitly
constitute a clan of the autochthonous determined to defend the
privileges they have acquired. Once again, however, they reluctantly
have to squeeze in a bit further and make more room. The two
once-outsider passengers, promoted to the ranks of the neo-autoch-
thonous, show no solidarity towards the new arrivals, obliged to
confront the same rejection, the same resistance, that they had
themselves experienced and should, therefore, remember.

What happens in the train compartment – and it is not an
experiment, but rather an experience which many people have
been through – is telling in many regards. First of all, it comes to
light that proximity is not a state, but reason for 'concerns'.[75] The
pigheaded defence of the 'territory' as soon as it has been occupied

– a defence that is absurdly repeated, first once, then another time – is astonishing. It is as if the compartment were not a temporary sojourn, a site of passage that is used in order to reach another place and is thus itself devoted to change and mobility. This does not stop the silent stubbornness with which the passengers defend their precarious abode. The paradox reaches its pinnacle when one considers that the passenger is the negation of the sedentary. Yet those who enter the compartment not only overlook the precarity of the territory that has been conquered but rapidly forget that they were themselves unfamiliar to the others, as they proudly and arrogantly present themselves as autochthonous. Here emerges the strong sense of unfamiliarity awakened by the arrival of each set of new passengers.

This also allows us to consider an element that ought not to go unremarked, especially in the globalized world. The other for whom space is made is a stranger who is almost never seen. It is not necessary either to know her or to like her, or even to have the slightest link with her, in order to be bound to welcome her. The ethics of space stand above either sympathy or aversion; these ethics are ignorant of the other's qualities or defects. This is why, paradoxically, proximity with the stranger is, simultaneously, both so simple and such a commitment.

To make space for those who arrive means stepping back a bit, moving aside a little. With the risk, perhaps, of disturbance or a loss of comfort. This is all the more true wherever there is a lack of space, where the members of a group feel that they are being squeezed against one another in a body that is already full. But outside of this immunizing vision, which removes that space which always subtends the common, there opens up the non-identitarian logic of the included third party. Rather than proceed with the aprioristic exclusion that stems from the 'common sense' [*buon senso*], and closed to the divisions between within and without, friend and enemy, this latter shows that the self and the other are not opposed but rather imply one another. Even to the point of swapping sides, like the passengers in the compartment who considered themselves autochthonous but then discovered themselves to be strangers, and vice versa. To make space for the other means, then, on each occasion to open up common spaces: the immunized space can more easily crystallize and become a new front. Even within a train carriage, a border can be set up.

This applies to an even greater degree in the landscape of globalization, where proximity with the unfamiliar is an everyday phenomenon. Many have noted this, recently including Bauman.[76] Till not so long ago, everyday life held few encounters in store; and these were circumscribed to familiar or already-known individuals. The arrival of a foreigner was thus something of an event. On the contrary, today walking through any city – and not necessarily a global metropolis – one will surely come across a large number of unknown persons who may well remain as such even after this chance encounter. The network of information, from the telephone to the web, has enormously empowered this effect. Given that 'every human community' has entered into the global network, each person can 'realistically imagine contacting any other of our six billion conspecifics'.[77] In the global tribe, mobility and density have changed human cohabitation.

13 What does cohabiting mean?

The political accusation that Arendt directed against Adolf Eichmann in the final part of her controversial essay *Eichmann in Jerusalem: A Report on the Banality of Evil* has often gone unremarked. Perhaps because the accusation is not articulated with due clarity or elaborated in all its aspects; perhaps because it is put in the shadows by other, no less serious, critiques; or perhaps, lastly, because it appears in the concluding, awesomely severe passage in which Arendt calls for the death penalty for the Nazi criminal.

It is worth remembering that when Himmler established the Reichssicherheitshauptamt (RSHA; Central Office for the Reich's Security) in 1939, he entrusted its Fourth Section to Eichmann. This section was a particularly delicate operation, which was meant to concern itself with the 'elimination of enemies' as well as the 'evacuation of minorities'. Another expression used, here, was 'the forced emigration of peoples'. Moreover, even in previous years, Hitler had outlined a 'negative demographic policy', whose main goal – far from any traditional idea of conquest – was to create a *volkloser Raum*, a 'space without peoples', a de-inhabited area where Germans could then settle. Before he became the plenipotentiary of the genocide in the occupied territories, Eichmann was, therefore, the emigration minister. It would thus be an error, Arendt warns, to consider the measures taken against the Jews – be they Germans or from the East – only as the product of anti-Semitism. This error of interpretation pushes us, still today, to see in the Shoah a high-powered pogrom – the paroxysmal outcome of a centuries-long persecution – and prevents us from grasping the peculiarites of this extermination. On closer inspection, the 'final solution' was the final phase of an emigration policy that was meant to 'cleanse' Germany again.

It can thus be understood why Arendt made such an effort to establish the interconnections between the Nuremburg laws of 1935 and the subsequent mass expulsion. First, the Reich legislated for discrimination against the Jewish minority, thus perpetrating an internal, 'national' crime; subsequently, it moved on to forced immigration, and thus perpetrated a crime that went beyond the frontiers and also involved other nations. Indeed, the displaced now had to seek refuge in countries that were not always well disposed to taking them in. In both cases, though, it is possible to indicate modern historical precedents. The genuinely new crime took form when the Nazi regime decided not only to expel all the Jews from Germany, but to eliminate the Jewish people from this Earth. This planetary crime, later defined as a 'crime against humanity' – for it was a crime committed against the human condition – was, for its part, without historical precedent.[78]

Arendt's reasoning is explicit enough in scope – namely, to criticize the Jerusalem court's pretension to judge a crime which, though carried out on the bodies of the Jewish people, moreover involved humanity itself and thus required an international tribunal. Beyond this judgement of Arendt's, it is also worth remarking on the continuity which she attempts to demonstrate between the three phases of this 'negative demographic policy'. What thread links discrimination, expulsion and genocide? The book ends with an epilogue in which there appears a sort of verdict that the judges ought to have had the courage to pronounce, and which is, ultimately, the verdict issued by Arendt herself:

> You admitted that the crime committed against the Jewish people during the war was the greatest crime in recorded history, and you admitted your role in it.... You told your story in terms of a hard-luck story, and, knowing the circumstances, we are, up to a point, willing to grant you that under more favorable circumstances it is highly unlikely that you would ever have come before us or before any other criminal court. Let us assume, for the sake of argument, that it was nothing more than misfortune that made you a willing instrument in the organization of mass murder; there still remains the fact that you have carried out, and therefore actively supported, a policy of mass murder. For politics is not like the nursery; in politics obedience and support are the same. And just as you supported and carried out a policy of not wanting to share the earth with the Jewish people and the people of a number of other nations – as though you and your superiors had any right to determine who should and who should not inhabit the

world – we find that no one, that is, no member of the human race, can be expected to want to share the earth with you. This is the reason, and the only reason, you must hang.[79]

The expressions Arendt uses are 'inhabit' and also 'share the earth'. Behind these English terms, it is not difficult to make out two German words of no little philosophical importance for this pupil of Heidegger: *Erde* and *Wohnen*. If Arendt was not familiar with all Heidegger's lectures, she did know both the reflection contained in *Being and Time* and that elaborated in the *Letter on 'Humanism'*, in which Heidegger dwells on the Greek term *éthos*, the source of 'ethics', or, better, 'the originary ethic'.

Already, before this, Heidegger had pointed to this otherwise forgotten or omitted connection, in his lecture course on Heraclitus. He translated the fundamentally important term *éthos* as *Aufenthalt*, 'sojourn', and *Wohnung* as 'habitation'. In so doing, he took his cue from Heraclitus' fragment 78. *Éthos* is 'man's sojourn', his 'habitating'. 'Ethics', then, means reaching an understanding on this *éthos*.[80] If, for Kant, it is human dignity that constitutes the basis of any ethical obligation, for Heidegger dignity or humanity can come about only on condition of the safeguarding of this sojourn, in whose opening, as ek-sistance unfolds, the world comes to light. In his *Letter on 'Humanism'*, explicitly invoking the famous passage in *Being and Time* in which he had interpreted existence as being-in, Heidegger links ethics to habitation. And he does this precisely after having recognized *Heimatlosigkeit* as a 'global fate'.[81] In the disorientation of each person, it is necessary to go back to the source of ethics, where it is connected not with moral customs and habits but rather with habitation and sojourning. Ethics resides in the human stay on this Earth.

Arendt attempts to grasp the specificities of the Nazi extermination, which might otherwise appear only as the most terrible pogrom in Jewish history, and to search for the thread that links expulsions to the gas chambers. To this end, she imposes a new political sense on the theme of habitation, which for good reason also here becomes the theme of cohabitation. This allows her to point to the crime in all its incalculable monstrosity: to have purported to establish with whom one would cohabit.

In this sense, Nazism was the first project for the biopolitical remodelling of the planet. The 'negative demographic policy' did not aim at a simple persecution; rather, it was guided by the idea that there should no longer be any place on Earth for the Jewish people. This had never happened before. Arendt rightly sees in this the very presupposition of the genocide, the prelude for the Hitlerite workshops of death. Eichmann and his associates had reworked the principle of cohabitation to the extreme point of devising a plan for cleansing, expulsion and annihiliation. This plan aimed at ethnic homogeneity and thus struck against all the heterogeneous, the allogeneous, the foreigners: the disabled, the sick, homosexuals, dissidents, communists, the Roma and the Sinti, and Jews. In short, all those whose existence jeopardized the homogeneity of the nation would have to be eliminated.

Even before this, Arendt had written that 'The fundamental deprivation of human rights is manifested first and above all in the deprivation of a place in the world.'[82] Here she echoes the theme of the *éthos*, of the human stay on this Earth. In her personal sentence against Eichmann, however, everything became sharper: not only had the victims been deprived of any 'place in the world', but this happened within a political project that was conceived and realized by those who held that they could make the sovereign choice to decide with whom they would share the Earth. This was a crime against humanity in two ways, both because it deprived these others of a place in the world, and – above all – because of the pretension that a human being can arrogate to himself the right to decide with whom to cohabit. It was precisely this decision that made the crime so enormous as to require the death penalty.[83]

The point is that Arendt recognizes a troubling continuity, which provides the backdrop that the genocidal extermination project stands out from. First of all, this is a continuity with the nation-state which, already as such, in basing itself on an ideal of homogeneity, is driven to expel – mercilessly to spit out – those who do not belong to the nation, as if they were rubbish, undesirable scum, of which it erases any trace and dissipates any memory, such that it can conserve its own clean and uncorrupted history. This explains the recurrent production of masses of refugees, a production destined to increase in scope. Hence Arendt's insistence on the nexus between expulsions and extermination. In her view, since nationalism did not end after the Holocaust, the nation-state now represented an even more worrying threat. For Arendt, the nation-state faced with the growing mixing among people within its borders would in any case seek to make nation coincide with state, even using violent means to this end. The refugees could expect difficult days ahead.

But the continuity also regards the future. What remains of Hitlerism? The idea that it is possible to choose with whom to cohabit. Arendt does not clearly say this. But between the lines one can note her apprehension and fear about a project which, once it had been introduced into history, was liable to repeat itself. The final outcome of the extermination ought not to be allowed to mask the political constellation in which it was conceived. Cohabitation cannot be a choice – or, still less, a free one. Thanks to liberalism's fiction of the voluntarily stipulated contract, the idea has spread that one can decide who to admit or who to exclude with a similar autonomy. Arendt was not mistaken. This legacy persisted and it shines through from those liberal theses on immigration that re-propose the principle of freedom of cohabitation, often without reflecting on the consequences to which this has led in the past. But to demand this freedom for oneself is already to head off down the path towards a politics of genocide. The immunizing principle underlying it is the same.

It ought to be emphasized – with Arendt and beyond Arendt – that the mutual bond precedes any accord, any voluntary act, and it cannot, therefore, be reduced to these latter. An unwanted proximity and an unchosen cohabitation are the preconditions of political existence. Long before sealing any contract, each person is always bound to the other, ineluctably tied to so many others who have never been known and never been chosen, on whom her existence depends and whose own existence, therefore, demands to be preserved and defended. This applies beyond any possible sense of belonging. Cohabiting on this Earth imposes the permanent and irreversible obligation to coexist with all the others, who have equal rights to it, no matter how unfamiliar or heterogeneous they may be. One can choose who to live with, with whom to share one's own roof, or one's own neighbourhood, but one cannot choose with who to cohabit. To generate confusion in this regard is a grave error. In this sense, cohabitation, the being-with that stands at the basis of each and every tie, and characterizes human existence itself, precedes any political decision. Indeed, such decisions must necessarily safeguard cohabitation, unless they are to set off down a hazardous slope.

The discriminatory act asserts its own exclusive claim to place. Whoever carries out this act sets himself up as a sovereign subject. Claiming a supposed identity between himself and this place – fantasizing that he is at one with it – he asserts his rights of ownership over it. Concealed within this claim is an ancestral violence. This sovereign subject, be it an 'I' or a 'we', and whether it proclaims itself in the singular or the plural, is but a usurper bent on substituting himself for the other, kicking her out and erasing any trace of her. It is as if the other, who had always-already preceded him in this very place, had no right there – or, rather, had never even existed. Thus, as well as erasing the other, this sovereign subject erases any ethics. For no one has ever been chosen; she temporarily has a place on this Earth in which another had earlier lived. This is, therefore, a place which she can hardly claim to possess. When one instead recognizes that another came first, in the place which one happens to inhabit, this is to open oneself up not only to an ethic of proximity but also to a politics of cohabitation. The co- in cohabitation should be understood in its broadest and deepest sense, indicating not only participation but also simultaneity. It is not a matter of rigidly standing next to one another. In a world crisscrossed by the combined paths of so many exiles, to cohabit means to share spatial proximity in a temporal convergence – one in which the past of each can be articulated in the common present, indeed within the perspective of a common future.

14 Resident foreigners

The foreigner risks becoming ossified as a limit-figure. Even when one looks beyond a state-centric perspective to that of the open city, the stateless end up at most finding a place in the dichot- omous conjunction 'foreigners *and* citizens'. Perhaps that would be better put as citizens *and* foreigners, given that the citizens are supposedly by definition the beating – and hospitable – heart of the city. Even to resort to the term 'denizen', which (negatively) emphasizes the inadequacy of 'citizen', does not transcend this dichotomy.[84] Centring, this old logical-territorial ordering of things, makes the foreigner the not-yet-urbanized dweller of the periphery, as it pushes her out into the slums. Any prospect of the foreigner being able to undo this concentric, self-centred order is enormously restricted. This owes not only to the popular and populist xenophobia that she comes up against. In political terms, she is relegated to the slums; but these slums may also prove to be metaphysical ones.

Paradoxically, this also applies to those philosophies that write Foreigner with a capital F as a mark of their own will to accom- modate. Idealized, sublimated, exalted, the foreigner becomes the 'absolute arrivee' who brings with her a singular, ethical test. Yet, after this test, those who ought to welcome her, having in turn scrutinized their own deep extraneousness and thus confessed their familiarity with the stranger, end up recognizing that hospitality is impossible. The Foreigner, the absolute arrivee, proves impossible to play host to, if not with a unique, exceptional, boundless, hyperbolic act. The gap between law and justice becomes more acute; the split is an irreparable one. Fundamentally, justice emerges defeated from this. It thus abdicates its role and, unable to translate itself into practice, gives way to law, though it also continues hot on its heels.

Having admitted that it is itself wholly apolitical, justice allows politics to speak instead. But in so doing, it consigns the Foreigner, who cannot be hosted, into the hands of law and makes her into an out-law foreigner, an illegal immigrant.

This is the existential effect that the gap between hospitality and migration has produced, even if inadvertently. As if it were sufficient to assert the ethical purity of hospitality and avoid dirtying one's hands with the problem of migration. This approach has left itself open to all sorts of denigratory attacks on 'do-gooder' humanism. As if, faced with the proliferation of boats making their arrival, it were instead preferable to hold firm to the question of the 'absolute arrivee'. If, indeed, the migrant ought to be recognized as a foreigner – or, better, resident foreigner – it is also necessary to avoid overlooking the migrant, her concreteness, her corporeity, her bare life, and to avoid extracting from her only the mythologized and aura-like essence of the Foreigner.[85]

But the metaphysical slums where the migrant marks the limit of politics, beyond which hangs opens the impolitical, are also threatened by another looming danger which is in many aspects opposite to the previous one. This is the danger of essentializing bare life. This would have grave consequences, for, stripped of her rights, no longer urbanized, outside of the *pólis*, the migrant would risk tumbling into an apolitical abyss from which she could not resurface. The slums would, then, represent not a temporary political indigence, but rather the ante-chamber of an ineluctable expulsion from humanity itself.

John Steinbeck described, perhaps better than anyone else, the drifting of the migrant who gradually regresses from the semi-civil state back to the wild one. This is the story of the Joads, an American family constrained, like other families, by the 1929 crisis to move to the West in the attempt to survive. This is, therefore, a discussion of internal migration, which is, however, no less bitter and distressing. As their moral conditions worsen in tandem with their material ones, the migrants succumb to an animalistic fury that pushes them to transgress one rule after another, thus becoming outlaws. At first, they spark compassion, then disgust, and finally only hatred. Expelled from the civil collective, without being able to put up any resistance other than their blind rage, their dark affliction, they resign themselves to taking leave first from the status of citizens and then from the human condition itself. The others consider them 'domestic barbarians', nomads doomed to the 'state of nature' because they have not grasped the wellbeing of settled existence.[86] For Steinbeck, this reveals itself as the fatal outcome of migration.

An analogous inclination comes out in Arendt's thinking. Her attitude towards foreigners, the excluded and the pariahs, who populate her pages, often seems ambivalent. The question particularly concerns the stateless, who are exposed to an inexorable regression precisely on account of their statelessness. Underlying this reading is the schema of long tradition which counterposes culture to nature. The trap – and even Arendt herself does not avoid it – is that of applying this same schema to those excluded from the political community, who are thus supposedly spat out into a wild state, into a merely biological condition of existence. The stateless would, then, no longer be a *zôon politikón* [political animal], but would instead be reduced to a human being in her 'abstract nakedness' and 'mere existence'. Perhaps because Arendt looks above all at the concentration camps, where there operates a 'total domination' in its absolute capacity to destroy the human species, she identifies the final step in the irreversible passage from biographical existence to mere biological life, from *bíos* to *zoe*. Yet this not only unbinds existence from any relationships and any connections, but ends up essentializing biological life itself. She thus carries out two abstractions, which do not have a basis even in the *lager* – the testimonies from which (and not only Primo Levi's) instead evidence quite the opposite. Moreover, it could well be asked where a human life reduced to biological naturalness, outside of any relations, could indeed play out.

This interpretative drift, which leads to the essentialization of 'bare life', appears to be a risk present in some currents of biopolitics, in which the figure of the *Homo sacer* is seen only as a denizen, a non-citizen stripped of any human grouping, doomed to death, isolated in her mute nudity, overwhelmed by a tragic fate. Here, it seems, this figure is unable to put up any resistance and lacks any capacity for revolt. Yet through her extraneousness, which is nonetheless always a relation, the excluded does not tumble into the abyss, is not submerged in the whirlpool. Rather, she has the advantage of being on the margin, the virtue of that heterotopia that gives her a clearer view of the city.

So, she remains foreign. But she is a foreigner who, as such, does not stand opposed to the citizen. Rather, she has a lot in common with this latter. This is not only an existential commonality, in which we detects in the other the extraneousness that also divides ourselves deep within and, thus awakening us to our familiarity with the stranger, drives us to hospitality. Rather, once the citizen thus recognizes that she is herself troublingly exposed, without refuge in the planetary exile, the commonality is also a political one. And the figure who brings this to light is the resident foreigner. It is she who opens the gates of a city where it no longer makes sense to speak of a 'right to asylum' and where the question of 'hospitality' disappears. For this is a city where no one resides *except as* foreigners. This is the political–existential condition of each inhabitant, who is at the same time both foreigner *and* resident.

Here, a politics of separation has recognized that to inhabit does not mean to establish oneself, to move in, to settle in, to acquire a *status*, to become the state. Inhabitation understood as a possession of place constitutes the criterion for the partition of land, the rise of fatherlands, the erection of frontiers and the confrontation among nation-states. Confined to the soil, nailed to the immanence of power, jealous of its own sovereignty, the state is founded on the exclusion of the foreigner.

The irruption of the resident foreigner is a violation of the *nomos* over the land, a fracturing of the state-centric order of the world. For the resident foreigner evokes the immemorial exile of each person, reminding herself and others that, on this inappropriable, inalienable Earth, all are temporary guests and tenants. There is no archaeology that holds: no one is autochthonous. Thus, the origin myths are unmasked and the pretence to autochthony is disavowed. And this points to the abyss over which stands the community, whose *munus* is nothing other than this inhabitation.

The resident foreigner breaks apart the *arché*. For she recognizes that she has always-already been preceded in this place by others, acknowledges that she is not 'of this place' and, similarly, that it is not her own possession. She is thus testament to the possibility of another form of inhabiting – one that is distinguished not only by its spatial-temporal instability, and which is not, therefore, only a matter of migration. For this form is not reducible to the passage from being settled-in to wandering errantly. The foreigner is a resident – but even as she resides here also remains separate from the land. Through its embrace of extraneousness, this non-identitarian relationship with the land lifts the veil on a cohabitation that is not defined by rootedness. It instead corresponds to the development of a citizenship that is unbound from the possession of territory. It corresponds to a hospitality that presages another way of being in the world, and another world order.

Notes

Notes to Chapter 1

1 Franz Kafka, *Amerika, The Man Who Disappeared*, trans. with Introduction by Michael Hoffmann, London: Penguin, 1996, p. 3.
2 For the history of Ellis Island, see V. J. Cannato, *American Passage: The History of Ellis Island*, New York and London: Harper, 2010.
3 J. Q. Whitman, *Hitler's American Model: The United States and the Making of Nazi Race Law*, Princeton and Oxford: Princeton University Press, 2017, pp. 34ff. and 59ff.
4 In 2001, an American Family Immigration History Center opened on the island. For more on Ellis Island, see Emanuele Crialese's 2006 film *Nuovomondo*.
5 See Art. 13 of the Universal Declaration of Human Rights signed on 10 December 1948, and Art. 12 of the International Covenant on Civil and Political Rights of 16 December 1966.
6 Art. 33 of the 28 July 1951 Geneva Convention Relating to the Status of Refugees.
7 See Hobbes, *De cive*, V, 9.
8 See Hobbes, *Leviathan*, xxx.
9 See R. Ashley, 'The Powers of Anarchy: Theory, Sovereignty, and the Domestication of Global Life', in *International Theory: Critical Investigations*, ed. J. D. Derian, London: Macmillan, 1995, pp. 94–128.
10 See D. Harvey, *The Condition of Postmodernity*, Oxford: Blackwell, 1989; J. Habermas, *Die postnationale Konstellation. Politische Essays*, Frankfurt: Suhrkamp, 1998.
11 Even in the few cases in which this term does appear, it most of all takes on sociological hues. See 'Migrazioni' in the collective work *Enciclopedia filosofica*, VIII, Milan: Bompiani, 2006, pp. 7436–7. Conversely, it is wholly missing from J. Ritter (ed.), *Historisches Wörterbuch der Philosophie*, 13 vols., Basel: Schwabe, 1971–2007.
12 M. T. Cicero, *De divinatione et De fato libri*, Frankfurt, 1828, p. 24.
13 M. T. Cicero, *The Political Works of Marcus Tullius Cicero: Comprising*

his Treatise on the Commonwealth; and his Treatise on the Laws. Translated from the Original, with Dissertations and Notes in Two Volumes, London: Edmund Spettigue, 1841–2, 'Commonwealth', VI, 9. Philo of Alexandria also spoke of *apoikia*, migration in a metaphysical and theological sense.

14 See K. Röttgers, 'Kants Zigeuner', *Kant-Studien*, 88, 1997, pp. 60–86.

15 *A Theory of Justice*, Cambridge, MA: The Belknap Press of Harvard University Press, 1999, p. 9.

16 See 'Immigration' (revised 2015 version) in *Stanford Encyclopedia of Philosophy*, https://plato.stanford.edu/entries/immigration.

17 See A. Cassee, M. Hoesch and A. Oberprantacher, 'Das Flüchtlingsdrama und die Philosoophie', *Information Philosophie*, 3, 2016, pp. 52–9. For an interesting panorama, see the collective volume A. Cassee and A. Goppel (eds.), *Migration und Ethik*, Münster: Mentis, 2014.

18 The award-winning articles were published in T. Grundmann and A. Stephan (eds.), *'Welche und wie viele Flüchtlinge sollen wir aufnehmen?' Philosophische Essays*, Stuttgart: Reclam, 2016.

19 See T. Schramme, 'Wenn Philosophen aus der Hüfte schießen', *Zeitschrift für Praktische Philosophie* 2, 2, 2015, pp. 377–84.

20 Lucretius, *On the Nature of Things*, trans. Cyril Bailey, Oxford University Press, 1948, II, 1, p. 65.

21 See H. Blumenberg, *Schiffbruch mit Zuschauer*, Frankfurt: Suhrkamp, 1997.

22 See B. Pascal, *Pensées*, Harmondsworth: Penguin, 1995, § 223, p. 530.

23 H. Arendt, *The Life of the Mind: The Groundbreaking Investigation on How We Think*, 2 vols., New York: Harcourt, Brace & Co., 1981, I, p. 45.

24 Aristotle, *Politics* 1324a 16. See Arendt, *The Life of the Mind*, cit. I, p. 53.

25 Arendt, *The Life of the Mind*, cit. I, p. 12.

26 Ibid., cit. I, p. 96.

27 H. Arendt, *Lectures on Kant's Political Philosophy*, ed. R. Beiner, University of Chicago Press, 1982, p. 45.

28 See Plato, *Laws*, 735e–736c. On this, see also ch. 3.6.

29 On the exile, see section 2.7.

30 Martin Heidegger, *'The Age of World Picture': The Question Concerning Technology and Other Essays*, trans. by William Lovitt, New York; Harper and Row, 1977, pp. 115–54.

31 See P. Sloterdijk, *Globes: Macrospherology,* Cambridge, MA: Semiotext(e), 2014, II.

32 A. Pigafetta, *Il primo viaggio intorno al mondo con il trattato della sfera*, ed. M. Pozzi, Vicenza: Neri Pozza, 1994, p. 126.

33 See S. Benhabib, *The Rights of Others: Aliens, Residents and Citizens*, Cambridge University Press, 2004, pp. 49ff.

34 See G. Agamben, *Homo sacer: Sovereign Power and Bare Life*, Stanford University Press, 1998, pp. 75ff.

35 H. Arendt, 'We Refugees', in *The Jewish Writings*, ed. J. Kohn and R. H. Feldman, New York: Schocken, 2007, pp. 264–74.

36 Ibid., p. 266.

37 Ibid., p. 271.
38 Ibid., p. 272.
39 See H. Arendt, *The Origins of Totalitarianism* [1951], New York: Harcourt Brace & World, 1979, p. 267.
40 See G. Agamben, *Al di là dei diritti dell'uomo*, in *Mezzi senza fine. Note sulla politica*, Turin: Bollati Boringhieri, 1996, p. 24.
41 Arendt, *The Origins of Totalitarianism*, p. 282.
42 Ibid.
43 Ibid., pp. 293–4.
44 Ibid, p. 284.
45 Ibid., pp. 296–7.
46 Ibid., p. 286.
47 C. Mouffe, *The Democratic Paradox*, London: Verso, 2005.
48 Perhaps, however, democracy began elsewhere, as Spinoza suggests. On this point, I refer the reader to D. Di Cesare, 'De Republica Hebraeorum. Spinoza e la teocrazia', *Teoria* 2, 2012, pp. 213–28.
49 E. Balibar, *Nous, citoyens d'Europe? Les frontières, l'Etat, le peuple*, Paris: La Découverte, 2001, p. 175.
50 See F. G. Whelan, 'Democratic theory and the boundary problem', in *Liberal Democracy*, ed. J. R. Penock and J. W. Chapman, New York University Press, 1983, pp. 13–47.
51 I. Kant, *The Metaphysics of Morals*, in *Toward Perpetual Peace and Other Writings on Politics, Peace and History*, New Haven: Yale University Press, 2006, A 166/B 196, II, I, § 46, p. 113.
52 See C. Lefort, 'Droits de l'homme et politique', in *L'invention démocratique*, Paris: Fayard, 1981, pp. 45–83.
53 See A. Abizadeh, 'Democratic theory and border coercion: no right to unilaterally control your own borders', *Political Theory*, 1, 2008, pp. 37–65; Abizadeh, 'Closed borders, human rights, and democratic legitimation', in *Driven From Home: Protecting the Rights of Forced Migrants*, Washington, DC: Georgetown University Press, 2010, pp. 147–65.
54 Toni Negri has observed as much, with regard to that constituent power which exists only for the sake of its own disappearance. See his *Il potere costituente. Saggio sulle alternative del moderno*, Rome: Manifestolibri, 2002.
55 See M. Walzer, *Spheres of Justice: A Defense of Pluralism and Equality*, New York: Harper Collins, 1983, pp. 31–63.
56 See M. Walzer, 'The distribution of membership', in *Global Justice: Seminal Essays*, ed. T. Pogge and D. Moellendorf, St Paul: Paragon House, 1995, pp. 159–62; 'Universalism, equality and immigration: interview with H. Pauer-Studer', in *Constructions of Practical Reason: Interviews on Moral and Political Philosophy*, ed. H. Pauer-Studer, Stanford University Press, 2003, pp. 194–210. For an Italian reading of the English-language debate, see E. Greblo, *Etica dell'immigrazione. Una introduzione*, Milan: Mimesis, 2015.
57 M. Walzer, *Spheres of Justice*, p. 32.
58 Ibid.
59 Ibid, p. 39.
60 Ibid, p. 41.

61 Ibid., p. 43.
62 Ibid. p. 39.
63 On this, see J. Habermas, 'Staatsbürgerschaft und nationale Identität', in Habermas, *Faktizität und Geltung. Beiträge zur Diskurstheorie des Rechts und des demokratischen Rechtsstaats*, Frankfurt: Suhrkamp, 1992, pp. 632–60, p. 656.
64 D. Miller, *Strangers in Our Midst: The Political Philosophy of Immigration*, Cambridge, MA: Harvard University Press, 2016, pp. 63, 69.
65 See P. C. Meilaender, *Towards a Theory of Immigration*, Basingstoke: Palgrave, 2001, p. 163.
66 See C. H. Wellman, 'Freedom of association and the right to exclude', in *Debating the Ethics of Immigration: Is There a Right to Exclude?*, ed. P. Cole and C. H. Wellman, Oxford University Press, 2011, pp. 11–155; for a first formulation of this argument, see Wellman, 'Immigration and freedom of association', *Ethics*, 119, 1 (2008), pp. 109–41.
67 Wellman, 'Freedom of association and the right to exclude', p. 13.
68 See ibid., p. 110.
69 The Third Reich is a past example of a state that was illegitimate on account of the crimes it committed, but the present also abounds with illegitimate states.
70 See ibid., p. 123.
71 See J. Habermas, *Die Einbeziehung des Anderen. Studien zur politischen Theorie*, Frankfurt: Suhrkamp, 1996, pp. 131–63.
72 See Habermas, 'Staatsbürgerschaft und nationale Identität', p. 659.
73 See section 3.6.
74 See, for instance, L. C. Becker, *Property Rights: Philosophical Foundation*, London: Routledge, 1977.
75 See R. Pevnick, *Immigration and the Constraints of Justice: Between Open Borders and Absolute Sovereignty*, Cambridge University Press, 2011, pp. 28–30.
76 Kant, *Toward Perpetual Peace*, p. 82.
77 See J.-J. Rousseau, *Œuvres complètes*, vol. III: *Du contrat social – écrits politiques*, Paris: Gallimard, 1964, pp. 262ff.
78 T. Hobbes, *Leviathan*, Oxford University Press, II, XVII, 8, pp. 134 ff.
79 See Psalms, 115, 16.
80 J. Locke *Two Treatises of Government*, London: Thomas Tegg, 1823, II, V, § 32.
81 See ibid., §§ 35–6, p. 118.
82 T. More, *Utopia*, New York: Dover, 1997, 'Of their traffic', p. 38.
83 See M. I. Finley, 'Le colonie: un tentativo di tipologia', in M. I. Finley and E. Lepore, *Le colonie degli antichi e dei moderni*, pp. 2–28, p. 17.
84 Kant, *Toward Perpetual Peace*, §§ 7, 10, AB68, AB77, pp. 65, 73.
85 Kant, *Metaphysics of Morals*, p. 131.
86 Ibid., § 17, p. 84.
87 Ibid., § 1, p. 41.
88 Ibid., § 6, p. 45.
89 Ibid., § 9, p. 50; § 17, p. 83.

90 See Ibid., § 15, p. 82.
91 See A. de Saint-Exupéry, *The Little Prince* [1943], London: Penguin, 2010.
92 See C. R. Beitz, 'Cosmopolitan ideals and national sentiment', *Journal of Philosophy*, 80, 10, 1983, pp. 591–600.
93 See J. Carens, 'Aliens and citizens: the case for open borders', *Review of Politics*, 49, 2, 1987, pp. 251–73. This essay became a chapter in the thick, indeed comprehensive, recent volume J. Carens, *The Ethics of Immigration*, Oxford and New York: Oxford University Press, 2013. A similar position is taken by A. Cassee, *Globale Bewegungsfreiheit. Ein philosophisches Plädoyer für offene Grenzen*, Berlin: Suhrkamp, 2016.
94 Carens, *The Ethics of Immigration*, p. 225.
95 Ibid., p. 289.
96 See A. Sachar, *The Birthright Lottery: Citizenship and Global Inequality*, Cambridge, MA: Harvard University Press, 2009, pp. 7ff.
97 On the left-libertarians' arguments, see H. Steiner, *An Essay on Rights*, Oxford: Wiley-Blackwell, 1994.
98 R. Nozik, *Anarchy, State and Utopia* [1974], New York: Harper Collins, 2013, pp. 26ff.
99 Rawls, *A Theory of Justice*, pp. 118ff.
100 See Carens, 'Aliens and citizens', pp. 263ff. On this, see also M. Mona, *Das Recht auf Immigration. Rechtsphilosophische Begründung eines originären Rechts auf Einwanderung im liberalen Staat*, Basel: Helbing & Lichtenhahn, 2007.
101 See C. Beitz, *Political Theories and International Relations*, Princeton University Press, 1979, pp. 129–36.
102 See J. Nida-Rümelin, *Über Grenzen denken. Eine Ethik der Migration*, Hamburg: Köber-Stiftung, 2017, pp. 95ff. While Nida-Rümelin is involved in the SPD, the Social-Democratic Party, in Germany, the new Right has been successful in reviving all the anti-immigrant slogans. One example is the book by the popular, recently deceased journalist R. P. Sieferle, *Das Migrationsproblem, Über die Unvereinbarkeit von Sozialstaat und Masseneinwanderung*, Dresden: Tumult, 2017.
103 P. Collier, *Exodus: How Migration is Changing Our World*, Oxford University Press, 2015, p. 111.
104 See S. Allevi and G. Dalla Zuanna, *Tutto quello che non vi hanno mai detto sull'immigrazione*, Rome and Bari: Laterza, 2016, pp. 12ff.
105 P. Singer, *Practical Ethics* [1979], Cambridge University Press, 1999, p. 218.
106 See T. Pogge, *World Poverty and Human Rights: Cosmopolitan Responsibilities and Reforms*, Cambridge: Polity, 2008, 2nd edn.
107 On these classifications, see V. Beck, *Eine Theorie der globalen Verantwortung. Was wir Menschen in extremer Armut schulden*, Frankfurt: Suhrkamp, 2016.
108 M. Caparrós, *El hambre*, Barcelona: Anagrama, 2016, p. 3.
109 Habermas, *Faktizität und Geltung*, p. 682.
110 J. Habermas, 'Kampf um Anerkennung im demokratische Rechtsstaat', in *Die Einbeziehung des Anderen*, pp. 237–76.

111 Ibid., p. 270.
112 Ibid., p. 268.
113 S. Žižek, *Against the Double Blackmail*, Berlin: Ullstein, 2015, pp. 11ff.
114 See S. Mezzadra, *Diritto di fuga. Migrazioni, cittadinanza, globalizzazione*, Rome: ombre corte, 2006. See also P. Orchard, *A Right to Flee: Refugees, States, and the Construction of International Cooperation*, Cambridge University Press, 2014.
115 See E. Balibar, *Droit de cité*, Paris: Quadrige-Presses Universitaires de France, 2002, p. 8.
116 On this difference, see section 2.7.
117 On this difference, see section 3.9.
118 In the sense used by E. de la Boétie, *Discourse on Voluntary Servitude*, London: Hackett, 2012.
119 This is the thesis advanced by biologists and cognitivists. See, for example, V. Calzolaio and T. Pievani, *Libertà di migrare. Perché ci spostiamo da sempre ed è bene così*, Turin: Einaudi, 2016.
120 See C. Wihtol de Wenden, *Le droit d'émigrer*, Paris: CNRS Éditions, 2013.
121 T. Todorov, *La conquête de l'Amérique. La question de l'autre*, Paris: Seuil, 1982, p. 62.
122 J. Mair, *In secundum librum sententiarum, Distinctio*, Paris: Gallica, 1519, fo. CLXXVI. On this, see L. Baccelli, 'I diritti di tutti, i diritti degli altri. L'universalismo di Francisco de Vitoria', in *Paura dell'Altro. Identità occidentale e cittadinanza*, ed. F. Bilsancia, F. M. Di Sciullo and F. Rimoli, Rome: Carocci, 2008, pp. 85–98.
123 F. de Vitoria, *De Indis recenter inventis relectio prior*, in *De Indis et de jure belli relectiones* [1539], ed. E. Nys, New York: Oceana, 1964, III, 5, p. 260.
124 See G. Cavallar, *The Rights of Strangers: Theories of International Hospitality, the Global Community and Political Justice since Vitoria*, Aldershot and Burlington: Ashgate, 2002.
125 See J. Thumfart, 'On Grotius's "Mare Liberum" and Vitoria's "De Indis", following Agamben and Schmitt', *Grotiana*, 30, 2009, pp. 65–87.
126 H. Grotius, *The Free Sea*, Indianapolis: Liberty Fund, 2004, p. 40.
127 Ibid., p. 118
128 H. Grotii, *De iure belli ac pacis libri tres*, Amsterdami, apud Iohannem Blaeu, 1646, II, II, XVI.
129 See S. V. Pudendorf, *De jure naturae et gentium: libri octo*, Heidelberg: Junghans, 1672, III, III, IX.
130 See I. Kant, *Toward Perpetual Peace*, BA 41, p. 65.
131 On this famous etymology, see E. Benveniste, *Il vocabolario delle istituzioni europee*, 2 vols., Italian trans. M. Liborio, vol. I, Turin: Einaudi, 2001, pp. 64–5, 68–71.
132 Kant, *Toward Perpetual Peace*, p. 79.
133 Highlighted in a book dedicated to this theme: S. Chauvier, *Du droit d'être étranger. Essai sur le concept kantien d'un droit cosmopolitique*, Paris: L'Harmattan, 1996, pp. 176ff.
134 See J. Derrida, *Cosmopolites de tous les pays, encore un effort!* Paris: Galilée, 1997.

Notes to Chapter 2

1 See S. Castles, H. de Haas and M. Miller, *The Age of Migration: International Population Movements in the Modern World*, London: Macmillan, 2013, 5th edn, p. 13. See also C. Wihtol de Wenden, *La question migratoire au XXIe siècle. Migrants, réfugiés et relations internationales*, Paris: SciencesPo, 2013.

2 See United Nations, *International Migration Report 2015: Highlights*, www.un.org/en/development/desa/population/migration/publications/migrationreport/docs/MigrationReport2015_Highlights.pdf.

3 The best and most reliable source of data is the UNHCR website (www.unhcr.org).

4 The great philosopher of language Wilhelm von Humboldt made major steps in this direction. His ideas were picked up by Franz Rosenzweig in the insightful theological–political grammar introduced in his *The Star of Redemption*. These are the two valuable – yet often unknown and overlooked – sources of Martin Buber's reflection on the 'you' (singular).

5 See L. L. Cavalli Sforza and D. Padoan, *Razzismo e noismo. Le declinazioni del noi e l'esclusione dell'altro*, Turin: Einaudi, 2013, pp. 54ff.

6 For an overview of this question, M. Theunissen's *Der Andere. Studien zur Sozialontologie der Gegenwart*, Berlin: De Gruyter, 1977, remains a point of reference.

7 E. Carrère, *À Calais*, Milan: Adelphi, 2016.

8 P. Kingsley, 'The Death of Alan Kurdi: One Year on, Compassion Towards Refugees Fades', *Guardian*, 2 September 2016.

9 On this, see D. Di Cesare, *Terrore e modernità*, Turin: Einaudi, 2017, pp. 185ff.

10 Emblematic in this regard is the interview Peter Sloterdijk gave in January 2016, in which he asserted the need for closed borders: P. Sloterdijk, 'Es gibt keine moralische Pflicht zur Selbstzerstörung', *Cicero*, 20 January 2016 (http://cicero.de/innenpolitik/peter-sloterdijk-ueber-merkel-und-die-fluechtlingskrise-es-gibt-keine-moralische).

11 G. W. F. Hegel, *Lessons on the Philosophy of History*, Cambridge University Press, 1975, p. 169.

12 See C. Schmitt, *Der Nomos der Erde im Völkerrecht des Jus Publicum Europaeum*, Berlin: Duncker & Humblot, 1997; *Land and Sea*, New York: Telos, 2015.

13 P. Valéry, *The Graveyard by the Sea*, trans. David Pollard, http://intranslation.brooklynrail.org/french/the-graveyard-by-the-sea.

14 On the philosophical definition of the Jew as a basis for the Nuremburg laws, I refer the reader to D. Di Cesare, *Heidegger e gli ebrei. I 'Quaderni neri'*, Turin: Bollati Boringhieri, 2016, pp. 188ff.

15 See the multi-author volume Grundmann and Stephan (eds.), *Welche und wie viele Flüchtinge sollen wir aufnehmen?* pp. 7–12.

16 Paradigmatic in this regard is K. Ott, *Zuwanderung und Moral*, Leipzig: Reclam, 2016, pp. 15, 47.

17 See J. Roth, *Reise in Russland*, in Roth, *Werke*, vol. III, Cologne: Allert de Lange – Kiepenheuer & Witsch, 1976.

18 See *Définir les réfugiés*, ed. M. Agier and A.-V. Madeira, Paris: Presses Universitaires de France, 2017.
19 See E. Haddad, *The Refugee in International Society: Between Sovereigns*, Cambridge University Press, 2008.
20 Ibid.
21 See J. Conrad, *Amy Foster*, Whitefish: Kessinger, 2010.
22 On exile understood as an existential and political condition, see section 3.1–2.
23 See E. W. Said, *Reflections on Exile and Other Essays*, Cambridge, MA: Harvard University Press, 2000, p. 222.
24 On this, see *Exil, Wissenschaft, Identität. Die Emigration deutscher Sozialwissenschaftler 1933–1945*, ed. I. Srubar, Frankfurt: Suhrkamp, 1988.
25 T. W. Adorno, *Minima moralia. Reflexionen aus dem beschädigten Leben*, Frankfurt: Suhrkamp, 1951, p. 21.
26 See Bemidbar/Numbers 35, 15–25. 'Refuge cities' operate in an even more complex way than *asila*, introducing subtle criteria of distinction. See § 4.7.
27 M. Foucault, *History of Madness*, Oxford: Routledge, 2006, p. 62.
28 A. Sayad, *La double absence*, Paris: Seuil, 1999, pp. 162ff.
29 On this, see A. Dal Lago, *Non-persone. L'esclusone dei migranti in una società globale*, Milan: Feltrinelli, 2004, pp. 48ff.
30 R.W. Ellison, *Invisible Man*, New York: Random House, 1952, p. 2.
31 See Plato, *Republic*, 358a–360d.
32 See J. Rancière, *Xénophobie et politique, entretien avec Yves Sintomer*, in Rancière, *Et tant pis pour les gens fatigués*, Edition Amsterdam, 2009, pp. 192ff.
33 On more recent phenomena linked to this failure, and particularly radicalization, I refer the reader to Di Cesare, *Terrore e modernità*, pp. 97ff.
34 See G. le Blanc, *Dedans, dehors. La condition de l'étranger*, Paris: Seuil, 2010, pp. 77ff.; É. Pestre, *La vie psychique des réfugiés*, Paris: Payot, 2010.
35 Such an entry is always almost missing. See, for example, *The Cambridge Dictionary of Philosophy*, Cambridge, New York and Melbourne: Cambridge University Press, 1995, where it appears only in the entry 'Alienation' on p. 20.
36 Aristotle, *Physics*, 207a 8.
37 Plato, *Apology*, 17b.
38 See Plato, *Sophist*, 241d.
39 H. Joly, *Études Platoniciennes. La question des étrangers*, Paris: Vrin, 1992, p. 78.
40 See Sophocles, *Oedipus Rex* and *Oedipus at Colonus*.
41 G. Simmel, *The Sociology of Georg Simmel*, Glencoe: Free Press, 1950, p. 402.
42 Ibid.
43 See A. Schütz, 'The Stranger: An Essay in Social Psychology', in *Collected Papers*, vol. II: *Studies in Social Theory*, ed. A. Brodersen, The Hague: Nijhoff, 1964, pp. 91–105.
44 See E. Husserl, *Husserliana*, vol. XI: *Analysen zur passiven Synthesis*.

Aus Vorlesungs- und Forschungsmanuskripten 1918–1926, ed. M. Fleischer, The Hague: Nijhoff, 1966, p. 138.

45 See Schütz, 'The Stranger', p. 91.

46 Unconvincing in this choice of terms is the word 'radicalism' and its metaphorical allusion to roots. See B. Waldenfels, *Grundmotive einer Phänomenologie des Fremden*, Frankfurt: Suhrkamp, 2006, p. 56.

47 On the theme of birth, see A Cavarero, *Tu che mi guardi, tu che mi racconti. Filosofia della narrazione*, Milan: Feltrinelli, 2001, pp. 29ff.

48 See J. Kristeva, *Étrangers à nous-mêmes*, Paris: Fayard, 1988.

49 Waldenfels, however, stops at its existential consequences.

50 See M. Foucault, 'Des espaces autres', in *Dits et Écrits: 1954–1988*, ed. D. Defert, F. Ewald and J. Lagrange, vol. IV: *1980–1988*, Paris: Gallimard, 1994, pp. 752–62.

51 M. Foucault, *Histoire de la folie à l'âge classique*, Paris: Gallimard, 1972, p. 23.

52 See G. Bachelard, *La poétique de l'espace*, Paris: Presses universitaires de France, 1957, p. 178.

Notes to Chapter 3

1 See D. Di Cesare, 'Esilio e globalizzazione', *Iride* 54, 2008, pp. 273–86.

2 Bereshit/Genesis 12, 1.

3 On the ancient city, see F. de Coulanges, *La cité antique*, Paris: Flammarion, 1984; *La città antica. Guida storica e critica*, ed. C. Ampolo, Bari: Laterza, 1980.

4 F. Engels, *On the Housing Question* [1872], in *Marx–Engels Collected Works*, vol. XXIII, London: Lawrence & Wishart, 1988.

5 See M. Cortelazzo and P. Zolli, *Dizionario etimologico della Lingua italiana*, Zanichelli: Bologna 1979, p. 35.

6 See M. Heidegger, *Sein und Zeit*, Tübingen: Niemeyer, 1967, § 12, p. 54.

7 M. Heidegger, 'Bauen – Wohnen – Denken', in his *Vorträge und Aufsätze*, GA 7, Frankfurt: Klostermann, 2000, pp. 150, 163.

8 Ibid., p. 164.

9 See M. Heidegger, *Der Spruch des Anaximander, Holzwege*, GA5, Frankfurt: Klostermann, 1977, pp. 321–75, pp. 328, 339.

10 Cicero, *De re publica*, VI, 9.

11 M. Heidegger, 'Brief über den Humanismus', in his *Wegmarken*, Frankfurt: Klostermann, 1976, pp. 313–64, p. 343; see also his *Hölderlin's Hymn 'Der Ister'*, Bloomington: Indiana University Press, 1996, p. 33.

12 On the patterns of otherness in Heidegger's discussion of space, see A. A. Vallega, *Heidegger and the Issue of Space: Thinking on Exilic Grounds*, University Park, PA: The Pennsylvania State University Press, 2003, pp. 65ff.

13 *Hölderlin's Hymn 'Der Ister'*, p. 30.

14 Ibid., p. 35.

15 Heidegger, *Sein und Zeit*, p. 252.
16 This is the difference between *Heimkunft* and *Heimkehr*. See M. Heidegger, 'Andenken', in his *Erläuterungen zu Hölderlins Dichtung*, GA 4, Frankfurt: Klostermann, 1981, pp. 79–151, p. 121.
17 Heidegger, *Hölderlin's Hymn 'Der Ister'*, p. 7.
18 Ibid., p. 10.
19 Ibid., p. 5.
20 Ibid., p. 36.
21 Ibid., p. 180; 'Andenken', p. 79.
22 Heidegger, *Hölderlin's Hymn 'Der Ister'*, p. 28.
23 Heidegger, 'Andenken', p. 137.
24 Heidegger, *Hölderlin's Hymn 'Der Ister'*, p. 48. The terms that Heidegger uses to indicate settlement are *Siedlung* and *Einsiedlung*.
25 W. Benjamin, *Kurze Schatten*, II, in his *Kleine Prosa Baudelaire–Übertragungen, Gesammelte Schriften*, vol. IV/1, ed. T. Rexroth, Frankfurt: Suhrkamp, 1991, pp. 425–38, p. 428.
26 Heidegger, 'Bauen – Wohnen – Denken', p. 150.
27 Heidegger, *Hölderlin's Hymn 'Der Ister'*, p. 137.
28 M. Heidegger, '...dichterisch wohnet der Mensch...', in his *Vorträge und Aufsätze*, pp. 189–208, p. 206.
29 M. Heidegger, 'Hölderlin und das Wesen der Dichtung', in his *Erläuterungen zu Hölderlins Dichtung*, pp. 33–48, pp. 41–2; *Hölderlind Hymnen 'Germanien' und 'der Rhein'*, GA 39, Frankfurt: Klostermann, 1980, pp. 257–8
30 M. Heidegger, 'Hebel – der Hausfreund', in his *Aus der Erfahrung des Denkens 1910–1976*, GA 13, Frankfurt: Klostermann, 2002, pp. 133–50, 147.
31 See G. Dumezil, *Le Festin d'immortalité. Esquisse d'une étude de mythologie comparée indo-européenne*, Paris: Geuthner, 1924, pp. xv–xvi.
32 See Hesiod, *Theogony*, 372, 564, 755.
33 See Plato, *Statesman*, 270e–271c.
34 See Herodotus, *Histories*, VIII, 73.
35 See Demosthenes, *Epitaph*, 4.
36 Plato, *Menexenus*, 237b–c.
37 Ibid., 238e–239a.
38 See A. Brehlich, *Gli eroi greci. Un problema storico religioso*, Milan: Adelphi, 2010, p. 138.
39 See Plato, *Politics*, 262d–e.
40 See Herodotus, *Histories*, VII, 161.
41 Plato, *Menexenus*, 245c–d. W. R. M. Lamb's translation overlooks the counterposition of *sunoikoûsin* ('they cohabit') and *oikoûmen* ('we inhabit').
42 On the etymology, see P. Gauthier, 'Métèques, périèques et paroikoi: bilan et points d'interrogation', in *L'étranger dans le monde grec*, ed R. Lonis, Presses universitaires de Nancy, 1988, pp. 24–46, p. 27. See also D. Kamen, *Status in Classical Athens*, Princeton and Oxford: Princeton University Press, 2013.
43 See Aristotle, *Politics*, trans. H. Rackham, 1275a 7.
44 See E. Benveniste, 'Deux modèles linguistiques de la cité', in *Échanges et*

communications: mélanges offerts à Claude Lévi-Strauss, ed. J. Pouillon and P. Maranda, Paris and The Hague: Mouton, 1970, pp. 589–96.

45 See Dionysius of Halicarnassus, *Roman Antiquities*, II, 16–17.

46 See C. Nicolet, *Le métier de citoyen dans la Rome républicaine*, Paris: Gallimard, p. 176; A. Sherwin-White, *The Roman Citizenship*, Oxford: Clarendon Press, 1973, especially pp. 147–53.

47 On the ambivalence of this immigration policy, see A. Barbero, *Immigrati, profughi, deportati nell'Impero romano*, Bari: Laterza, 2006.

48 On the theme of *origo*, see Y. Thomas, *'Origine' et 'commune patrie'. Étude de droit public romain (89 av. J.-C. – 212 apr. J.-C.)*, Paris and Rome: EFR, 1996.

49 See Cicero, *De legibus*, II, 5.

50 G. Du Mezil, *La religion romaine archaïque*, Paris: Payot, 1966, has contributed to an interpretation of these myths.

51 See F. Dupont, *Rome, la ville sans origine*, Paris: Gallimard, 2011, pp. 28ff.

52 See Dionysius of Halicarnassus, *Roman Antiquities*, I, 4, 2; Livy, *Ab urbe condita*, I, 8, 5–7.

53 See Dionysius of Halicarnassus, *Roman Antiquities*, I, 10.

54 A certain reading of the texts of Paul of Tarsus has also contributed to this.

55 Shemot/Exodus 12, 49.

56 See Shemot/Exodus 12, 47–9; Vayikra/Leviticus 18, 26; so, too, 16, 29; 17, 15; 24, 16–22.

57 Shemot/Exodus 22, 20; 23, 9.

58 Devarim/Deuteronomy 24, 14–15.

59 Shemot/Exodus 20, 10.

60 Bamidbar/Numbers 15, 29 – but also Shemot/Exodus 12, 19; Bamidbar/Numbers 9, 14, 19, 20.

61 Bamidbar/Numbers 35, 15.

62 Devarim/Deuteronomy 24, 17–22.

63 Devarim/Deuteronomy 14, 29. See also Devarim/Deuteronomy 16, 11; 26, 13.

64 As the verse 'any foreigner residing in your towns' is interpreted in the Hebrew tradition; see Shemot/Exodus 20, 10.

65 S. Trigano, 'La logique de l'étranger dans le judaïsme. L'étranger biblique, une figure de l'autre?' in *La fin de l'étranger? Mondialisation et pensée juive*, ed. S. Trigano, Paris: Éditions In Press, 2013, pp. 95–104, p. 101.

66 Ibid.

67 The Book of Ruth is, in a certain sense, the charter of Jewish sovereignty.

68 Bereshit/Genesis 2, 7; 2, 15.

69 See Shemot/Exodus 12, 38.

70 See C. Bultmann, *Der Fremde im antiken Juda. Eine Untersuchung zum sociale Typenbegriff 'ger' und seinem Bedeutungswandel in der alttestamentlichen Gesetzgebung*, Göttingen: Vandenhoeck & Ruprecht, 1992, p. 22.

71 Devarim/Deuteronomy 17, 15.

72 1 Kings 3, 18.

73 Vayikra/Leviticus 19, 34.

74 Vayikra/Leviticus 25, 23.
75 This is the objection that Rashì advances in his comment on Bereshit/ Genesis 23, 4, where Abraham declares himself *ger vetoshàv*, 'I am a stranger and a sojourner among you.'

Notes to Chapter 4

1 O. Weber, *Frontières*, Paris: Éditions Paulsen, 2016, p. 273.
2 For a historical view, albeit one lacking in a more properly philosophical–political reflection, see C. Quétel, *Murs. Une autre histoire des hommes*, Paris: Perrin, 2012.
3 See section 2.3.
4 See W. Brown, *Walled States, Waning Sovereignty*, New York: Zone Books, 2010.
5 See M. Foucher, *L'obsession des frontières*, Paris: Perrin, 2007 (2nd edn, 2012); *Le retour des frontières*, Paris: CNRS Editions, 2016. See also M. Graziano, *Frontiere*, Bologna: il Mulino, 2017.
6 See A. L. Amilhat Szary, *Qu'est-ce qu'une frontière aujourd'hui?* Paris: Presses Universitaires de France, 2015, pp. 21ff.
7 The sculpture is the work of the artist Mimmo Paladino. The project was supported by the NGOs Amani Onlus, Alternativa Giovani Lampedusa and Arnoldo Mosca Mondadori. At the bottom of the sea next to Lanzarote, in the Canary Islands, stands an underwater Museo Atlántico. The artist Jason deCaires Taylor created a sculpture then placed there, *The Raft of Lampedusa*, which depicts a dinghy with thirteen refugees lost at sea. It is inspired by the *Raft of Medusa* by French painter Théodore Géricault.
8 On Lampedusa and migrant reception, see D. Camarrone, *Lampaduza*, Palermo: Sellerio, 2014.
9 Badiou's *De quoi Sarkozy est-il le nom?*, published in English as *The Meaning of Sarkozy*, London: Verso, 2010.
10 See G. Marramao, *Passaggio a Occidente. Filosofia e globalizzazione*, Milan: Bollati Boringhieri, 2003, pp. 86–8, 202–5.
11 The term *Grenze* assumed an important philosophical value already in Kant, who distinguished it from *Schranke*. On this, see D. Di Cesare, *Ermeneutica della finitezza*, Bologna: Guerini & Associati, 2004, pp. 28ff. On the concept of the limit, see R. Bodei, *Limite*, Bologna: il Mulino, 2016.
12 See J. Attali, *L'homme nomade*, Paris: Arthème Fayard, 2003, p. 453.
13 See M. Augé, *A Sense for the Other: The Timeliness and Relevance of Anthropology*, Stanford University Press, 1998.
14 See M. Augé, *Pour une antropologie de la mobilité*, Barcelona: Gedisa, 2007.
15 See R. Debray, *Éloge des frontières*, Paris: Gallimard, 2010.
16 Another exception is J. Butler, *Precarious Life: The Power of Mourning and Violence*, London and New York: Verso, 2004.
17 See M. Agier, *Gérer les indésiderables. Des Camps de réfugiés au gouvernement humanitaire*, Paris: Flammarion, 2008; see also the contributory volume that brings together an overall topography of this

question: *Un monde des camps*, ed. M. Agier, Paris: La Découverte, 2014.

18 These themes cannot, therefore, be properly dealt with within a philosophy of migration.

19 Arendt, *The Origins of Totalitarianism*, p. 445.

20 J. Kotek and P. Rigoulot, *Le siècle des camps*, Paris: Jean-Claude Lattès, 2000, p. 22.

21 Agamben, *Homo sacer*, p. 166.

22 For an updated map, see Migreurop (www.migreurop.org).

23 See M. Foucault, *Security, Territory, Population (Michel Foucault, Lectures at the Collège de France)*, London: Palgrave Macmillan, 2009.

24 See J. Torpey, *The Invention of the Passport: Surveillance, Citizenship and the State*, Cambridge University Press, 2000, pp. 4ff. See also T. Claes, *Passkontrolle! Eine kritische Geschichte des sich Ausweisens und Erkanntwerdens*, Berlin: Vergagangenheisverlag, 2010.

25 See V. Groebner, *Der Schein der Person: Steckbrief, Ausweis und Kontrolle im Mittelalter*, Munich: Beck, 2004.

26 See L. A. L. de Saint-Just, *Oeuvres complètes*, Paris: Champ libre, Édition Gérard Lebovici, 1984 (address to the Convention of 26 Germinal year II – 15 April 1794); S. Wahnich, *L'impossible citoyen, l'étranger dans le discours de la révolution française*, Paris: Albin Michel, 1997.

27 See F. Faloppa, *Razzisti a parole (per tacere dei fatti)*, Rome and Bari: Laterza, 2011.

28 See P.-A. Taguieff, *Le racisme*, Paris: Flammarion, 1997.

29 See D. Sibony, *Le 'racisme', une haine identitaire*, Paris: Seuil, 1997.

30 Paul of Tarsus, Epistle to the Ephesians 2, 19. It is worth noting that the Greek term used by Paul is *paroikós*, a translation of the Hebrew *ger* which, contrary to what some interpretations argue, does preserve its meaning.

31 See J. Derrida, *Voyous. Deux essais sur la raison*, Paris: Galilée, 2003, p. 64.

32 J. Derrida, *Force de loi: le 'fondement mystique de l'autorité'*, Paris: Galilée, 1994, p. 34.

33 On his political engagement in these years, see C. Ramond, 'Présentation. Politique et déconstruction', *Cités*, 30, 2007, pp. 11–16.

34 See J. Derrida, *Le droit à la philosophie du point de vue cosmopolitique*, Paris: Éditions UNESCO / Verdier, 1997.

35 See Derrida, *Cosmopolites de tous les pays*.

36 See J. Derrida and A. Dufourmantelle, *Of Hospitality*, Stanford University Press, 2000, p. 127.

37 See J. Derrida, *Ghostly Demarcations*, ed. M. Sprinker, London and New York: Verso, 1999, p. 253.

38 J. Derrida, *Adieu to Emmanuel Lévinas*, Stanford University Press, 1999, p. 49.

39 E. Lévinas, *Ethics as First Philosophy* in *The Levinas Reader*, Oxford: Blackwell, 1989, pp. 75–87, p. 78.

40 See E. Lévinas, *Totality and Infinity*, trans. Alphonso Lingis, The Hague, Boston and London: Martinus Nijhoff Publishers and Duquesne University Press, pp. 152ff.

41 J. Derrida, 'Une hospitalité à l'infini', in *Autour de Jacques Derrida. Manifeste pour l'hospitalité – aux Minguettes*, ed. M. Seffahi and M. Wieviorka, Grigny: Paroles d'Aube, 1999, pp. 97–120, p. 100.

42 Derrida and Dufourmantelle, *Of Hospitality*, p. 25.

43 Ibid., p. 77.

44 Ibid., p. 75.

45 See J. Derrida, *Séminaire: La bête et le souverain*, vol. I: *2001–2002*, Paris: Galilée, 2008.

46 See the interview with Thomas Assheuer, Chief Editor of the German daily *Die Zeit*: J. Derrida 'Non pas l'utopie, l'im-possible', *Die Zeit*, 5 March 1998, reproduced in *Papier machine: le ruban de machine à écrire et autres réponses*, Paris: Galilée, 2001, pp. 357–9.

47 J. Derrida, 'Responsabilité et hospitalité', in *Autour de Jacques Derrida*, ed. Seffahi and Wieviorka, pp. 121–4.

48 On this theme, I refer the reader to D. Di Cesare, *Utopia del comprendere*, Genoa: Il melangolo, 2003, pp. 61ff. The model of translation is also adopted by P. Ricoeur, 'Le paradigme de la traduction', in *Sur la traduction*, Paris: Bayard, 2004; 'Étranger, moi-même', in *L'immigration. Défis et richesses,* Paris: Bayard, 1998, pp. 93–110.

49 J. Derrida, *Sur parole. Instantanés philosophiques*, Paris: Éditions de l'Aube, 2002, p. 63.

50 See Plato, *Protagoras*, 337c.

51 Diogenes Laërtius, *Lives and Opinions of Eminent Philosophers*, VI, 63.

52 Zeno, SVF 1, 54, 6 ff.; see Plutarch, *De Alexandri Magni fortuna aut virtute*, I, 6, 329.

53 See D. Zolo, *Cosmopolis. La prospettiva del governo mondiale*, Milan: Feltrinelli, 2002; D. Archibugi, *Cittadini del mondo. Verso una democrazia cosmopolitica*, Milan: Il Saggiatore, 2009.

54 See H. Arendt, 'Jaspers as Citizen of the World?' in *Men in Dark Times*, San Diego, New York and London: Harcourt Brace & Co., 1968, pp. 81–94.

55 Habermas, 'Staatsbürgerschaft und nationale Identität', p. 632.

56 Ibid., p. 637.

57 Ibid., p. 652.

58 See S. Benhabib, *Another Cosmopolitanism: Hospitality, Sovereignty, and Democratic Iterations*, Oxford University Press, 2006, pp. 13–80.

59 See C. Joppke, *Citizenship and Immigration*, Cambridge: Polity, 2010.

60 It is worth noting that a charter of civil rights is also granted in certain European cities – for instance, Amsterdam. See 'Toward a converging cosmopolitan project: dialogue between Seyla Benhabib, Daniele Archibugi', ed. M. Croce, *Cahiers philosophiques*, 122, 3, 2010, pp. 115–27.

61 J. Derrida, *Inconditionnalité ou souveraineté. L'Université aux frontières de l'Europe*, Athens: Patakis, 2002, p. 30. On the use of 'mondialisation', see C. Resta, *La passione dell'impossibile. Saggi su Jacques Derrida*, Genoa: Il melangolo, 2016, pp. 200ff.

62 See J. Derrida and B. Stiegler, *Écographies de la télévision. Entretiens filmés*, Paris: Galilée, 1996, p. 36.

63 See Derrida, *Voyous*, p. 108.

64 See E. Lévinas, *L'au-delà du verset*, Paris: Minuit, 1982, pp. 51–70.

65 Derrida, *Cosmopolites de tous les pays encore un effort!* pp. 43–4.

66 Unaware of the model of the Biblical city, Derrida thus instead turned to refuge-cities.

67 See R. Esposito, *Categories of the Impolitical*, New York: Fordham University Press, 2015.

68 See R. Esposito, *Communitas. Origine e destino della comunità*, Turin: Einaudi, 2006.

69 See R. Esposito, *Immunitas. Protezione e negazione della vita*, Turin: Einaudi, 2015 (new edn).

70 See R. Esposito, 'Il proprio e l'estraneo tra comunità e immunità', in *Hospes. Il volto dello straniero da Leopardi a Jabès*, ed. A. Folin, Venice: Marsilio, 2003, pp. 261–7.

71 See Aristotle, *Politics*, 1327b 20–33.

72 I refer the reader to D. Di Cesare, 'Die Heimat der Verschiedenheit. Über die plurale Identität Europas', in *Die philosophische Idee Europas*, ed. W. Stegmaier, Berlin and New York: de Gruyter, 2000, pp. 109–22.

73 Pascal, *Pensées*, para. 64.

74 This anecdote is employed in H. M. Enzensberger, *Die große Wanderung. Dreiunddreißig Markierungen mit einer Fußnote*, Frankfurt: Suhrkamp, 1992, pp. 4ff.

75 E. Lévinas, *Autrement qu'être ou au-delà de l'essence*, The Hague: Nijhoff, 1978, p. 103.

76 See Z. Bauman, *Strangers at Our Doors*, Cambridge: Polity, 2016, p. 50.

77 K. A. Appiah, *Cosmopolitanism: Ethics in a World of Strangers*, New York and London: W. W. Norton & Co., 2006, p. v.

78 See H. Arendt, *Eichmann in Jerusalem: A Report on the Banality of Evil*, London: Penguin, 1963, p. 269.

79 Ibid., p. 252.

80 M. Heidegger, *Heraklit*, GA 55, Frankfurt: Klostermann, 1979, p. 206.

81 Heidegger, 'Brief über den Humanismus', pp. 339–57.

82 Arendt, *The Origins of Totalitarianism*, p. 296.

83 Here I will not discuss Arendt's question any further. On this, see J. Butler, 'Hannah Arendt's death sentences', *Studies in Comparative Literature*, 48, 3, 2011, pp. 280–95. Butler has herself confronted the theme of cohabitation, but in the different context of the Israel–Palestine conflict. See J. Butler, *Parting Ways: Jewishness and the Critique of Zionism,* New York: Columbia University Press, 2012.

84 See T. Hammar, *Democracy and the Nation State: Aliens, Denizens and Citizens in a World of International Migration*, Aldershot: Avebury, 1990.

85 This is again a case of confusing the exile with the foreigner. In his final years, Derrida thus made an – albeit fleeting – reference to the gap between hospitality and immigration, without, however, confronting this problem.

86 See J. Steinbeck, *The Grapes of Wrath*, London: Penguin, 1997.